Cooperation and Governance in
International Trade

Cooperation and Governance in International Trade

THE STRATEGIC ORGANIZATIONAL APPROACH

Beth V. Yarbrough and
Robert M. Yarbrough

PRINCETON UNIVERSITY PRESS

PRINCETON, NEW JERSEY

Copyright © 1992 by Princeton University Press
Published by Princeton University Press, 41 William Street,
Princeton, New Jersey 08540
In the United Kingdom: Princeton University Press, Oxford

Library of Congress Cataloging-in-Publication Data

Yarbrough, Beth V.
Cooperation and governance in international trade : the
strategic organizational approach / Beth V. Yarbrough and
Robert M. Yarbrough.
p. cm.
Includes bibliographical references (p.) and index.
1. Commercial policy. 2. International relations. 3.
Organizational behavior. I. Yarbrough, Robert M. II. Title.
HF1411.Y337 1992 382'.3—dc20 91-43290

ISBN 0-691-04263-2

This book has been composed in Linotron Sabon

Princeton University Press books are printed on acid-free paper,
and meet the guidelines for permanence and durability of the
Committee on Production Guidelines for Book Longevity of the
Council on Library Resources

Printed in the United States of America

1 3 5 7 9 10 8 6 4 2

CONTENTS

ABBREVIATIONS

AD   antidumping duty
ASEAN   Association of Southeast Asian Nations
BIT   Bilateral Investment Treaty
CAP   Common Agricultural Policy
COCOM   Coordinating Committee for Multilateral Export Controls
CVD   countervailing duty
EC   European Community
ECSC   European Coal and Steel Community
EES   European Economic Space
EFTA   European Free-Trade Association
FCN   Friendship, Commerce, and Navigation Treaty
FIRA   Foreign Investment Review Agency
GATT   General Agreement on Tariffs and Trade
GSP   Generalized System of Preferences
ITC   International Trade Commission
MFN   most favored nation
NAFTA   North American Free-Trade Area
NEO   new economics of organization
NTB   nontariff barrier
OPEC   Organization of Petroleum Exporting Countries
PTA   preferential trade agreement
SEA   Single Europe Act

PREFACE

THIS BOOK examines trade liberalization, past, present, and future. It focuses less on when and why trade liberalization occurs and more on the form in which it occurs. The institutional forms of trade liberalization have varied dramatically over the last one hundred and fifty years, and we present a simple theoretical framework to explain those shifts. However, the issues addressed are not merely of historical interest. The proliferation of unilateral, bilateral, multilateral, and minilateral approaches to trade is at the center of current policy debates. The key point of what we call *the strategic organizational approach* to international trade institutions is that institutional variety reflects alternate governance structures used to organize and enforce agreements.

Most of the attention devoted to international trade policy focuses on the choice between free trade and protectionism. Our central question, the form of liberalization, often is implicit or neglected entirely. A look at modern trade history reveals at least four types of institutions—unilateral, multilateral, bilateral, and minilateral. The nature and benefits of these forms have received surprisingly little attention, and the bulk of it has been normative, suggesting which "lateralism" should be pursued. Remarkably, as far as we have been able to ascertain, neither economics nor political science has ever produced a theory explaining the historically observed forms of trade-policy institutions. Such a theory seems a necessary first step, preceding the normative questions of whether or why one form should be chosen over another. Taking that first step is the purpose of this book.

Our primary aim is not to settle or even rehash historic disputes. We do, however, try to provide a simple, clear, comprehensive framework that integrates different pieces of evidence and theoretical debates. We hope the approach will interest scholars working in international trade, international politics, and international relations (including both economists and political scientists), scholars studying institutions more broadly defined, and trade policymakers.

We began working on international trade institutions in 1983, inspired initially by trade theorist Robert Baldwin and economic historians Charles Kindleberger and Douglass North. We first wrote a paper examining hegemonic cooperation using Bengt Holmstrom's principal-agent logic; that paper later evolved into "Free Trade, Hegemony, and the Theory of Agency" (*Kyklos* [1985]). A second paper, an explanation of the move to bilateralism, used insights from Oliver Williamson's then-new

credible commitments framework, Lester Telser's self-enforcing agreements, and Robert Axelrod's "Tit-for-Tat." A nontechnical version of
that paper later became "Reciprocity, Bilateralism, and 'Economic Hostages': Self-enforcing Agreements in International Trade" (*International
Studies Quarterly* [1986]). There were also papers on customs unions and
other hybrid institutional forms. As we researched the topics, we realized
that the methods of economic theory alone would not be sufficient to
explain the history or future path of trade relations, especially if we
wanted to understand not just why free trade or protection triumphed at
a particular time, but why policy took the institutional *forms* it did. We
began to explore the political science and international relations literatures, initially reading the work of Bob Keohane, Steve Krasner, Robert
Gilpin, and John Conybeare.

As yet, we had not thought with much sophistication about the con-
nection between our papers on hegemony and bilateralism. That changed
when Bob Baldwin invited us, in 1985, to a National Bureau of Economic
Research conference on "The Political Economy of Trade Policy," organized jointly by Baldwin and Bob Keohane. He suggested we write a conference paper combining the two papers, which he had seen only in their
1984 working-paper form. With necessity motivating invention, we developed a story integrating our analyses of hegemon-enforced multilateralism and self-enforcing bilateralism. The framework explained well the
history of trade policy and even anticipated major moves like the European Community's push toward economic integration by 1992 and the
formation of the Canada-U.S. Free-Trade Agreement. Realization of
those subsequent events encouraged us to shore up deficiencies in our understanding and fine-tune our multidisciplinary approach, which eventually became the strategic organizational approach. After many conversa-
tions, papers, and seminars, the result is this book.

This volume presents for the first time the complete framework of the
strategic organizational approach to trade institutions. Bits and pieces of
the approach were sketched out in the two articles already mentioned,
plus two articles in *International Organization* (1987a; 1990b), one in
The Journal of Law, Economics, and Organization (1987b), and one in
The Journal of International Economic Integration (1990a).

Along the way, we benefited from the encouragement and support of
many individuals. Their generosity was remarkable, since none of them
had been our graduate teachers or advisers. New friendships with political scientists were particularly gratifying to two neoclassically trained
economists. We presented some of the ideas here in many forums, including annual meetings of the American Economic Association, American
Political Science Association, Southern Economic Association, the NBER
conference mentioned above, and seminars at McGill University, Colum-

bia University, Amherst College, and the University of California-Berkeley. We cannot list all who commented on those ideas. We must, however, mention Bob Baldwin (who also steered Jack Repcheck of Princeton University Press our way), Olly Williamson, Dave Richardson, Steve Krasner, Joanne Gowa, Bob Keohane, and Steve Brams. For a productive year (1989–90) spent as Visiting Scholars in Economics at Berkeley and in Political Science at Stanford, we owe special thanks to Oliver Williamson and Steve Krasner. Jack Repcheck was the perfect editor—patient and impatient at all the right times. Amherst College, thanks to Dick Fink, Ron Rosbottom, Ralph Beals, and Peter Pouncey, provided financial support through a Trustee Faculty Fellowship, as well as generous assistance with travel and research materials. M.R.V. and S.L.V. proved unfailingly patient and supportive, as always.

Cooperation and Governance in International Trade

Chapter One

INTRODUCTION

The Question

The arena of modern international trade policy provides an intriguing set of puzzles.[1] Although country names, product categories, and specific disputes have changed, many fundamental issues and debates have remained remarkably constant for centuries.[2] Because of their direct impact on standards of living and their linkages to other aspects of international relations—including war, peace, and international cooperation—few questions of international trade policy have escaped attention. In this book we focus on one question that has, however, received relatively scant analysis: *What can explain the historically observed institutional variety in efforts to liberalize or open the world trading system?* In other words, we are interested less in whether, when, or where (that is, in which industries or countries) trade liberalization occurs than in how and in what form trade liberalization occurs.[3] Liberalization can be unilateral,

---

[1] *Modern* refers to the period since (i) the ground rules for international commercial law were set and (ii) income taxes relieved international trade policy of major fiscal responsibility and reduced the role of tariffs to protectionism. The first criterion was satisfied by the mid-nineteenth century (Lipson [1985, especially pp. 4, 8]), and the second more recently. The first comprehensive British income tax was instituted in 1799 but was short-lived (off and on until 1816); a permanent income tax was not in place until 1842 (Kindleberger [1975]; and Levi [1988, pp. 140–144, 176–177]). The U.S. income tax began in 1913. Modern analyses often overlook the revenue role of tariffs; but see Stein (1984, especially pp. 360–364) on Britain and Hansen (1990) on the United States. Use of income taxes is not totally exogenous and may be systematically related to tariffs; see Baack and Ray (1985a, 1985b).

[2] Discussion of many current trade issues dates back at least to Plato; see, for example, "First Principles of Social Organization," in *The Republic*.

[3] This type of question—concerning the organizational form of international activities—has received more attention in studies of international investment (for example, Hymer's [1976] analysis of why capital flows sometimes take the form of direct operational control) and in studies of protection (for example, Aggarwal, Keohane, and Yoffie's [1987] analysis of organizational variety across industries in the evolution of negotiated protectionism) than in examinations of trade liberalization. Haggard and Simmons (1987, especially pp. 496–497 and 508) highlight the trade literature's relative neglect of organizational issues. Major exceptions are the works of John H. Jackson (1987a, 1987b, 1990), and John Gerard Ruggie (1983). Detailed studies of particular sectors (for example, Aggarwal [1985]) tend to devote more attention to institutional and organizational questions, but the resulting insights often prove difficult to generalize. Organizational concerns have long been important in the security area (Waltz [1964]; Deutsch and Singer [1964]; Snyder and Diesling [1977];

multilateral, bilateral, or minilateral and accompanied by varying degrees of bargaining, threats, harmony, discord, or explicit cooperation. Why has trade liberalization historically taken such different forms?

Even a casual glance at the key episodes of the last one hundred and fifty years of trade reveals glaring differences in the institutional form of nations' attempts to liberalize trade.[4] Figure 1.1 highlights one obvious difference.[5]

Mid-nineteenth-century Britain followed what could be called a *unilateral* trade policy.[6] Following the Industrial Revolution and a long period of protectionism under the doctrine of mercantilism, Britain autonomously lowered its trade barriers, including the famous Corn Laws. Some other countries also liberalized trade, while others continued protectionist policies. In most cases each nation made its trade policy choice independently—not as part of explicit international negotiations or agreements.[7]

Figure 1.1: Observed institutional variety in the liberalization of international trade.

Bueno de Mesquita [1978]; Duncan and Siverson [1982]; and Snyder [1984]). Gowa (1989a) ties international organization along security lines to trade policy. Keohane (1990, p. 736) concurs on the importance of organizational questions.

[4] The historical episodes mentioned briefly here will be examined in greater detail, along with the relevant literatures, in Chapters Three through Five. We characterize each period by the dominant form of trade policy used by the major industrial countries, although lesser elements of many forms can be found in each period.

[5] Lake (1988, especially pp. 44–59), adopts the unilateral, multilateral, and bilateral terminology and uses it in a very different model from ours.

[6] McKeown (1983); Stein (1984); and Irwin (1988, pp. 1149) document the unilateral character of Britain's trade policy. Recently, the word *unilateralism* has become identified with arbitrary protectionism (for example, Hathaway and Masur [1990, pp. 4, 20]; and Bhagwati [1990]). Here, *unilateralism* refers merely to trade policy undertaken autonomously by a single country.

[7] There were exceptions to the unilateral character of Britain's policies, for example, the 1860 Cobden-Chevalier treaty with France.

In contrast, the post–World War II period of extensive trade liberalization, was characterized by the creation of international institutions, including the General Agreement on Tariffs and Trade (GATT), that served as a set of international rules for trade policy. The cornerstone principles of the GATT, nondiscrimination and most-favored-nation (MFN) status, required that all member countries be treated equally in trade.[8] The GATT system, under which all members have been subject (at least in principle) to the same set of rules, provides an example of *multilateral* trade policy.[9] The rounds of tariff-reduction negotiations conducted under the auspices of the GATT stand in stark contrast to Britain's earlier unilateral policy, although both historical episodes were periods of significant trade liberalization characterized by the presence of a single dominant political-economic power. Ikenberry and Kupchan have characterized the difference between the two periods of liberalization as a contrast in "norms"—with British hegemony dominated by "free trade" and U.S. hegemony by "liberal multilateralism."[10]

The multilateral, rule-based GATT approach dominated international trade policy for about twenty years following World War II. Beginning around 1965, trade policy decisions increasingly occurred outside the multilateral GATT framework. Negotiations and agreements among pairs or small groups of countries proliferated, indicating a trend toward *bilateral* rather than multilateral trade policy. This trend away from multilateralism has given rise to widely varying interpretations and prognoses. On the one hand, bilateral negotiations permit like-minded countries to bargain over the issues most relevant to their trade and to reach a level of liberalization permissible within the context of the countries' overall relationship.[11] On the other hand, a bilateral system appears inherently less open than the multilateralism of the GATT and raises the specter of a world trading system divided into conflictual blocs or "fortresses."[12]

[8] See Dam (1970) on the GATT. The nondiscriminatory character of the GATT rules came largely at the insistence of the United States, as argued by Culbert (1987).

[9] Keohane (1990, p. 731) defines *multilateralism* as any coordination involving three or more states. He argues that multilateralism is on the rise. Most discussions by trade policy experts suggest, in contrast, that multilateralism as traditionally defined has declined since about 1965 and been replaced by bilateral or minilateral policies. Keohane's unusually broad definition of the word *multilateralism* is at least partially responsible for the differing perception of events. His usage of the word has the disadvantage of not distinguishing between small agreements (for example, the free-trade agreement among Chile, Brazil, and Argentina) and much larger ones such as the GATT. For a useful discussion of multilateralism, see Martin (1991).

[10] Ikenberry and Kupchan (1990, p. 285n).

[11] See, for example, Wonnacott (1987); John H. Jackson (1987a); Dornbusch (1990); and Hathaway and Masur (1990).

[12] See, for example, Wolf (1986); Banks and Tumlir (1986); Hart (1987); Snape (1988); and Bhagwati (1990). Buzan (1984) questions whether regional trading blocs are necessarily conflictual.

Early indications[13] are that the late 1980s and early 1990s represent a continuation of the trend toward small-group negotiations, but with an important development—regional integration involving increased use of supranational dispute-settlement institutions—that we refer to as *minilateralism*.[14] Previous forms of regional integration (for example, the 1957 Treaty of Rome creating the European Community) typically involved weak or nonexistent supranational institutions—a fact attributable to the perceived conflict between such institutions and national sovereignty. However, more recent forms of regional integration, including the Canada-U.S. Free-Trade Agreement and most notably the European Community's Single Europe Act, involve the potential for efficacious supranational institutions to govern trade.

This brief sketch of trade history, summarized in Figure 1.1, obviously is painted with a very broad brush. Nonetheless, it raises fundamental questions about our understanding of international trade policy. The questions are not only of historical interest. The relative roles of unilateral, multilateral, bilateral, and minilateral approaches to trade are at the center of current policy debates, as evidenced by the following excerpt from a recent newspaper editorial:

> We were sorry to see it happen, but the collapse of the trade talks [the Uruguay Round] does finally clear the air on free trade. Perhaps we can even start to understand that the best policy for a nation is to pursue free trade not multilaterally or bilaterally, but unilaterally. . . .
>
> The apparent death of multilateral negotiations ought to increase odds that some country, preferably the United States, will see the advantages of

---

[13] Final characterizations must await the results of the Uruguay Round of GATT negotiations, one goal of which is to stop or slow the drift of trade policy decisions away from the GATT. For a midterm "report card" on the Uruguay Round, see Schott and Hufbauer (1991).

[14] In Yarbrough and Yarbrough (1986a, 1987a,b) *bilateralism* and *minilateralism* were used interchangeably to denote self-enforcing agreements among small groups of countries (but not necessarily only two). Here, we wish to distinguish between two types of arrangements among small groups of countries. In one type, agreements are self-enforcing; these we call *bilateral* although they may involve more than two countries. Allowing bilateralism to encompass arrangements with more than two parties is consistent with trade policy literature that refers to any non-GATT-based trade policy as bilateral. In the other type, agreements are based on third-party enforcement by a supranational institution (for example, the European Community under the Single Europe Act); these we call *minilateral*, although such an agreement could involve only two countries. In other words, *bilateralism* and *minilateralism* are used here to distinguish the type of enforcement mechanism—not the number of parties. Richardson (1987, p. 289) uses *minilateral* to denote less-than-multilateral agreements among more than two countries. For our purposes, the term *regionalism* is potentially confusing because regional agreements can be either bilateral or minilateral in our sense, and some agreements (for example, the U.S.-Israel Free-Trade Area Agreement) are not regionally based. For comparison of our usage with that of Keohane (1990), see footnote 9 above.

lowering its trade barriers regardless of reciprocity. While it now sounds he-
retical, unilateral free trade has at times been practiced to great advantage. . . .

The best test of unilateral free trade . . . occurred in 19th-century Britain. . . .

The decades since developed countries abandoned unilateral free trade
have taught some important lessons, including most importantly that trade
wars do not free trade. Everyone also understands that interdependent economies require open trading. . . . The question now is which country will be
the first to embrace unilateral free trade and reap its considerable rewards.[15]

The relative merits of various arguments can hardly be judged without
an understanding of why different approaches have dominated different
historical periods. It is common to: (i) assert the superiority of multilateralism and (ii) attribute moves toward bilateral or minilateral arrangements to biases created by GATT rules that prohibit tariffs and force
countries to adopt alternate, nonmultilateral means of protection.[16] Most
analyses identify, either explicitly or implicitly, the extent of multilateralism in the trading system with the degree of openness or protectionism.
However, such a view leaves unexplained most periods of trade liberalization, except that following World War II. Another puzzle also remains:
the failure of trade to decline in the 1970s and 1980s, as predicted by the
proponents of multilateralism.[17] The distinction between openness and
multilateralism is only slowly being recognized; for example, McKeown
notes that the "degree of protection and of multilateralism in the trading
system are two distinct properties."[18]

Our focus, therefore, differs from the most frequently addressed question of international trade policy research, that is, the question of free
trade versus protectionism. Instead, we examine why trade policies have
at times been instituted unilaterally and at other times been undertaken
multilaterally, bilaterally, or minilaterally.

FREE TRADE VERSUS PROTECTIONISM

Neoclassical Economic Trade Theory

The traditional neoclassical economic theory of international trade has
little to say about our organizational or institutional question concerning
the form of trade liberalization. However, that theory does provide a

[15] *Wall Street Journal* (1990b).

[16] Among numerous possible examples, see Dixit (1987, p. 245); Deardorff and Stern
(1987, p. 25); and Hathaway and Masur (1990, p. 22).

[17] *Wall Street Journal* (1986b); Bergsten and Cline (1983); Strange (1985); and McKeown
(1991, p. 151).

[18] McKeown (1991, p. 153).

powerful demonstration of the potential gains from international specialization and trade according to comparative advantage.[19] Given a few basic assumptions, unrestricted international trade maximizes total world income from a fixed quantity of available resources and technology.[20] Even if one or more of the model's assumptions is violated, restrictions on international trade generally are a second-best remedy.[21]

By ignoring transaction and adjustment costs associated with trade liberalization, this traditional view posits trade as a situation of almost perfect harmony—a positive-sum game with little role for strategy, negotiation, or disagreement among countries.[22] If nations acted in accord with the theory, each country, in its individual self-interest, would liberalize trade unilaterally; and total world income would be maximized as an (unintended) result.

Given the dissonance between the prescriptions of neoclassical trade theory and observations of international trade policy, it is hardly surprising that economists have centered their attention on the apparent free trade-protection dichotomy rather than more subtle issues concerning institutional forms of trade liberalization.[23]

Economists' primary explanations of the failure of free trade to emerge hinge on distribution issues. Trade, while it enhances the size of the available pie, also recuts and reallocates the pieces.[24] Typically, trade provides dispersed benefits (lower prices to many consumers) and concentrated costs (reduced rewards to the owners of resources in a country's comparative disadvantage industries).[25] The "political economy of trade" argu-

[19] Jones and Neary (1984); and Yarbrough and Yarbrough (1991b, Chapters Two and Three) provide overviews.

[20] The primary assumptions include competitive output and factor markets, absence of external effects in production or consumption, and absence of economies of scale.

[21] Bhagwati and Ramaswami (1963); Corden (1984); Richardson (1990); and Yarbrough and Yarbrough (1991b, Chapter Nine).

[22] An exception is the nationalistic "optimal" tariff. The optimal tariff maximizes the gains from trade for a large country, that is, a country with enough market power to improve its terms of trade by imposition of an import tariff. See Conybeare (1984, 1987); and Yarbrough and Yarbrough (1991b, pp. 286–288).

[23] There are exceptions. See, for example, Destler (1986); Aggarwal, Keohane, and Yoffie (1987); and Jackson (1990). The characterization of the relationship between international trade theory and practice as one of "dissonance" comes from Cohen (1990, p. 261).

[24] Corden (1984); and Yarbrough and Yarbrough (1991b, Chapter Four).

[25] The precise allocation of benefits and costs depends on the mobility of factors of production among industries. The specific-factors model implies owners of an immobile factor gain (lose) from trade if the factor is employed specifically in a comparative advantage (disadvantage) industry. The Stolper-Samuelson theorem states that if all factors are mobile among industries, owners of a factor gain (lose) from trade if the factor is used intensively in producing a good in which the country has a comparative advantage (disadvantage). See

ment suggests that this pattern of costs and benefits biases policy out-comes toward protectionism. According to this view, a free-trade initiative would pass in a direct referendum with costless voting, but not in a referendum with costly voting or in a representative system. Positive voting costs or a representative system pulls the outcome toward the po-sition in which costs or benefits are concentrated rather than dispersed; in the case of trade, the result is protectionism.[26] The likelihood of this outcome increases with the possibility of rent seeking, in which individ-uals, firms, and industries invest in lobbying as a means to obtain protec-tion from foreign competition.[27]

The result is an ongoing tension between the gains from open trade and distribution-based pressures for protection. The obvious questions from this perspective are the following: Why is the trading system relatively open at some times and not others? Why do some countries follow rela-tively open trade policies, while others are much more protectionist? Why is trade in some industries more heavily restricted than trade in others? These are the questions on which trade policy research has centered. Commonly suggested answers tend to cluster in three literatures: busi-ness-cycle theories, political power or voting theories, and hegemony-based theories. As in neoclassical trade theory, the focus of each literature is the free trade-protectionism continuum represented in Figure 1.2; each attempts to explain positions or movements along the continuum. By concentrating on the free trade-protectionism choice, each perspective provides useful insights into trade policy decisions; however, none is well suited to address our primary question concerning the *form* of trade lib-eralization.[28]

Business-Cycle Theories

In the simplest terms, business-cycle theories of trade hypothesize that a country's trade policy will be more open when unemployment is low and less open when unemployment is high.[29] Outstanding examples that ap-

Yarbrough and Yarbrough (1991b, Chapter Four). For the original presentations, see Sam-uelson (1971); Jones (1971); and Stolper and Samuelson (1941). Rogowski (1989) uses these models to build a theory of domestic political coalitions.

[26] Robert E. Baldwin (1982, 1985).

[27] Krueger (1974); Tollison (1982); Colander (1984); and Magee, Brock, and Young (1989).

[28] Milner and Yoffie (1989) make a related observation concerning existing theories' in-ability to explain some firms' preferences for strategic or contingent trade liberalization over unilateral free trade or protection.

[29] A range of perspectives can be found in Temin (1976); Takacs (1981); McKeown

Theories	<Free Trade<	>Protectionism>
Neoclassical trade theory	<Efficiency gains<	>Distribution-based pressure>
Business-cycle theories	<Boom<	>Bust>
Political power/voting theories	<Politically powerful gainers from trade<	>Politically powerful losers from trade>
Hegemony-based theories	<Hegemon<	>No hegemon>

Figure 1.2: Theories predicting movements along the free trade-protectionism continuum.

pear to fit the business-cycle scenario include the Smoot-Hawley tariffs passed by the United States during the Great Depression and the restrictive trade measures applied to many U.S. industries (for example, steel and automobiles) during the recession of 1980–1983.

Business-cycle theories predict international trade policy largely on the basis of domestic considerations, in particular on fluctuating political pressures for protection. Such theories are quite flexible. They can be used to predict or explain changes over time in one country's trade policy choices or differences in policy choices across countries at a point in time. Similarly, they can be used to predict changes in the protection accorded a particular industry as it moves through the business cycle or changes in a country's overall level of protection.[30]

Political Power/Voting Theories

Political power/voting theories posit that the allocation of domestic political power or votes determines the point a country chooses on the free trade-protectionism continuum.[31] If politically powerful groups can gain

---

(1983, 1984); Gallarotti (1985); Conybeare (1986, especially p. 170); Cassing, McKeown, and Ochs (1986); Cooper (1987); and Magee and Young (1987).

[30] A recent variant suggests that pressure for protection rises during periods of unexpectedly high trade volume; see Bagwell and Staiger (1990).

[31] Taussig (1931); Schattschneider (1935); Caves (1976); Pincus (1977); Baack and Ray (1983); Lavergne (1983); and Robert E. Baldwin (1985). Baldwin (1984b) surveys the rel-

from trade (for example, business owners and unions in the U.S. steel and automobile industries of the 1950s), policy tends to move in a free-trade direction, or to the left in the schematic in Figure 1.2. If, instead, politically powerful groups are in a position to lose from trade (for example, farmers in France or Japan), policy moves in a protectionist direction.

Modifications in the extent of suffrage or reassignment of policymaking prerogatives between legislative and executive branches of government produce different trade policy outcomes by altering the balance of political power or the efficacy of pressure from various interest groups. For example, the English Reform Bill of 1832 extended the franchise to skilled male factory workers and played a role in the eventual repeal of the Corn Laws, which had favored the landed gentry over the factory owners and workers. (Before the Reform Bill, the landed gentry had controlled the vote.)[32] Similarly, transfers of policymaking responsibility from the legislative branch to the executive branch, whose broader national base better insulated it from protectionist interest groups, helped establish the United States as the leader in twentieth century moves toward an open trading system.[33]

Like business-cycle theories, political power or voting theories typically attribute trade policy choices largely to domestic political considerations rather than characteristics of the larger international system. Also, like business-cycle theories, political power/voting theories are ill suited to explain why trade liberalization has been undertaken so differently in terms of its organization or institutions.[34]

---

evant literature, both theoretical and empirical. Two recent contributions are by Milner (1988b,c) on the export interests of firms as a mitigating force on protectionist pressures and by Rogowski (1989) on the relationship between trade and domestic political coalitions.

[32] Anderson and Tollison (1985) examine various interest groups' roles in the 1846 Corn Law repeal. Schonhardt-Bailey (1991) demonstrates that landowners' diversification into industry also played a crucial role in lessening support for agricultural protection after 1830.

[33] Destler (1986).

[34] Institutions are the formal and informal rules or constraints that shape human interaction and structure incentives in exchange, whether political, economic, or social. Like institutions, organizations structure human interaction and may be political, economic, or social. North (1990) discusses these issues at length; Keohane (1990) uses similar definitions. In many contexts, the terms *institution* and *organization* can be used interchangeably; in other contexts, one term may be preferable. Often, the word *organization* is used to denote an entity, body, or group, where *institution* carries no such connotation. For example, in the industrial organization literature, a firm is an organization with legal status (Masten [1988]). A firm may also be an institution, with formal and informal political, economic, and social rules that enable and constrain human interaction (Leibenstein [1987]). Firms have an organizational form (for example, competitive or monopoly, single- or multi-divisional) with institutionalized patterns of exchange (arm's-length market exchange, or nonstandard contracts). In this case, we typically speak of the institutional or organizational

Hegemony-Based Theories

Hegemony-based explanations, in contrast to business-cycle and political power/voting theories, are explicitly international views of trade policy.[35] Their fundamental prediction, also illustrated in Figure 1.2, is that the trading system will be relatively open in the presence of a hegemonic country (that is, mid-nineteenth-century Britain or the postwar United States) and more closed without a hegemon.[36] In two versions of the hegemonic stability hypothesis, a hegemonic country is able either (i) to force other countries to be open for the benefit of the hegemon or (ii) to absorb the costs of running an open system that benefits all.[37] In either case, existence of a hegemonic country is both a necessary and a sufficient condition for a liberal trading system.[38]

Empirical Evidence

The empirical evidence for all three classes of theories is mixed.[39] Even the "classic" examples of each are not without dispute.[40] The hegemonic stability hypothesis, in particular, presents problems for empirical verifi-

---

form as institutionalized exchange between organizations (firms). Those firms, in turn, are composed of individuals engaged in institutionalized patterns of nonmarket exchange (Williamson [1985a]; Leibenstein [1987]). See Yarbrough and Yarbrough (1988) and the discussion of the agent-structure problem in Chapter Six.

[35] Footnote 37 below contains the classic citations. The basics of the hegemonic stability hypothesis have been extended in several ways. Lake (1988) suggests that the particular configuration of non-hegemonic countries in the international system also is an important consideration in determining trade policy outcomes. Stein (1984, pp. 383, 385) suggests that the efficacy of hegemony for assuring openness may depend on the state of the business cycle, since severe downturns reduce the hegemon's willingness to forgo retaliation against other countries' protectionist policies.

[36] The criticisms of this view will be dealt with at length later. Conybeare (1984); and Grunberg (1990, especially pp. 437–438) argue that hegemons should not be expected necessarily to favor free trade.

[37] Kindleberger (1973); Krasner (1976); Wallerstein (1980); Kindleberger (1981); Cox (1983); Keohane (1984); and Gilpin (1987) represent the range of views. For analyses, see Snidal (1985); Onuf and Klink (1989); and Grunberg (1990, pp. 439–442 and 444–445). Snidal (1985, p. 581) argues that only the case where the hegemon absorbs the costs of running a system that benefits all is properly termed *hegemonic stability*.

[38] Keohane (1984) dissents from this view.

[39] Baldwin (1984b) surveys empirical tests of several variants of the political power/voting theories. Conybeare (1983); Cowhey and Long (1983); and McKeown (1991) test alternate hypotheses.

[40] To cite just a few examples, Vernon (1982, pp. 486–487) questions the standard business-cycle explanation of the Depression-era tariffs. Conybeare (1984) and McKeown (1983) point out weaknesses of the hegemonic stability hypothesis as an explanation of British and American trade policies. James and Lake (1989) provide an alternate, hegemony-based interpretation of the Corn Law repeal.

cation. The two biggest problems are the existence of only two clear-cut modern cases and the difficulty of unambiguously dating each period of hegemony.[41]

Of course, there is little reason to expect one theory to explain all of observed trade policy. It would be difficult to argue that any one of the proposed explanations—business cycles, domestic political power, or the structure of the international system—is irrelevant to trade policy choices. Of more immediate relevance here is the fact that all three theories focus on the tension between trade liberalization and protectionism; that is, they predict or explain positions or movements along the continuum in Figure 1.2.[42] All largely ignore institutional form (as does neoclassical trade theory); and none focuses explicitly on distinctions among the unilateral, multilateral, bilateral, and minilateral forms noted in the time-line in Figure 1.1. *At most,* the theories can explain the rise and fall of openness over time, across countries, or among industries; they cannot explain why moves toward openness have taken different forms at different times. This is the issue we address.

The view taken here, which we call the strategic organizational approach to trade policy, builds on insights from a variety of perspectives, including economics, political science, law, and organization theory.[43] The fundamental ideas are quite simple. The benefits from trade agreements depend on the pattern and extent of compliance; and different kinds of trade are differentially susceptible to problems of noncompliance. Countries considering trade liberalization are aware of these problems and attempt to deal with them in the design of agreements. Thus, the form of any trade agreement reflects, among other factors, a governance structure aimed at securing the cooperation embodied in the agreement. Before we expand on this idea, some background concerning the special character of international trade relations may be helpful.

Trade Liberalization as Cooperation under Anarchy

It has been argued that the absence of the enforcement mechanism of the state makes international economic relations more insecure and obviously discordant than economic relations within a single nation. The

[41] McKeown (1983); Keohane (1984); Stein (1984, p. 357); Russett (1985); and Strange (1987) address the problem of dating.

[42] As McKeown (1991, p. 151) emphasizes, international trade history reads quite differently depending on whether one studies actual trade patterns or policy measures.

[43] Chapter Six outlines links between our strategic organizational approach to trade policy and the new economics of organization (NEO). Readers with a special interest in the NEO or issues regarding its application to international relations may wish to read Chapter Six before Chapter Two.

same concept of sovereignty (that is, authority over citizens with no recourse to higher law) that contributes to domestic stability and order also contributes to international "anarchy," since states have little recourse to higher law in their dealings with one another.[44] The relationship of states to international law is quite different from that of citizens to the law of a single state: "A higher propensity to deny the rule of law . . . and to resort to coercion is a characteristic distinguishing international from domestic politics. . . . Organs of state are, international lawyers remind us, immune from international law."[45]

Because of the absence of a supranational sovereign, states find it difficult to guarantee they will keep their promises. Compared with the domestic scene, the international system lacks agreed-upon procedures for dispute resolution, a coherent set of predictable sanctions, and the backing or support of uniform culture and ideology.[46] The result is a substantial role for self-help in international relations, including international trade. Elements of all these aspects of anarchy combine to hamper cooperation, even when it could potentially benefit all.[47] In other words, states face severe problems in contracting.

Contracts are agreements legally enforceable by the state. Each nation's contract law specifies the conditions under which contractual nonperformance may be met with state enforcement and the permissible punishments (for example, monetary damages or specific performance). The enforcement institutions embodied in a state's contract law obviously are valuable in facilitating transactions, economic and otherwise. The transactions supported by contracts are mutually beneficial to parties involved since the contractual relationship must, by definition, be voluntary.[48]

Despite the *ex ante* mutuality of benefits under a contract, breach is sometimes advantageous to a party *ex post*. A transaction that would be mutually beneficial if all parties abided by their commitments may not be mutually beneficial if one or more parties reneges. Were it not for the enforcement and remedy available in contract law, many potential mutually beneficial transactions might not be undertaken due to the parties' perceived vulnerabilities to breach.

Contract law is just one of many complex social institutions designed

[44] Stoessinger (1981, p. 26).

[45] Conybeare (1980, pp. 325–326).

[46] Lipson (1985, p. 11).

[47] Milner (1988a) explores the various facets of anarchy and their role in the international political economy. See also Waltz (1979, especially Chapter Six).

[48] Contracts must be mutually beneficial *ex ante*; for example, contractual promises extracted through duress, fraud, or undue influence may be exempt from enforcement. In many cases, some degree of *ex post* mutual benefit may be required as well for legal enforcement of a contract.

to prevent and compensate for breach by providing a transactional governance structure. When nonperformance is a hazard, obtaining the mutual benefits from the transaction requires designing a governance structure to control nonperformance. In everyday economic transactions, these governance structures include such common arrangements as collateral to prevent non repayment of loans, brand names to convey quality information, Better Business Bureaus to provide information about the reliability of firms, automobile "lemon" laws to protect car buyers from opportunistic dealers, and product guarantees to compensate for unpleasant quality surprises. By making transactions more secure, each of these arrangements allows mutually beneficial transactions that otherwise might not be undertaken. Each arrangement is an example of the cooperation necessary because of the possibility of nonperformance; deliberate or opportunistic nonperformance introduces an element of conflict into the parties' commonality of interests.[49]

The same basic problem arises in international trade liberalization. A trade agreement consists merely of policy commitments by the signatory countries, each of which faces continual pressure from domestic special-interest groups for protection. One country, by ignoring or cheating on its commitment to liberalization while other countries abide by theirs, may be able to gain at the expense of its trading partners.[50] Such a policy (that is, protection violating a negotiated commitment to liberalization) can be called *opportunistic protectionism*.[51]

The goal of opportunistic protectionism generally is not to halt trade. Instead, a threat to halt trade attempts to force a renegotiation with more favorable terms for the opportunistic country (in the same sense that the goal of blackmail is not to reveal the secret but to transfer resources from the victim to the blackmailer).[52] When opportunistic protectionism presents a hazard, potential disharmony requires cooperation if trade liberalization is to occur.[53]

[49] With no element of conflict, cooperation would be unnecessary; with no commonality of interest, it would be impossible. On conflict, harmony, and cooperation, see Keohane (1984).

[50] On the enforcement problem in trade agreements, see McMillan (1990).

[51] Deardorff and Stern (1987, p. 38) refer to policies that allow one country to gain at the expense of its trading partners as "exploitative intervention." Our concept of opportunistic protection is a subset of exploitative intervention; it includes only policies that deliberately renege on agreements to take advantage of a trading partner's vulnerability in the relationship.

[52] Rhodes (1989, especially p. 281) provides a useful discussion.

[53] This is consistent with Rhodes' (1989, p. 297) interpretation of the Canada-U.S. auto industry dispute that led to the 1965 Auto Pact. On harmony, disharmony, and cooperation more generally, see Keohane (1984).

Cooperation under Anarchy and the Institutional Structure of Trade Liberalization

Recognition of the opportunism problem in international trade relations has important implications for the expected institutional structure of trade liberalization. International trade often involves transactions that make the parties vulnerable to one another's opportunistic actions. For any agreement, each party must consider not only the effect of compliance on the country as a whole and on domestic distributional patterns, but also the likelihood and impact of opportunism.

Central to the strategic organizational approach is the fact that trade agreements are not exogenously defined entities to be accepted or rejected; rather, parties craft agreements with careful attention to and negotiation over specific terms. In particular, if parties to a potential agreement are aware of the scope for *ex post* opportunism, that awareness will be reflected *ex ante* in the form of the agreement. This can happen in three ways. First, if it is obvious to all parties that no agreement could be enforced given the incentives for opportunistic protectionism, no agreement may be reached despite existence of mutual gains from trade. This outcome is the trade analogy to the school of arms-control thought that sees meaningful arms control as impossible, despite mutual gains from arms control, because it cannot be mutually verifiable and enforceable. In this case, cooperation does not emerge.

The second possible outcome is that efforts may be channeled into negotiation of naive agreements that ignore the possibility of opportunism. Such agreements are difficult to reach and short-lived, so the implications of this second possibility are like those of the first: gains from trade cannot overcome the contracting problems. The arms-control analogy would be a simple mutual promise to eliminate all weapons, with no monitoring or enforcement mechanism. The Anglo-Hanseatic trade wars (1300–1700) provide a prime example of this behavior in international trade. The two sides repeatedly negotiated agreements to liberalize trade, but the agreements repeatedly broke down. The result: four hundred years of recurring trade wars.[54]

The third possibility is to use an understanding of the incentives for opportunism to construct enforceable agreements. This is a costly process; but in a world of transaction costs and opportunism, the relevant choice is not between protectionism and an ideal, costlessly enforced trade agreement—just as the arms-control choice is not between an uncontrolled arms race and an ideal, costlessly enforced arms-control pact. Instead, the relevant choice is to forgo the benefits of trade or design gov-

---

[54] Conybeare (1987, especially pp. 152–158).

ernance structures that facilitate effective trade agreements. The greater the hazard of opportunism in a particular transaction, the stronger the governance structure required to reach an agreement. This link between the degree of hazard of opportunistic protectionism and the benefits to particular institutional arrangements implies that *different forms of international trade liberalization will be successful under different conditions.* Our task, then, is to match the possible institutional forms of liberalization with the conditions under which we would expect each to be successful. This can be accomplished by viewing the possible institutional forms as alternate governance structures, which is a key perspective of what we call *the strategic organizational approach* to international trade policy.

The Strategic Organizational Approach in a Nutshell

Self-interest demands that parties not accept vulnerabilities to others' opportunism without the security of some type of governance structure. However, all trade transactions are not equally susceptible to opportunistic protectionism, and the form of cooperation should reflect the extent of the threat. There are four basic types of governance structure, two of which rely on self-help and two on third-party enforcement mechanisms.[55] Figure 1.3 summarizes the four.

With no effective third-party enforcement, agreements must be self-enforcing; that is, the only punishment a victim of opportunism can impose

Institutional form	Enforcement	Example	Chapter
Unilateral	Self-help	Mid-19th-century Britain	Three
Bilateral	Self-help	U.S.-Israel Free-Trade Area Agreement	Four
Minilateral	Third-party	Post-1985 European Community	Five
Multilateral	Third-party	Postwar GATT (1945-65)	Three

Figure 1.3: Governance structures in international trade.

[55] The possibility of both self-help and third-party-based governance structures is consistent with Keohane's (1984, p. 246) admonition that "it is misleading, therefore, to evaluate regimes on the basis of whether they effectively centralize authority."

is withdrawal from the relationship.[56] If low-cost withdrawal is a viable alternative in a particular trading relationship, trade policy can be *unilateral*. Each country liberalizes trade or imposes protection independently, as did mid-nineteenth-century Britain. Those that choose to liberalize rely on their ability to withdraw from a trading relationship to discipline their partners against opportunism. Such unilateral liberalization will be viable when the nature of transactions between the parties places no special premium on the continuity of the relationship. The option of low-cost withdrawal implies that neither party can successfully "hold up" the other.

However, if continuity matters in a relationship, unilateral withdrawal is costly and no longer provides an adequate means of self-help or defense against potentially opportunistic trading partners. Agreements may still be based on self-help, but cooperation requires a stronger governance structure. When continuity is important, self-enforcement requires issue linkages so that the benefits of cooperation to each party offset the costs and deter opportunism. Self-enforcement also may require parties to provide hostages in order to create deliberate vulnerabilities (as opposed to those inherent in the transaction itself) and signal the hostage-provider's good intentions.[57] These characteristics of self-enforcing agreements limit such agreements to small groups; in our terminology, they dictate that agreements be *bilateral*. The 1985 free-trade agreement between the United States and Israel is one of many examples.

One way to avoid the requirements for a self-enforcing agreement is to authorize some type of third-party enforcement mechanism. This is particularly problematic in international trade because of the actual or perceived conflict with national sovereignty. During periods of economic and political hegemony by a single country, such as the postwar era dominated by the United States, third-party enforcement may be viable on a large scale if the hegemon is willing and able to provide a governance structure for international agreements. *Multilateral* trade policy institutions such as the GATT are then feasible. Without a hegemon, multilateralism of the type exemplified by the early postwar GATT, while still possible, is much less likely to be the dominant form of international trade policy. Effective third-party enforcement is then likely to be limited to smaller groups, such as the European Community (EC), and to issue areas where the high efficiency costs of self-enforcement offset fears of reduced national sovereignty. *Minilateral* groups such as the post–1985 EC create dispute-settlement institutions that act as third-party governance devices for their respective groups.

To summarize the key proposition of the strategic organizational ap-

---

[56] Chapter Four discusses the details of self-enforcing agreements.

[57] The analysis of hostages to support exchange is from Williamson (1983).

proach to trade policy: *Institutional variety in trade liberalization reflects the efficacy of alternate governance structures for different types of trade transactions in different political and economic environments.* The two key elements are these: (i) Can a party withdraw at low cost from a relationship in response to a partner's opportunistic behavior, or is continuity of specific relationships highly valued? If withdrawal from a relationship imposes little cost, few demands are placed on the relationship's governance structure, and unilateral trade policy is likely to be viable. If withdrawal imposes high costs, governance demands are higher, and unilateralism is likely to fail. (ii) Is the international system, or an appropriate subset of it, characterized by effective third-party enforcement of agreements? The absence of third-party enforcement necessitates bilateral trade institutions based on self-help mechanisms such as hostages and issue linkages. Presence of third-party enforcement on a broad scale can facilitate multilateral trade liberalization, and third-party enforcement on a more limited scale supports minilateral liberalization.

Chapter Two

STRATEGIC ORGANIZATION AND INTERNATIONAL TRADE INSTITUTIONS

TRADE POLICY AS A STRATEGIC ORGANIZATIONAL ISSUE

In a social exchange or transaction, parties may find themselves in harmony, where unilateral action suffices and only the simplest social institutions are required, or in actual or potential conflict, where different institutions hold varying levels of promise for achieving cooperation. In many diverse contexts, social organization faces a political-economic dilemma: actors within a group have common interests in expanding the size of the relevant pie, but conflictual interests in dividing it. Cooperation increases the size of the pie, but unilateral defection enables a party to capture a larger share of the smaller pie. The result—as in the classic Prisoners' Dilemma—can be mutual defection. Cooperation requires keeping concerns over division of the pie from interfering with increasing the size of the pie.

Agreements to cooperate are by necessity incomplete even under a well-developed legal system; the letter of any agreement necessarily falls short of the spirit. Strains are particularly acute when cooperation must extend through time.[1] Actors' required performances under an agreement may be nonsimultaneous, and nonperformance may leave an aggrieved party with little recourse. Legal enforcement may be problematic—nonexistent, costly, or otherwise imperfect. If so, the legal system will be unable to deter or compensate for breach of an agreement, leaving parties vulnerable and reliant on self-help. Bounded rationality and an uncertain future make it impossible to write long-term agreements that can govern a continuing relationship without periodic renegotiation; but the potential for opportunistic behavior makes adjustment and renegotiation problematic, since parties cannot be counted on to renegotiate in "good faith." Haggling over the division of gains may prevent potentially beneficial adjustments.[2]

---

[1] Kronman (1985) presents techniques of private ordering useful in nonsimultaneous exchange. Keohane (1984, pp. 13, 127–131, 180) emphasizes the importance of nonsimultaneous cooperation in international relations and argues that rules or regimes bind a government's future actions or those of its successors.

[2] These four elements—uncertainty, bounded rationality, imperfect legal enforcement, and opportunism—are the keys to Oliver Williamson's (1985a) approach to the new eco-

Despite the pull toward mutual defection, actors have incentives to establish institutions that can prevent a noncooperative outcome. The logic of the Prisoners' Dilemma clearly threatens to frustrate efforts to cooperate; but *ex ante* incentive structures can alter payoffs in ways that deter defection.[3] Even in a world of bounded rationality, opportunism, uncertainty, and imperfect legal enforcement of agreements, institutions can and do support mutually beneficial transactions that might otherwise fail due to contracting problems.[4] However, if actors can behave opportunistically—that is, deliberately conceal or disguise their preferences or actions to take advantage of others—some institutions, norms, and actions (such as the "always cooperate" strategy in Prisoners' Dilemma) are infeasible.[5] A major goal of social organization in such circumstances is to devise institutions that buttress cooperation by maintaining flexibility, safeguarding against opportunism, and forestalling and mediating disputes.

Keohane and Nye's recent characterization of the fundamental problems of international relations in a world of interdependence[6] strongly parallels the basic problems of social organization: (i) how individual governments can benefit from international exchange while maintaining as much autonomy as possible, and (ii) how a mutually beneficial pattern of cooperation can be generated and maintained in the face of competing efforts by governments and other actors to manipulate the system for their own benefit.[7]

Trade liberalization, for example, provides obvious and measurable group benefits, including increased availability of goods and services at lower prices. However, liberalization also constrains governmental autonomy in both obvious and subtle ways. With no tariffs, government

---

nomics of organization (NEO). Each is also undeniably important in international trade relations. Chapter Six examines the connections between our strategic organizational approach to trade policy and the new economics of organization. For readers with a special interest in the potential application of NEO to trade relations, Chapter Six can be read before Chapter Two.

[3] Williamson (1985a, pp. 204–205). Gowa (1986) similarly argues the limited relevance of Prisoners' Dilemma for international relations. One problem in applications of game theory, including Prisoners' Dilemma, to international relations and other areas is a failure to distinguish clearly between the structure of the underlying situation and the situation's structure once social norms, organizations, and institutions are superimposed. See also Keohane (1990, p. 738).

[4] Keohane (1984) argues that institutions reduce uncertainty and asymmetries of information, using Simon's (1978) definition of bounded rationality and Akerlof's (1970) treatment of asymmetric information.

[5] Williamson (1985a, pp. 56–59).

[6] Interdependence refers to relationships mutually costly to forgo; see, for example, David A. Baldwin (1979, especially pp. 175–177).

[7] Keohane and Nye (1987, p. 730).

revenue must come from domestic taxes;[8] and protection of domestic industries in response to rent-seeking must be limited.[9] The domestic political gains that come from responding to rent-seeking provide governments with an incentive to renege on their international commitments to liberalization. Trade agreements that would be mutually beneficial if all parties complied with their obligations may harm one or more if a party reneges.[10] As a result, achieving gains from trade—like other forms of international cooperation—hinges on successful contracting in a particularly demanding strategic environment.

Despite these difficulties, trade across national boundaries has expanded enormously.[11] Firms and states, individually and collectively, have developed both the capacity to organize production worldwide and the rules to protect traders in most circumstances. In this chapter, we view trade liberalization as a strategic organizational problem and suggest several considerations central in determining the form of organization that will be successful in liberalizing trade. These considerations are, first, the degree of vulnerability to opportunism;[12] second, the difficulty of detecting violations of an agreement; and third, the presence or absence of effective third-party enforcement.

OPPORTUNISM AND TRADE

Vulnerability to Opportunism: The Importance of Good Alternatives

In the Prisoners' Dilemma game often used to describe international trade problems, a cooperating party suffers more from a partner's defection than a defecting party does.[13] This vulnerability to opportunism, or cost of naiveté, renders defection the dominant strategy; defection is the only means of self-help available to avoid the worst payoff. The only defense against victimization is a good offense, that is, to defect. Even in a one-shot game, the two prisoners' histories link their future fates—neither

---

[8] Chapter One, footnote 1 contains references related to this revenue aspect of trade policy.

[9] Citations to the relevant literatures are in Chapter One, footnotes 24 through 33.

[10] On compliance, see Keohane (1984, pp. 98–100, 103–106); and McMillan (1990).

[11] Friedman (1977) and Wittman (1991a,b) argue that difficulties in transacting across national boundaries help determine countries' sizes.

[12] This is the amount that potential "victims" stand to lose should their trading partners renege on an agreement's terms.

[13] This aspect of the Prisoners' Dilemma typically is emphasized more in security-related issue areas than in trade; see Jervis (1988, p. 349). In Prisoners' Dilemma, the first party ranks outcomes (best to worst) as DC, CC, DD, CD, where C represents cooperation and D defection. For more on the classic story underlying the name of the game, see Chapter Three. Oye (1986b) provides a useful overview.

prisoner faces the option of unilaterally withdrawing from the relationship.

Both aspects of the Prisoners' Dilemma (that is, high cost of naiveté and inability to withdraw unilaterally) share a common element: each implies that neither party has good alternatives. The high cost of naiveté implies each prisoner's only means of self-help is to confess, but confession harms the confessor as well as the other prisoner. The inability to withdraw unilaterally from the relationship with the other prisoner eliminates the option of implicating the partner without implicating oneself.

The general importance of good alternatives, or the negative consequences of limited ones, goes beyond the single-play Prisoners' Dilemma game. An actor's alternatives are the ultimate constraint on partners' abilities to gain from opportunistic behavior. Therefore, the presence or absence of good alternatives is an important determinant of the severity of opportunism problems. This implies a key question in the strategic organizational approach to international trade liberalization: Can a victimized trading partner withdraw and find another equally beneficial relationship? Or is there a high premium on continuity of a particular relationship, even in the face of opportunism?

Before addressing this question directly, we inquire further into the nature and importance of opportunism in international trade relations. To provide an introduction, an analogy is useful. Then we discuss examples of transactions subject to opportunism and provide evidence that compliance and governance issues are extensive in international trade.

Opportunism in Trade: An Analogy

The possibility of opportunistic reneging on international agreements is most easily seen in actual or threatened expropriations of foreign direct investments such as oil fields, infrastructure developments, mines, or manufacturing facilities.[14] Typically, the foreign investor and host government agree *ex ante* on the terms of the relationship.[15] Once the investment is in place, the host state may expropriate the facility or, more commonly, use the "sunk" nature of the project to force a renegotiation with more favorable terms for the host.[16] The success of such an effort depends on several considerations, including the feasibility of continued profitable

---

[14] This discussion draws on Lipson (1985, pp. 121–126).

[15] Often, the host government that reached the initial agreement is no longer in power at the time of attempted expropriation. Similarly, sovereign debt repudiation most often occurs with the debts of a prior regime.

[16] Not all sunk costs provide a basis for expropriation or holdup. The asset must provide continuing value in the relationship and require duplication in any new relationship for the sunk character of the cost to support opportunism.

operation of the facility without cooperation of the original investor and the implications of opportunistic behavior for the host's future attempts to borrow or attract additional foreign investment.

Outright expropriations of foreign direct investments without compensation have always been rare. The 1960s, a period of rising nationalism among developing countries, saw a dramatic but temporary increase in such events.[17] In the years since, the character of opportunism against foreign direct investment has changed; outright expropriations, especially industry- or economy-wide ones, have again become extremely rare. Instead, more selective and subtle techniques of increased regulation of foreign investment enterprises, called "creeping" expropriations, have accomplished the task of altering *ex post* the terms between foreign investor and host state.[18]

For our purposes, an even more revealing development is the frequency with which these subtle and partial expropriations have involved a continuing relationship between opportunist and victim. In other words, host behavior has revealed that the purpose underlying the expropriation policies is *not* to eliminate foreign investments. In fact, many host governments have actively encouraged new investments and engaged in "creeping" expropriations simultaneously. Instead, the goal has been to force a renegotiation of terms. The post–renegotiation relationship has continued to benefit both parties, but the terms have shifted in favor of the host and against the foreign investor. Not only have many such relationships continued, but the parties often have negotiated the expropriations on explicitly mutual terms. Such opportunism can be "customized" to exploit the particular nature and magnitude of the foreign investor's vulnerability and is, therefore, more profitable on average than less sophisticated across-the-board expropriations.[19]

What types of foreign direct investments are most vulnerable to holdup? The key to answering this question—and therefore the extent to which parties are vulnerable to one another's opportunism—is the relative value of parties' alternatives. Evidence suggests that the most vulnerable investments are those with large immobile facilities that can operate profitably without continued involvement of the original investor; examples include Chilean copper mines and Exxon's La Brea y Pariñas oil fields in Peru.[20] The large immobile facility limits the investor's alterna-

[17] Kobrin (1984).

[18] Kobrin (1980, 1984).

[19] See Lipson (1985, p. 183n). On customized versus standardized relationships between host governments and foreign firms more generally, see Encarnation and Wells (1985).

[20] The examples come from Lipson (1985, p. 264n*). However, Shafer (1983) suggests, based on analysis of copper expropriations in Zaire and Zambia, that even in extractive

tives. Moving to another location is not an option; the only choice is to renegotiate the current relationship or abandon the facility. The host's ability to continue operating limits the original investor's only counter-vailing threat: *to abandon a facility that the host cannot use profitably.* These considerations explain the high rate of expropriations in natural resource industries relative to high-tech ones.[21] Natural resource indus-tries typically involve immobile facilities and standardized technologies that do not require continuing input from the original investor for prof-itable operation. High-tech industries, in contrast, rely less on large site-specific assets and more on a continuing stream of technologically inno-vative inputs from the foreign investor.

Opportunism of this type is not limited to foreign direct investment. Vulnerability to forced renegotiations and the importance of good alter-natives for preventing such holdups apply much more broadly—indeed, *any relationship involving relation-specific investment raises the specter of opportunism.*

Relation Specificity: The Loss of Alternatives

By definition, relation-specific investment is undertaken to be used in spe-cific transactions with a specific partner; the value of such assets in alter-nate uses is low.[22] Therefore, partners in relationships involving relation-specific assets suffer a loss of alternatives. International trade leads to such investment by altering the pattern of production and investment in the participating economies.[23] Types of relation-specific investment in in-ternational trade include (i) locationally specialized trade facilities (for example, the Soviet-European gas pipeline); (ii) specialized vertical pro-duction linkages across national boundaries (for example, Canadian-U.S. links in the North American automobile industry); and (iii) dedicated as-sets in the form of export capacity (for example, Japanese automobile capacity designed to service the U.S. market).

The simplest and most obvious examples are transportation facilities specialized locationally to handle trade-oriented transport. Once such fa-cilities are built, one party may attempt to alter the terms of exchange, leaving the other with little alternative due to the investment's nonsal-vageable character. Consider the Soviet-European gas pipeline. Europe-

---

industries host governments may underestimate the importance of continuing services (or "insulation") provided by foreign investors.

[21] Lipson (1985, pp. 29, 130–131).

[22] Williamson (1985a, pp. 52–56). Relation-specific investment can occur in any durable asset, including human skills. The term *investment* is used merely to denote durability, an essential element of vulnerability to opportunism.

[23] Harris (1989, especially section 8.3) relates this to the idea of market access.

ans have exchanged technology to build the pipeline for a promise of
future Soviet natural gas exports. Once completed, the pipeline is susceptible to Soviet opportunism because the Soviets could reduce their gas
exports to Europe (for example, by a quota) and thereby reduce the value
of the pipeline to the Europeans. From the European perspective, the lack
of alternate uses for the pipeline (a relation-specific asset) implies they
could be forced to settle for less than the promised amount of gas. If pipeline maintenance requires European technology and personnel on a continuing basis, there could also be a hazard of European opportunism. It
could be possible for Europeans to demand more than the agreed-upon
quantity of Soviet natural gas exports in exchange for continued maintenance.

Note that the hazard of opportunism is *not* due to a traditional monopoly nor to the specialized purpose of the pipeline (that is, to carry natural
gas), but rather to the pipeline's specificity to a particular transaction or
relationship (Soviet-European trade in gas). The European countries do
not have a monopoly in the supply of pipeline technology, nor do the
Soviets in the supply of natural gas. *Ex ante* (before the construction of
the pipeline), many possible buyers and sellers existed. However, *ex post*
(after relation-specific investment in the pipeline), the Soviets and Europeans find themselves in a bilateral monopoly. The Soviets cannot use the
pipeline to provide non-European buyers with natural gas; and the Europeans cannot use the pipeline to obtain gas from non-Soviet suppliers.
Therefore, a breakdown of the existing relationship would cause a loss of
the asset's value. Relation specificity limits parties' alternatives even when
the transaction involves no *ex ante* monopoly based on technology or
control of unique resources.[24]

Note also that the role of asymmetry of interest or information is not
as simple as it might appear. The parties' vulnerabilities to holdup depend
on their alternatives as the relationship evolves. Identical size, interests,
and information at the beginning of an ongoing relationship do not guarantee that vulnerabilities will not emerge later. The alternatives of the
larger and apparently more powerful actor may even deteriorate more
than those of the smaller, apparently less powerful actor. If so, the pattern
of vulnerability will be different from the intuitively obvious one.[25]

[24] The appendix to this chapter compares the perspective presented here with the well-
known argument of Hirschman (1945).

[25] This occurred in the most studied example of a holdup in the new economics of organization literature. The case involved General Motors and an independently owned supplier
of auto bodies, Fisher Body. Changes in the nature of the industry altered the relationship
between the two firms in a way that allowed (small) Fisher Body to hold up (large) GM; the
resulting contractual problems led to a merger of the two firms. General Motors acquired
Fisher to control potential opportunism by the supplier. This case, one of many in which

Another example is Britain and France's joint construction of a trans-Channel tunnel. The initial contracting stage included an agreement over division of benefits and costs, both construction costs and operating expenses. Once the tunnel is operational, one country (say, France) might refuse to pay its agreed-upon share of costs or demand more than its agreed-upon share of benefits. Because the facility is relation specific, the scope for such opportunistic behavior is substantial. To exclude France from use of the tunnel, the victimized country (Britain) would have to bear alone the full operating cost of the facility. Otherwise, whatever payment it could coax from France would be better than nothing, and France's opportunism would be successful and unpunished.

Typically, countries form joint entities to manage such facilities (for example, Eurotunnel in the case of the trans-Channel tunnel). Such entities are an analogue of vertical integration and other nonstandard contracts used to handle relation-specific investments in domestic commercial transactions.[26] Although both the French and British governments refused to finance the tunnel from public funds, the project (even under strictly private funding) required a treaty between the two because of the potential for governmental opportunism.[27]

The concept of relation-specific investment is considerably broader than the pipeline and tunnel examples may suggest. A similar potential for opportunism arises if an industry in one country develops "upstream" (as an input supplier) or "downstream" (as a customer) to an industry in the trading partner.[28] If production in either industry involves relation-specific investment, one country may attempt to hold up the other. The most economically efficient location for processing ore from a mine in Country One may be across the border in Country Two. Once Country Two invests in a processing facility specialized to service One's mine, both countries face incentives to behave opportunistically. Country One may

potential opportunism affects the choice between intra-firm and market organization of transactions, is analyzed in Klein, Crawford, and Alchian (1978); Coase (1988); and Klein (1988).

[26] On nonstandard contracts, see Williamson (1985a).

[27] In addition to the usual incentives for opportunism, fears of the project being nationalized by a future British Labor Party government and of other, nongovernmental forms of opportunism also affected the negotiations. A number of design proposals were submitted, differing significantly in estimated cost. One of the primary cost determinants of various designs was whether they provided a road for automobile crossing in addition to rail crossing. Britain, long vulnerable to crippling rail strikes, favored the more costly projects that provided both automobile and rail facilities. France, on the other hand, viewed the automobile facility as too costly. The compromise calls for a rail tunnel with an option for future addition of automobile capacity. In the meantime, trains can carry automobiles across the Channel, but such capability does not alleviate the rail-strike problem.

[28] Reich (1991) provides several examples.

raise prices for its ore if the processing facility in Two has no alternate source of supply; similarly, Two may raise the price of its processing if One has no alternate processors available.[29] Note that this vulnerability is distinct from the foreign direct investment case, in which asset ownership actually crossed national boundaries. Assets, if relation specific, are vulnerable even if not located in the foreign country. The extensive vertical production linkages in the North American automobile industry, for example, required a treaty (the 1965 Auto Pact) between the United States and Canada to safeguard assets whose continuing value depended on continued cooperative production with assets across the border.[30]

The U.S. refusal (for political or security reasons) to provide replacement parts for military equipment sold to other countries presents a different example of relation-specific assets. The assets are relation specific in the sense that they must be maintained by continued trade with the United States to retain their usefulness. The United States, subsequently, has the option of exploiting its position by charging high prices for replacement parts or by providing the parts only in exchange for some concession. Of course, the United States also may refuse to provide parts on any terms, using its power in the transaction to keep the equipment out of use. Purchasers of the equipment could have bought similar non-U.S. equipment, and U.S. firms could have sold their equipment elsewhere; the initial relationship was not a monopoly *ex ante*. But once countries purchase U.S. equipment, an *ex post* bilateral monopoly results.

Relation-specific assets can take several forms; but for present purposes the most important are "dedicated assets" specialized to a particular relationship, whose loss would result in significant excess capacity and associated losses.[31] Dedicated assets are common in international trade, because the process of specialization according to comparative advantage involves investment in increased productive capacity designed to service export markets.[32] For instance, the United States computer industry has made a substantial specific investment in developing computer hardware and software capable of using Japanese *kanji* characters. The limited market for such a capability outside Japan makes Japan's ability to close its market to the technology a threat. Japan, on the other hand, has invested in capital equipment and skills necessary to produce automobiles meeting unique U.S. safety and pollution control standards. A complete closure of the U.S. automobile market to Japan could impose losses up to the value

---

[29] Alternatives always exist; the point is that they may be prohibitively costly.

[30] Acheson (1989); and Rhodes (1989) treat the Auto Pact case.

[31] Williamson (1985a, especially pp. 194–195). The view of trade liberalization based on dedicated assets is compared in the chapter appendix with the surplus-capacity hypothesis of Strange (1979) and others.

[32] See Harris (1989, especially section 8.3).

of those relation-specific assets. Such examples may sound trivial, but the sums involved can be substantial. Philips, the European electronics firm, estimated that, because of differing standards, an average of fifty to one hundred man-*years* of software engineering are required to rework computerized telecommunications exchange equipment to serve an additional European country.[33]

In each of these diverse cases, one country may be able to extract from the other an amount up to the difference between the value of the current transaction and that of the party's best alternative by threatening to withdraw from the relationship.[34] The best alternative involves a loss of at least part of the asset's value because the asset, by definition, is specific to a transaction between two particular parties. The lack of an approximately equal-valued alternative is the source of the potential for opportunism in each case.[35] A relation-specific asset renders the trading relationship irreversible, or reversible only at a cost equal to the value of the specific asset. These types of problems are particularly acute in international trade where location and geographic immobility can make investments nonsalvageable. In the presence of specific assets, opportunism poses a hazard, and cooperation (such as international trade liberalization) requires institutions to govern opportunism.

The Empirical Relevance of Relation-Specific Investment

In neoclassical trade theory, transactions occur at arm's length. If two states liberalize trade and firms in one country invest in capacity to service the other country's market, that investment can be easily dismantled or redirected should trade between the two break down. In such a world, opportunism poses no hazard, and trade liberalization requires little in the way of institutions to support cooperation. But once relation-specific assets enter, one party can hold up the other for an amount equal to the excess of the value of the current trading relationship over that of the party's best alternative.[36]

A country undertaking relation-specific investment for trade stands to lose the value of that investment should its partners impose opportunistic protection. The greater the potential return from such opportunism, the

---

[33] *Wall Street Journal* (1985, p. 32).

[34] Rhodes (1989, p. 281) outlines this type of noncooperative behavior.

[35] The analysis of relation-specificity highlights the general importance of defining no-agreement payoffs in strategic interactions (for example, are they the status quo, or worse?); see Hoekman (1989). With relation-specific investment, parties may be worse off if the relationship breaks down than if the relationship had never been undertaken.

[36] See, for example, Oye (1986b, pp. 9–11), and Rhodes' (1989, p. 297) discussion of the U.S.-Canadian relationship in the automobile industry.

stronger the safeguards (that is, assurances against opportunism) required for countries to enter liberalization agreements.

The concept of relation-specific investment generalizes vulnerability to opportunism beyond foreign direct investment and makes analysis of these issues much more important quantitatively to the study of international trade. In effect, *trade involving relation-specific investment blurs the line between trade and investment.* If such trade is widespread, this implies that the compliance and governance issues we raise are significant factors affecting institutional forms of trade policy. The broadening of the possibility for opportunism also blurs the distinction between political risks and commercial risks; but this is consistent with legal treatment of such matters.[37]

Even more importantly, such broadening is appropriate given the character of modern international trade, which is increasingly dominated by trade not conducted at arm's length.[38] Before accepting the assertion that relation-specific investment and the governance problems to which it leads influence the organizational form of international trade policy, consider some empirical evidence on the importance of such investment.

Ideally, one would like a reliable empirical measure of the magnitude of relation-specific investment in trade for each sector of the world economy and for each pair of trading partners. Unfortunately, such measures are not available and unlikely to become available. The reason for the paucity of data is evident from the definition of relation-specific investment. The concept does not lend itself to easy empirical quantification from statistics existing in either firms' accounting data or nations' balance-of-payments or national-income-accounts data. Measurement of relation-specific investment in a particular industry is a highly detailed process and, so far, has been heavily reliant on economists' efforts to gather survey data from production specialists in a given industry.[39]

Not only are the most obviously desirable data unavailable, but other "obvious" pieces of empirical evidence, while available, are potentially

---

[37] The distinction between political and commercial risk plays a central role in Lipson's (1985) analysis of the historical evolution of policies for protecting foreign capital. For example, the Hickenlooper amendment covering U.S. responses to foreign expropriations of U.S. private assets was explicitly amended in 1963 to include contract nullification as expropriation subject to the amendment's specified remedies (Lipson [1985, p. 211]).

[38] McKeown (1991, especially pp. 165–167) provides an excellent though brief overview of the important implications of non-arm's-length trade.

[39] The best-known estimates and analyses are for the automobile industry (Monteverde and Teece [1982]; Masten, Meehan, and Snyder [1989]), the aerospace industry (Masten [1984]), the electronic components industry (Anderson and Schmittlein [1984]), the aluminum industry (Stuckey [1983]), electric utilities and coal production (Joskow [1985, 1987, 1988]), petroleum coke (Goldberg and Erickson [1987]), natural gas (Mulherin [1986]), railroad shipping (Palay [1984, 1985]), and tuna fishing (Gallick [1984]).

misleading. It may seem that the importance of opportunism, compliance, and governance-structure issues could be ascertained by examining the incidence of "cheating" in various agreements.[40] However, if the strategic organizational approach is correct, cheating would not necessarily be observed. The key point of the strategic organizational argument is that when opportunism is a hazard *ex post*, parties will design agreements with governance structures sufficient to protect them from one another's opportunism. Therefore, opportunism will be observed only when the parties are "wrong" in one of three senses: (i) parties may have perceived incorrectly that opportunism would not be a problem in the particular transaction and proceeded to undertake the transaction with no safeguards; (ii) parties may have underestimated the potential for opportunism and created safeguards that proved to be insufficient; or (iii) parties may have overestimated the strength of the governance structure they created when entering the transaction. To the extent parties perceive threats *ex ante* and take those threats into account when designing their agreement, no *ex post* opportunism will be observed *even if the threat of opportunism is the deciding factor in the institutional form of the agreement.*[41] Thus, in seeking appropriate empirical measures, we must avoid inappropriate ones that may lead to erroneous conclusions.

Short of costly efforts to gather industry-level data of the type mentioned above, how can the empirical relevance of relation-specific investment in international trade be assessed? One way is to "piggyback" on the efforts of scholars working in industrial organization. A major finding of modern industrial organization is that relation-specific investment is a primary determinant of decisions by firms to integrate activities within the firm in place of market transactions.[42] When a given activity involves the firm in significant relation-specific investment, that activity tends to be integrated within the firm. By integrating the transaction, the firm reduces the hazard of opportunism below the level present in an arm's-length market transaction because both parties are brought under a common governance structure (one firm). This finding provides not only an explanation for much of domestic industrial organization, but also the

[40] Examples of attempts to gather and analyze such data are found in Keohane (1988b); Grieco (1990); and Haufler (1991).

[41] For example, banks usually require collateral for automobile loans to prevent opportunistic non-repayment. Although a very small proportion of automobile loans are not repaid, one would not want to claim that the rarity of non-repayment implied the potential for opportunism was not the primary motive for the institution of collateral.

[42] Williamson (1985a); and Joskow (1988). Citations to the famous General Motors-Fisher Body merger literature are in footnote 25; references to studies of other industries are in footnote 39. Further discussion can be found in Chapter Six.

central element in modern theories of multinationalism by firms.[43] It suggests that one indirect measure of trade involving relation-specific investment (and therefore the compliance and governance issues concerning us) is international trade that occurs within the firm, or what is known as *intra-firm trade*. Simply put, if transactions involving relation-specific assets tend to be integrated within the firm, such trade provides one indirect measure of the extent of relation-specific investment in trade.

Therefore, it makes sense to ask, how important is international intra-firm trade? According to McKeown, "Heterodox transactional forms—countertrade and intra-firm trade—have become a significant proportion of global trade. This development . . . seems to be the most noteworthy characteristic of the current era."[44] One set of estimates puts intra-firm trade as a share of total U.S. merchandise trade at 40.2 percent in 1977, 36.6 percent in 1982, and 38.2 percent in 1987.[45] If trade between parent firms and affiliates is defined more broadly, the figures rise to two-thirds of U.S. merchandise trade for 1987.[46] So between one-third and two-thirds of all U.S. merchandise trade over the last fifteen years has consisted of shipments between firms and their affiliates—shipments modern industrial organization theory and evidence suggest are motivated by relation specificity. Table 2.1 provides an alternate, but similar set of estimates for the United States, along with Japan and the United Kingdom. The evidence indicates a significant share of world trade contains elements of relation-specific investment substantial enough to cause firms to favor vertical integration over arm's-length market transactions and over nonstandard contracts.[47]

What are the implications? First, just as recognition of the importance of intra-firm organization has refocused modern industrial organization,

[43] Rugman (1981); Caves (1982); Casson (1987); Gatignon and Anderson (1988); Contractor and Lorange (1988); and Eden (1991). Milner (1988b,c) links intra-firm trade to multinationals and to trade liberalization, but does not address the source of or reason for intra-firm trade.

[44] McKeown (1991, p. 151).

[45] Hipple (1990a,b).

[46] *Wall Street Journal* (1990a).

[47] The possibility of using nonstandard contracts to protect vulnerable relation-specific assets implies that only *highly* vulnerable assets are integrated within the firm (Williamson [1985a]). Therefore, intra-firm trade is a *conservative* proxy for relation-specific investment in trade; that is, not all trade involving such investment is intra-firm trade. One less conservative proxy is intra-industry trade in intermediate products or components. Lake (1991, p. 116) argues that closure of intra-industry trade imposes lower costs than closure of intersectoral trade. This is true only if intra-industry trade takes the form of trade in highly substitutable products (for example, Saab automobiles for Volvos), but *not* if trade takes the form of vertical production linkages (for example, trade in unique auto components assembled in one country and exported as finished autos to countries from which the components came).

Country	Share of Intra-firm Transactions in International Trade
United States	
Exports	
1977	29.3
1982	23.0
1985	31.0
Imports	
1977	42.2
1982	38.4
1985	40.1
Japan	
Exports	
1980	25.8
1983	31.8
Imports	
1980	42.1
1983	30.3
United Kingdom	
Exports	
1981	30.0

Table 2.1: Intra-firm Transactions as a Share of International Trade for the United States, Japan, and the United Kingdom. *Source*: McKeown (1991); data from United Nations (1988, p. 92).

recognition of the intra-firm or non-arm's-length character of much of international trade has become essential to understand international trade policy. Second, transactions, trading partners, and historical periods become importantly unique, not identical as in neoclassical trade theory. History matters, and this includes the microanalytics of history as well as its broad scope.[48] Third, the issue of transparency of transactions

[48] Although this book focuses on the broad sweep of modern trade history, it reflects a

and trade policies becomes more crucial and complex. Rules may have to recognize the special character of unique ongoing trade relationships; in this case, a "one-size-fits-all" approach is no longer feasible. Finally, the degree of openness or protectionism becomes less obvious as institutions grow more varied and less transparent. Therefore, the growth of non-arm's-length trade carries important implications for the study of international trade policy.

Before analyzing the institutions of trade policy as responses to relation-specific investment and potential opportunism, we need to address the sources of opportunism in international trade.

Sources of Opportunism

A firm entering international trade requiring specific investment faces two potential levels of opportunism: (i) the trading-partner *firm* may threaten to halt trade to alter the prices at which trade occurs, and (ii) either *state* may alter the relationship by imposing trade restrictions. These sources of potential opportunism, private and state-sponsored, require two sets of institutional safeguards. As a result, adequate governance structures for international transactions require a more diverse and sophisticated range of institutions than otherwise comparable transactions within a single country.

In the case of private opportunism by firms, governance structures take the form of nonstandard contracting of the types studied intensively in the new economics of organization literature.[49] These private nonstandard contracts rely on issue linkages and hostages as safeguards and, in an international context, take forms such as joint ventures, long-term licensing agreements, and multinationalism.[50]

Private contractual arrangements between firms are of less use in limiting opportunistic changes in government policies.[51] Controlling this second layer or second source of opportunism requires analogous safeguards. Theoretically, a government could directly promise a firm or industry that no opportunistic trade restrictions or other policy manipulations would be attempted. However, the difficulty private parties have

---

first cut at research on a new question rather than a conviction that microanalytic details are unimportant.

[49] Major contributions are summarized in Williamson (1985a).

[50] Safeguards and securing contractual integrity are central to modern theories of multinationalism; see, for example, Rugman (1981); Caves (1982); Casson (1987); and Contractor and Lorange (1988).

[51] This is not to argue that firms have no effect on governmental policies. See Milner (1988b,c); and Milner and Yoffie (1989).

enforcing contracts against a sovereign state, especially a foreign one, limits the credibility of government-firm contracts.[52]

An obvious alternative to hard-to-enforce government-firm contracts is an agreement between governments concerning the aspects of policy that impact most directly on foreign trade. To guard against state-sponsored opportunism, states can enter the public-sector equivalent of private nonstandard contractual arrangements; the institutions providing this second set of safeguards are the focus here. The extent of the burden borne by these safeguards depends on the ease of detection of violations of agreements and on the availability of efficacious enforcement.

Detection

At first glance, the problem of detecting opportunistic violations of trade agreements appears trivial. After all, governments and international organizations collect mountains of trade statistics; tariff lists are publicly available; and the possibility of tracing goods through customs exists. However, several factors make this observation misleading.

First, there is no international consensus about whether a trade agreement automatically becomes domestic law in signatory countries. Usually, international agreements have no direct effects but must be converted into domestic law and enforced domestically.[53] This additional step introduces a chance for individual states to alter the terms of an agreement through definitional changes as well as explicit reservations about specific terms.[54] The result can be a signed agreement embodying differences among the signatories over acceptable behaviors under the (now multiple) terms. The U.S. Congress, for example, has periodically altered the domestic status of agreements reached through GATT negotiations.[55] Detecting violations under such conditions becomes a non-trivial problem.

---

[52] See, for example, Grandy (1989). Private firms can and do respond to state opportunism against both foreign direct investment and international trade, often preferring to negotiate quietly than to bring in the home government of the aggrieved party. In international law, the Calvo doctrine, elaborated by Argentinean jurist Carlos Calvo in 1868, asserts that foreign firms should be treated co-equally with domestic ones and should, therefore, be unable to enlist the assistance of their home-country governments in disputes with a host state (Lipson [1985, pp. xvi, 80, 122–123, 282]).

[53] See Piccioto (1984, p. 172); and Garrett (1990, p. 26) on the EC.

[54] Putnam (1988, p. 437n29).

[55] Baldwin (1984a). To cite just two examples: During the Kennedy Round of GATT talks, the United States signed a code on antidumping practices as an Executive Agreement. Congress objected it had not approved the code and passed a law directing the International Trade Commission to ignore it in making injury determinations in dumping cases (Robert E. Baldwin [1979, p. 13]). The 98th U.S. Congress considered a trade bill with provisions

Trade agreements, like domestic contracts, are not intended to be binding under all circumstances. A well-established principle of contract law recognizes situations in which, due to unforeseeable changes in circumstance, it is impossible or in no one's interest to honor a contract.[56] Failure to perform in such situations (for example, if an entertainer dies before a scheduled concert or a transportation strike makes timely delivery of promised goods impossible) is termed *discharge* rather than *breach*. Parties may disagree over whether performing is impossible (allowing discharge) or whether a party is claiming impossibility to breach the contract without punishment. For example, a country promising unrestricted imports of an agricultural product might later claim the product is tainted with a dangerous chemical, pesticide, or disease and close its market to imports. In a typical melodramatic episode between Canada and the United States during a period of depressed prices for most U.S. agricultural products, three northern states halted Canadian hog imports, claiming they had been treated with an unapproved antibiotic. Canadian producers denied use of the antibiotic, calling the states' action opportunistic protectionism; and U.S. producers had, in fact, been pressing for relief from the effects of Canadian exports. A similar dispute within the European Community hinged on members' rights to restrict British beef imports due to a 1990 outbreak of "mad cow disease." Detecting whether a country is acting opportunistically or in good faith in such circumstances may be difficult, costly, or impossible.

A third factor hampering detection of opportunistic behavior under trade agreements is more obvious: inability to define precisely behaviors that are or are not permissible. A brief list of recent trade disputes should suffice to illustrate this point. The United States and the European Community have a longstanding argument over which "domestic" policies are export subsidies and therefore proscribed under the GATT.[57] Do controlled natural gas prices in the United States constitute a subsidy to exported goods that use gas as an input? What about export credits at low interest rates, and at what levels do interest rates become "artificially" low? Is government subsidized or insured research and development an export subsidy for subsequently developed commercial products? Within the EC, different exchange rates to finance different activities, particularly agricultural trade at "green rates," causes disagreement, because an artificial exchange rate can have the same impact as an export subsidy. Non-

---

whose status was uncertain under existing international trade agreements; but an amendment preventing the bill from taking effect should it be found not to conform with those agreements was overwhelmingly defeated (Czinkota and Ronkainen [1988, p. 30]). Compliance problems are not new; Keohane (1988b) treats several historical examples.

[56] See, for example, Kronman (1978).

[57] On subsidies, see Hufbauer and Erb (1984); and Finger (1987a).

tariff barriers (NTBs), generally more opaque than tariffs, present particular problems since they are less adequately covered by the GATT and more intertwined with domestic policies and politics.

Transshipment under quantitative restrictions (that is, clandestine rerouting through unrestricted third countries) provides a classic case of another opportunistic violation that may be exceedingly difficult to detect or prove. For example, Britain has claimed Japan circumvented its voluntary restraint on automobile exports to Britain by shipping from Australia.[58] As firms increasingly undertake different stages of manufacturing in different countries, defining a good's country of origin becomes more difficult. Recent controversies over "screwdriver" plants illustrate this problem.[59] The intra-EC dispute over how to treat automobiles produced at the Honda plant in Britain is just one example of many.

Analogous detection problems plague disputes in the foreign investment area. Replacement of sudden, blatant, economy-wide nationalizations with selective, subtle, and "creeping" expropriation of foreign direct investments blurs the meaning of *expropriation* and taxes dispute-settlement procedures.[60] Even in portfolio lending, distinguishing reliably between genuine illiquidity or insolvency and subtle efforts to escape or postpone repayment opportunistically is difficult.[61]

After an opportunistic violation of an agreement is established, terminating the practice or imposing punishment remains a problem in the face of national sovereignty. The combined problems of detection and enforcement make opportunism a real threat to cooperation.

Enforcement

The negotiated reduction of trade barriers, like any form of contracting, is dependent on the availability of low-cost and effective enforcement. States typically have been unwilling to concede meaningful judicial or policy powers to international organizations, especially powers to impose punitive sanctions against opportunistic behavior. Because parties in trade disputes often are sovereign nations, limits on penalties are even more severe than contract enforcement problems among private contracting parties. For example, the GATT contracting parties have exhibited a persistent inability to agree on effective dispute-settlement procedures.[62]

[58] Cowhey and Long (1983, p. 178).

[59] Reich (1991) contains examples.

[60] Lipson (1985, pp. 122, 182).

[61] Lipson (1985, pp. 48–49).

[62] Ironically, the same enforcement problems that plague attempts at multilateral trade liberalization also hamper attempts at multilateral trade restrictions. The Coordinating Committee for Multilateral Export Controls (COCOM), which endeavors to keep strategic

These questions go to the heart of the nature of international law. States, by nature of their sovereignty, may declare disputes "political" rather than "legal" and thereby render them nonjusticiable and exempt from final legal settlement under international law. The legal principles of *pacta sunt servanda* (treaties are binding contracts and to be observed) and *rebus sic stantibus* (substantial changes in conditions negate treaty obligations) are potentially incompatible. Japan explicitly uses the latter doctrine in many of its commercial treaties.[63] This clause, permitting agreements to be broken if unexpected changes make honoring them undesirable, is unpopular with Japan's trading partners; and its status in international law is murky.

Moves in more blatant disregard of international law, especially if repeated, are likely to carry costs in a state system where relatively few actors engage in repeated interaction; state interests typically are not served by ignoring rules and norms.[64] Even political realists granted this long before the formal analysis of reputation appeared in the economic literature.[65] For example, Hans Morgenthau concluded that nations comply with their treaties because "a nation that has the reputation of reneging on its commercial obligations will find it hard to conclude commercial treaties beneficial to itself."[66]

Although important even in domestic contexts, questions related to reliance on formal law versus self-help or private ordering obviously become more troublesome in the international sphere. The extent to which even formal law rests necessarily on the foundation of a sovereign over all parties—or evolves spontaneously as needed by contracting parties—has yet to be explicated fully.[67] However, it is easy to overemphasize the domestic-international dichotomy, since doctrines of impossibility, unconscionability, or duress that allow discharge rather than breach are central to controversies in domestic contract law.[68]

---

and high-technology Western goods away from the East, is a voluntary organization with no sanctioning power over its fifteen members for violations of agreed export bans. The result has been a notable lack of success in achieving the group's collective aim, even prior to easing East-West tensions. The U.S. Omnibus Trade and Competitiveness Act of 1988, in response to Toshiba Machine Company's violations, imposes mandatory sanctions for future violators of COCOM restrictions and permits the U.S. attorney general to sue violators for damages up to the cost of restoring U.S. military readiness.

[63] Millar (1984, p. 2).

[64] Keohane (1984, pp. 76–77, 258); and Hall and Ikenberry (1989, p. 95). See also Strange (1988, p. 40).

[65] Kreps and Wilson (1982); and Milgrom and Roberts (1982) provide formal analyses of the role of reputation.

[66] Morgenthau (1967 [1948], p. 283). On the role of reputation, see Keohane (1984, pp. 26, 105–106, 116).

[67] See Benson (1989); and Ellickson (1991).

[68] Williamson (1985a, pp. 397–401). Cooter and Ulen (1988, Chapters Six and Seven)

Absence of a simple, effective, low-cost "legal" framework within which trade disputes between sovereign states can be settled poses challenging contracting problems. In some circumstances, violation of a trade-liberalization agreement by one party may leave others worse off. To the extent parties recognize opportunism hazards *ex ante*, safeguards can be built into the structure of agreements; such practices should vary directly with the hazard of opportunism.[69] Based on this insight, the strategic organizational perspective offers the possibility of a unified, institutionally focused explanation of observed variety in international trade organization.

Opportunism, Safeguards, and Organizational Form

The link between the hazard of opportunism and benefits to particular trade-liberalization arrangements implies that different forms of trade institutions should be successful under different conditions.[70] These conditions reflect, first, the presence or absence of relation-specific assets and, second, the presence or absence of effective third-party enforcement, as illustrated in Figure 2.1.

		Specific Trade-Related Investment?	
		No	Yes
Effective 3rd-Party Enforcement?	No	No opportunism; Few safeguards	Opportunism problem; Internal safeguards
	Yes		Opportunism problem; External safeguards

Figure 2.1: Determinants of international opportunism and safeguards.

provide an economics-oriented discussion of contract enforcement and defenses against breach. Kronman and Posner (1979) present more analysis of the various doctrines.

[69] Williamson (1985a) argues that transactions must be "dimensionalized" according to the key characteristics of their vulnerabilities to opportunism and, therefore, the type of institutional arrangements that will support them. Similarly, North and Weingast (1988, p. 6) note the close match between incentive problems and kinds of institutional control.

[70] As a reminder, we are interested *not* in location along the free trade-protectionism continuum in Figure 1.2, but rather in the form of trade liberalization. Either liberalization or protection can take unilateral, bilateral, multilateral, or minilateral forms.

With little relation-specific investment, trade opportunism presents few problems, and safeguards can be minimal. The left-hand side of Figure 2.1 represents this situation. Lack of relation specificity implies that an attempted holdup would provide little bargaining power to the opportunistic party. The victim, on the other hand, possesses an effective means of self-help: unilateral withdrawal from the relationship, because continuity is not highly valued.

If relation-specific investment has been undertaken, a relationship becomes more subject to opportunistic behavior. With specific investment and no third-party enforcement (the upper right-hand corner of Figure 2.1), opportunism presents a significant problem. If conditions change, requiring adaptation of the relationship, each party has an incentive to hold out for more favorable terms. Because of the uniqueness of the relationship, unilateral action cannot provide either party with a satisfactory alternative in event of a breakdown. There is a high premium on continuity, so unilateral withdrawal as self-help no longer provides an adequate governance structure. The relationship is mutually beneficial, but each party can hold up the other for better terms. Strong safeguards are required; and, lacking effective third-party enforcement, the governance must be internal to the relationship. In particular, agreements must be structured in such a way to impose automatic punishment on violators. Possible arrangements involve three types of safeguards: (i) *ex ante* alignment of parties' incentives, using issue linkages and hostages;[71] (ii) creation of special damage-limiting governance structures, such as third-party arbitration, for dispute resolution; and (iii) deliberate "trading regularities that support and signal continuity intentions,"[72] of which the most common is reciprocity. These safeguards create a special relationship between the parties, with unique incentives, dispute-settlement procedures, and regularities or norms of behavior.

With specific investments and effective third-party enforcement (the lower right-hand corner of Figure 2.1), opportunism is a problem but safeguards can be external to the relationship because self-help is unnecessary.[73] A third party to adjudicate disputes reliably and impose appropriate sanctions allows agreements themselves to carry a much lighter burden.

The interplay of the safeguards, with the varying degrees of relation-specific investment involved in different transactions, provides the stra-

[71] Kronman (1985) provides an extensive discussion of the efficacy of hostages or bonds in a world of self-help or private ordering.

[72] Williamson (1985a, p. 34).

[73] Young (1978, pp. 256–258) discusses the potential for third-party enforcement in international relations.

tegic organizational explanation for observed organizational variety and, implicitly, institutional change.

STRATEGIC ORGANIZATIONAL FORM IN TRADE LIBERALIZATION

The general categories of organizational form in Figure 2.1 correspond to observed international trade policies in Figure 2.2. With little investment in relation-specific assets for trade (the left-hand side of Figure 2.2), opportunistic protection is unlikely, and *unilateral* liberalization is viable either with or without third-party enforcement. Arguably, such a situation characterized mid-nineteenth-century Britain, which pursued unilateral liberalization.[74]

With investment in specific trade-related assets (the right-hand side of Figure 2.2), liberalization takes on vulnerability characteristics reminiscent of a Prisoners' Dilemma, and *unilateral* liberalization is not viable. Cooperation or liberalization may still emerge in one of three forms represented in the right-hand side of Figure 2.2. Without effective third-party enforcement (for example, a hegemon or efficacious supranational enforcement institutions), cooperation can arise through self-enforcing agreements using issue linkages, hostages, and repeated play. These

		Specific Trade-Related Investment?	
		No	Yes
Effective 3rd-Party Enforcement?	No	UNILATERAL trade policy (e.g., 19th-century Britain)	BILATERAL trade policy (e.g., 1970-90)
	Yes		MULTILATERAL trade policy (e.g., 1945-65) OR MINILATERAL trade policy (e.g., Europe 1992)

Figure 2.2: Organizational variety in international trade in response to variations in specific trade-related investment and availability of effective third-party enforcement.

[74] The role of hegemony, along with the British and U.S. cases, is the subject of Chapter Three.

mechanisms strengthen capacities for self-help by automatically imposing costs on actors who behave opportunistically. The mechanisms themselves become unwieldy and ineffectual in large-group situations; thus they dictate what we call *bilateral* approaches to liberalization (the upper right-hand cell of Figure 2.2).[75]

The other two possibilities, represented in the lower right-hand cell of Figure 2.2 rely on third-party enforcement. In one case, a hegemon can enhance cooperation by acting as a third-party enforcement mechanism, as in the U.S. support of the *multilateral* GATT system following World War II.[76] Alternatively, small groups of countries can authorize supranational dispute-settlement institutions and create a form of *minilateral* cooperation such as that currently underway within the European Community under the Single Europe Act.[77]

Summary

This chapter suggests a unified strategic organizational explanation of observed institutional variety in international trade liberalization. International trade-liberalization agreements can present substantial contracting problems. If international specialization and exchange are potentially mutually beneficial, one may expect the development of institutions to support trade by assuring contractual integrity. Observed institutional variety can then be viewed as the reflection of alternate governance structures for international contracting. The strategic organizational approach focuses on the extent of relation-specific investments and the presence or absence of third-party enforcement mechanisms as determinants of contracting problems and, therefore, the form of successful trade agreements. The next three chapters explore the circumstances under which the strategic organizational perspective suggests unilateral, bilateral, minilateral, and multilateral liberalization in several episodes from trade history.

[75] Chapter Four treats bilateral approaches to trade liberalization. The defining characteristics of bilateral trade policy are in footnote 14 of Chapter One.

[76] Keohane's (1990) definition of multilateralism is much broader than the one used here; see footnote 9 in Chapter One.

[77] Chapter Five examines minilateral trade liberalization.

CHAPTER TWO APPENDIX

IN ATTEMPTING to make the strategic organizational argument clear and understandable, we have deliberately avoided lengthy digressions on the relationship between our argument and existing related literatures. This Appendix serves as partial remedy for that neglect. No single perspective can elucidate adequately the observed array of trade policies. We now turn to comparing and contrasting assumptions, strengths, weaknesses, and implications with several alternate approaches: Susan Strange's surplus-capacity explanation for protection, Albert Hirschman's national-power theory of trade policy, and Joseph Grieco's realist explanation of trade outcomes.[1]

RELATION SPECIFICITY VERSUS SURPLUS CAPACITY

Strange and others have put forward surplus capacity as an explanation for increased protectionist pressures and decreased momentum in trade liberalization.[2] They argue that when an industry's productive capacity exceeds demand at remunerative prices for a sustained period (not merely at a stage of the business cycle), anti-liberalization pressure rises. Proponents argue that surplus capacity has increased recently due to increases in the capital intensity of production, the number of industrialized or industrializing countries, and the pace of change in demands for manufactured products due to shocks such as changes in petroleum prices.[3]

As noted earlier, a major form of relation-specific investment in trade consists of dedicated assets—or productive capacity designed for trade with a specific partner so the loss of that market results in losses through excess capacity. Surplus capacity is similar to the presence of dedicated assets in that both imply a loss of asset value due to a loss of markets. The surplus-capacity literature emphasizes the tendency of industries that find themselves in a situation of surplus capacity to exert pressure for government assistance through trade barriers. In other words, the surplus-capacity perspective predicts that markets will be less open when important industries find themselves facing significant surplus capacity.[4]

---

[1] Chapter Three compares our perspective with the hegemonic stability hypothesis. Chapter Six examines the relationship between the strategic organizational approach and the new economics of organization.

[2] Strange (1979); Strange and Tooze (1980); Tsoukalis and da Silva Ferreira (1980); and Cowhey and Long (1983).

[3] Cowhey and Long (1983, p. 163).

[4] The surplus capacity argument is, in this sense, a longer-run version of the business-cycle theories of trade outlined in Chapter One.

With a primary interest in the perceived hazard of opportunism *ex ante* and its effect on the form of trade liberalization, the focus of the strategic organizational approach is different. The presence of dedicated assets in international trade implies the possibility of losing markets that would result in excess capacity. The possibility of such a future outcome becomes important since the prospect alone (whether or not it materializes) lessens willingness to enter certain types of trade-liberalizing agreements, in particular those that provide inadequate safeguards against opportunism by trading partners. So even if surplus capacity does not emerge, dedicated assets exert an influence on the trading system by altering the types of agreements to which countries are willing to commit.

STRATEGIC ORGANIZATION VERSUS NATIONAL-POWER TRADE POLICY

Hirschman examined national power as a goal of trade policy, implying the importance to each state of gains *relative* to other states.[5] The primary tool of a power policy, according to Hirschman, was fostering a monopoly position in one's exports (implying vulnerability of one's trading partners to trade stoppages) and avoiding a monopoly position in one's import suppliers (implying lack of vulnerability to stoppages). The ability to monopolize trade in certain products was viewed as technologically determined, with market size also being an important consideration.

There are three major differences between our strategic organizational analysis and the national-power analysis of Hirschman. First, the assumed purpose of international trade differs. Hirschman explored the possibility of a power-oriented international trade policy that could involve steps inconsistent with wealth- or income-maximization. We do not wish to argue here over the pros and cons of the wealth-maximization goal versus the power goal. Nonetheless, the distinction is important in comparing our argument with that of Hirschman.

The strategic organizational perspective assumes that trade liberalization increases total world income, implying that, in a world of zero transaction costs, all countries could agree to eliminate trade barriers. Of course, transaction costs are positive; and, as a result, domestic special-interest groups exert pressure for protection. States' responses to these domestic political realities raise hazards of opportunistic protectionism. When such opportunism occurs, the "victimized" country may be worse off than without the liberalization agreement. This will be true if the country invested in relation-specific assets for trade that provide the partner country with the basis for a holdup. Neither country can credibly

---

[5] Hirschman (1945). For a critique, see Wagner (1988). Also see Powell (1991), and Snidal (1991).

promise *ex ante* not to behave opportunistically; and this barrier can prevent a mutually beneficial transaction (that is, trade liberalization) from occurring. The goal, then, is to arrive at some type of institutional arrangement for credible commitments to compliance and remove the block to completing the mutually beneficial transaction. The vulnerability to opportunism inheres in the desired activity (liberalization) and the goal in the strategic organizational view is to *break* the link.

The Hirschman perspective is quite different. The goal of the power policy is to *foster* partners' vulnerabilities in order to act opportunistically. The trade involved in such a power policy might not itself be beneficial, but merely serve to create a dependency that could then be exploited. If the goal of trade were solely to foster exploitable dependency, trade presumably would impose costs on the opportunist during the "setup" period, and expected subsequent power gains would have to offset these costs. This limitation is important, because any power gains are short-lived—based on the victim's inability to find alternate sources of trade, a condition that would not last forever.

This point suggests a second distinction between our argument and that of Hirschman. The deliberate fostering of dependence that can then be exploited requires an asymmetry of information between the parties about the relationship. The intended victim must be either unaware of the danger being plotted or so desperate to trade with the opportunist that the potential danger is ignored. The strategic organizational framework, on the other hand, does not rely on such an asymmetry of information.[6] Both parties are assumed to be aware of potential opportunism that might result from a particular agreement. The point is that when the potential for opportunism exists and is known *ex ante*, the agreement will take a form that can secure against the opportunism. For a mutually beneficial transaction, parties have an incentive to design arrangements to bolster the agreement, just as lenders and borrowers use arrangements (for example, collateral) to deter opportunistic non-repayment.

A third, more subtle difference is in the assumed source of asset specificity. For Hirschman, a country wants to be a monopolist in its export markets and a competitor in its import markets. Technology, along with the relative sizes of markets, determines these market structures. Relation-specific investment is a broader category than technology-based monopoly. As noted earlier in the Soviet-European pipeline example, specific investment can transform *any* relationship into a bilateral monopoly. The importance of these issues is larger in the strategic organizational ap-

---

[6] We do not deny the importance of information asymmetry, but we minimize reliance on it as an explanation because it tends to lead to nonrefutability. On the role of deception as a result of asymmetric information, see Keohane (1984, pp. 92–95).

proach than it would appear based on the few true technological monopolies of strategic minerals, unique patents, and such. As noted earlier in
the chapter, evidence indicates that relation-specific investment is important in between one-third and two-thirds of U.S. trade. Relation-specific
investment transforms an otherwise competitive situation into a monopoly subject to opportunism.

Neoliberal Institutionalism versus Realism

In the longstanding debate between realists and neoliberal institutionalists over the nature of and prospects for international cooperation, Joseph
Grieco argues that neoliberal institutionalism cannot explain trade policy
outcomes.[7] He asserts that a realist perspective is required, one which
recognizes that "states are fundamentally concerned about their physical
survival and their political independence."[8] Each state is then a "defensive
positionalist," unwilling to enter agreements that might provide *relative*
benefits to trading partners in spite of absolute benefits to itself.

In support of his thesis, Grieco examines the codes negotiated as part
of the Tokyo Round of GATT talks. He characterizes the various code
provisions as successful or unsuccessful and correlates the success or lack
thereof with United States-European Community cooperation in the negotiations.[9] The extent of U.S.-EC cooperation depends on (i) the perceived allocation of expected benefits and (ii) the sensitivity to any perceived imbalance in that allocation (that is, realist considerations). Grieco
dismisses the possibility of differential vulnerability to opportunism in the
various issue areas (or "cheating," in his terminology) as a potential explanation—an example of the inferiority of neoliberal institutionalism
compared with realism.[10]

However, the neorealist perspective as articulated by Grieco has several
disadvantages. Except in the unusual circumstance in which benefits are
allocated on a precise fifty-fifty basis, there will be a relative gainer and
loser in each agreement. This implies that the only feasible agreements are
(i) those that satisfy the fifty-fifty criterion (either naturally or based on

[7] Grieco (1990). Despite this central point, many of Grieco's "realist" conclusions (particularly those in the book's final chapter) are exactly those of neoliberal institutionalism.
Major works in the realist tradition include Carr (1964); Waltz (1959, 1979); Morganthau
(1967 [1948]); and Gilpin (1975, 1981); recent developments are discussed in Keohane
(1986a). Contributions in the neoliberal institutionalist tradition include Axelrod (1984);
Keohane (1984); and Oye (1986a).

[8] Grieco (1990, p. 10).

[9] A wide spectrum of analysts characterize the code provisions covering customs valuation and import-licensing procedures as successful and those covering subsidies, technical
trade barriers, and government procurement as unsuccessful.

[10] Grieco (1990, p. 19).

side-payments) and (ii) those in areas where the parties are insensitive to distribution of gains. Agreements in class (i) are presumably few, and Grieco states explicitly that those in class (ii) are few, if any.[11] Such a perspective appears to underestimate substantially the potential for co-operation in the trade area. In addition, Grieco's realist perspective is unable to explain the key phenomenon of interest here, that is, not why free trade sometimes prevails and protection sometimes prevails, but rather, why trade liberalization takes such different forms.

Grieco's dismissal of the institutional perspective seems premature. The successful codes, those covering customs valuation and import licensing, cover well-specified trade procedures in which deviations from the specified rules would be relatively easy to detect.[12] The ease of detection and the definitional, across-the-board character of the rules limit potential reneging on these codes. Holding out from compliance would be unlikely to produce more favorable terms, because the changes introduced in the codes deal primarily with harmonization issues in relative isolation from specific industries and interest groups. Because of these characteristics, even the relatively weak enforcement mechanisms within the post–hegemony GATT are sufficient to support cooperation in the customs-valuation and import-licensing codes.

The less successful codes, on the other hand, attempt to cover issues that offer much greater potential for opportunism. Subsidies, technical barriers, and government procurement do not lend themselves to clear, definitional rules. Lines dividing policies that do or do not comprise subsidies are notoriously difficult to draw because subsidies can occur at any stage of the production process, be indirect, and even occur through use of different exchange rates. Technical barriers to trade are subject to manipulation because of their foundation in "domestic" policies; for example, how does one decide whether a trade restriction is based in "legitimate" domestic regulatory or safety concerns or in a desire for subtle protection? Government procurement is infamous for its lack of transparency, even in a strictly domestic context. Government contracts often involve large relation-specific investments in research and development, prototype production, and technological innovation to meet unique standards. Combined with security-based restrictions on information, sealed bidding procedures, and long-term relationships between government agencies and the few firms producing many of the relevant goods, large relation-specific investments imply that international rules for government procurement face enormous compliance-based problems. These

---

[11] Grieco (1990, pp. 46–47).

[12] This is not to say that disputes cannot arise under these codes. For a case dealing with customs valuation, see Yarbrough and Yarbrough (1991b, pp. 231–233).

codes, then, attempt to cover issues that present more serious governance problems than do the customs-valuation and import-licensing codes.[13] The result has been relatively weak agreements, reflecting the unwillingness of parties to commit themselves to stronger terms without more effective detection and enforcement mechanisms. All this evidence is consistent with the strategic organizational approach.

The strategic organizational approach is, in Grieco's terminology, a neoliberal institutionalist one: States find it hard to cooperate in trade liberalization because, in the environment in which they operate, detection of opportunism is difficult and enforcement is problematic. When trade involves relation-specific investments, trading partners are vulnerable to one another's opportunism. Holdups can alter *ex post* the agreed-on terms of an agreement. States recognize these vulnerabilities and are unwilling to enter agreements that fail to provide adequate safeguards against such *ex post* reallocations. Nevertheless, international institutions, by providing the needed safeguards, can improve the prospects for cooperation (for example, by making agreements self enforcing).

We do not argue that states will pursue free trade; the realities of domestic politics with transaction costs dictate nontrivial levels of protection, even when free trade could maximize national income. Neither do we argue that states are indifferent to the allocation of benefits from agreements, particularly when the initially agreed-on allocation is vulnerable to *ex post* alteration. In some situations and some issue areas, states may be unable or unwilling to cooperate, and inability to agree on a distribution of the available gains may be a major source of problems.

We argue instead that, in those areas in which states *do* choose to liberalize trade, they do so in ways that recognize the special strategic organizational problems they face. The precise nature of these problems differs across issue areas and so, therefore, will the institutional responses. Many institutional roles that Grieco characterizes as uniquely realist (for example, setting boundaries on the relative allocations of gains that can evolve under an agreement, providing side-payments to reach mutually acceptable terms, sponsoring periodic reviews and renegotiations) are exactly the responses on which neoliberal institutionalists focus.[14]

---

[13] This is but one instance of the general phenomenon that nontariff barriers to trade tend to raise more governance difficulties than do tariff barriers.

[14] For example, the arrangements mentioned by Grieco are precisely the focus of Williamson (1985a). Chapter Six includes more discussion of "neoliberal institutional" approaches.

Chapter Three

HEGEMONY AND INTERNATIONAL TRADE:
UNILATERAL OR MULTILATERAL LIBERALIZATION?

THE ECONOMIC theories of international trade and comparative advantage associated with Adam Smith, David Ricardo, Eli Heckscher, Bertil Ohlin, and Paul Samuelson treat countries anonymously and symmetrically.[1] However, several recent politically focused perspectives embody a special role for a single country. The theories associated with Robert Gilpin, Charles Kindleberger, Robert Keohane, Stephen Krasner, and others emphasize the role of a hegemonic country in creation and maintenance of open international trade and monetary regimes.[2]

A hegemon is a state that is dominant in its leadership in the world economy. Among other attributes of leadership, such a country may be willing and able to act as an arbitrator in disputes and to support international cooperative institutions such as the General Agreement on Tariffs and Trade. However, if it is to lead, the hegemon must do so on terms that convince other states to follow or defer to its leadership. The leadership role of the hegemon has been viewed by various writers as one of providing international stability, security, and rules of behavior, stabilizing expectations, and enforcing rules.

HEGEMONIC STABILITY VERSUS HEGEMONIC COOPERATION

The most common hegemony-based theory, called the *hegemonic stability hypothesis*, views an open trading system as a public good that must be provided by a hegemonic country.[3] Nonhegemonic countries are free-riders that face inadequate incentives to contribute to the maintenance of a liberal trading system.[4] The analogy with standard public goods theory is clear and direct: just as non-rivalry and non-excludability of domestic

---

[1] The original presentations are Smith (1937 [1776], Books I and IV); Ricardo (1971 [1817], Chapter Seven); Heckscher (1919); Ohlin (1933); and Samuelson (1939). These works are the foundation for modern economic trade theory.

[2] See, for examples, the citations in Chapter One, footnotes 35 through 38.

[3] Keohane (1984, Chapter 3, and pp. 210–214) provides criticisms of the "crude" version of the hegemonic stability hypothesis.

[4] The appropriateness of the public-good characterization is a matter of debate. Examples include Conybeare (1984); Snidal (1985); Russett (1985); Yarbrough and Yarbrough (1985a,b); Gowa (1988, 1989b); and Grunberg (1990, pp. 442–443).

public goods may require government intervention, so potential free-riding in the international economic system requires hegemonic intervention.[5]

The main source of disagreement among analysts in the hegemonic stability tradition concerns the extent of benevolence or exploitation by the hegemon.[6] In the view of some, the hegemon is benevolent—overcoming other countries' incentives to free-ride by bearing the burden of system-maintenance with little direct reward. For others, the hegemon is exploitative and coercive—forcing other countries into openness that serves primarily, if not exclusively, the interests of the hegemon.

The hegemonic stability hypothesis predicts a hegemon is both necessary and sufficient for an open trading system and is instrumental in bringing it about. Full historical support for the hypothesis would find first hegemonic Britain and then the hegemonic United States actively and successfully promoting a cooperative, open trading system; it would also find movements away from such an open system at all other times. The actual empirical evidence is mixed.[7] Although the two periods of hegemony *were* relatively open, Britain did *not* pursue worldwide liberalization very actively; and non-hegemonic periods have *not* been characterized uniformly by a lack of openness.

Besides the ambiguous empirical evidence, the "hegemonic provision of a public good" explanation of international trade policy has encountered two theoretical criticisms. First, it is not clear that trade liberalization embodies the two essential characteristics of publicness: non-rivalry in consumption and non-excludability.[8] Second, the hegemonic view seems to rest on the assumption that a hegemon's first-best policy is free trade. The economic theory of international trade, on the other hand, suggests that a "large" country (that is, one with monopoly and/or monopsony power in world markets) is more likely than a small one to gain

[5] The standard works on public goods include Samuelson (1954, 1955); Olson (1965); Buchanan (1965); Frohlich, Oppenheimer, and Young (1971); Stigler (1974); Hardin (1982); and Cornes and Sandler (1986). However, see Ostrom (1990).

[6] Snidal (1985); James and Lake (1989); and Grunberg (1990, pp. 439–442, 444–445). Charles Kindleberger is uncomfortable with the range of behaviors now described as hegemonic: "Political science has now transmuted the concept of leadership into 'hegemony,' a word that makes me uncomfortable because of its overtones of force, threat, pressure. I think it is possible to lead without arm-twisting, to act responsibly without pushing and shoving other countries. . . . The word *hegemon* means leadership in Greek, to be sure, but my *Columbia Encyclopedia* associates it with the Peloponnesian Wars and the struggle for dominance between Athens and Sparta" (1986, pp. 841–842).

[7] The evidence, especially regarding the periods of British and U.S. hegemony, is examined later in the chapter. The first attempt at a multi-period test of the hypothesis was Krasner (1976).

[8] See the citations in footnote 4 above.

from trade restrictions.[9] These two criticisms, if accepted, seriously weaken the hegemonic stability explanation of liberal international trade regimes. In the view of the critics, free trade would not require a hegemonic provider; and a hegemon probably would not choose to pursue free trade as its first-best policy. Finally, as noted above, even proponents of hegemonic stability theory do not agree whether the hegemon benefits directly from providing a liberal regime or is merely willing and able to bear the costs of a regime for others.

The strategic organizational view of hegemonic cooperation taken here involves a related but slightly different role for the hegemon in trade liberalization.[10] This alternate view has two advantages over the traditional hegemonic stability hypothesis: (i) it avoids several theoretical criticisms, and (ii) it appears more consistent with the (admittedly limited and sometimes ambiguous) empirical evidence. We focus on two issues that Robert Keohane highlights as inadequately addressed by the hegemonic stability literature: the hegemon's incentives to lead and other countries' incentives to defer to the hegemon's leadership or to defect.[11] The strategic organizational approach to hegemonic cooperation also helps in the scientific problem of evaluating a theory with only two modern cases (Britain and the United States).[12] By attempting to say something about the particular *form* trade liberalization would take under different conditions, this perspective also advances additional, potentially refutable implications.

The strategic organizational perspective on hegemonic cooperation suggests that both the proponents of hegemonic stability theory and their critics are partially correct. First, trade liberalization does have characteristics that may sometimes involve a special role for the hegemon, but these characteristics are not best described as publicness. Second, the hegemon may not pursue (and historically has not pursued) completely free trade and yet still may play a catalytic role in a liberal trade regime. In fact, manipulation of its own trade policy is one mechanism by which the hegemon performs its role. Finally, the hegemon's role cannot be summarized as *either* collecting the gains from an open regime *or* bearing its

---

[9] This is true both in "traditional" trade theory, based on models of perfect competition, and in the "new" trade theory, based on models of imperfect competition and strategic behavior. On the differences between the two approaches, see Krugman (1983, 1987); Stegemann (1989); and Richardson (1990). Grunberg (1990, p. 436) argues that Robert Gilpin's work on hegemony is internally inconsistent in its view of the relationship between hegemony and preferences for free trade.

[10] For a more formal model, see Yarbrough and Yarbrough (1985a). The terminology *hegemonic cooperation* is from Keohane (1984, p. 55).

[11] Keohane (1984, pp. 39, 44–46).

[12] Keohane (1990, p. 757) makes a related comment about the number of integration cases.

costs; the hegemon must do both.[13] The relevant description of the hegemon is as a "principal" or "residual claimant" in the world trading system.[14] Perhaps closest to our interpretation of the hegemon as principal is a statement by Robert Baldwin, "In effect, the United States redistributed to other countries part of the economic surplus reaped from its unusually favorable export opportunities to enable those countries to support the establishment of an open trading regime."[15]

One dictionary defines hegemony as dominance of leadership. This definition is appropriate to the interpretation of the hegemon as the principal of the trading system. The hegemon is dominant in its leadership; but leadership requires followers, and the hegemon's success depends upon its ability to lead on acceptable terms. Trade liberalization is a cooperative activity. A hegemonic country cannot singlehandedly create an open trading regime.[16] Such a country can, however, provide the governance structure necessary for successful trade agreements.

To avoid reneging on liberalization agreements and the costs of associated protectionism, individual countries' incentives for participating in the world trading system must discourage opportunism. Gains from opportunistic protectionism come at the expense of one's trading partners; hegemonic cooperation focuses on the hegemon's role in providing a reward or governance structure to discourage beggar-thy-neighbor opportunism.[17]

There are two aspects of the hegemon's role in easing cooperation. *Ex ante*, an acceptable allocation among countries of the costs and benefits of liberalization must be achieved if a trade agreement is to be reached. This negotiation stage aligns the incentives of the participating countries and forms the "carrot" aspect of the hegemon's role. *Ex post*, the hegemon must be willing and able to monitor countries for compliance with their commitments and to apply agreed-on punishments in the case of opportunism. This monitoring stage forms the "stick" of the enforcement

---

[13] This is consistent with Keohane's (1984, p. 138) statement that, "simplistic notions of hegemony as either complete dominance or selfless, dedicated leadership hinder rather than promote historical understanding."

[14] This terminology comes from principal-agency theory; useful treatments are Holmstrom (1982); MacDonald (1984); and Pratt and Zeckhauser (1985).

[15] Baldwin (1984a, p. 11).

[16] Stein (1984) emphasizes this point.

[17] A hegemon possesses overall political-economic dominance in the world economy and acts as a large player in many international markets. However, presence of a hegemon does not rule out the existence of other "large" countries, that is, countries able to affect their terms of trade in some markets. Periods of hegemony do not imply that all other countries act as "small" countries unable to affect their terms of trade. Therefore, countries other than the hegemon may be tempted to impose protectionism for terms-of-trade as well as distribution reasons. In addition, relation-specific investment for trade in particular markets can make transactions subject to holdups, providing still another reason for threats to impose protection. See Harris (1989, especially section 8.3) on market access.

mechanism. The threat to each country is that, should it act opportunistically, the hegemon will alter its trade policy to punish defection. Under a successful hegemonic-cooperation system, the "stick" will be applied rarely because an effective hegemon can persuade other countries to follow rather than relying on force.[18]

The reward to each country for compliance under hegemonic cooperation must be sufficient to compensate it for forgoing opportunistic protection; that is, the reward must at least cover the perceived adjustment costs incurred by the country because of its liberalization. The hegemon must absorb these costs and pay each country an additional side-payment to assure compliance. The larger the side-payments, the stronger the incentives provided to nonhegemonic participants, but the higher the costs to the hegemon of the side-payments. Bargaining between the hegemon and other countries determines the side-payments. There are two constraints on bargaining: (i) side-payments must be positive to convince countries to cooperate, and (ii) residual gains from trade (the reward for the hegemon's efforts) must be positive for the hegemon to perform its role.

The enforcement power of the hegemon depends on its ability to impact a large share of world trade through its own policies, including retaliation and control of access to its market.[19] The hegemon's trade policies are therefore a *response* to the policies of other countries; a hegemon would not necessarily be expected to pursue free trade. Ironically, the hegemon's pivotal role within the trading system constrains its own trade policies. A country's willingness and ability to perform the principal's role and accept the implied policy constraints may be limited. The hegemon will only act as principal as long as the protectionism that would follow from lack of enforcement would reduce the total gains from trade sufficiently to make the enforcement role the hegemon's best outcome. The hegemon shares the gains from openness with other countries to achieve their cooperation; but net gains remain for the hegemon. The benefits to the hegemon of the open trading system more than compensate for the payments that must be made to achieve the cooperation of other countries. Should this cease to be the case, the hegemon would no longer perform its role in the world trading system.[20]

The argument over whether the hegemon is benevolent or exploitative

---

[18] This is consistent with the observation in a military context that actual use of force is evidence of a breakdown of power, or impotence, rather than strength; see Garnett (1981, p. 71). One implication is that empirical evidence from periods of hegemony will consist more of carrots than sticks. During periods of hegemonic decline, sticks would become more prevalent as "deterrence" fails.

[19] On market access, see Harris (1989); and Keohane (1984, p. 33).

[20] For a more detailed examination of the incentives facing the hegemon in its bargaining with other countries, see Yarbrough and Yarbrough (1985a, 1989).

becomes more subtle in this view. A system of open trade supported by hegemonic cooperation is mutually beneficial to all participants; however, there is no reason to expect the gains to be distributed evenly. The hegemon is breaking a Prisoners' Dilemma-like problem that results from countries' inability to make binding precommitments to avoid opportunistic protectionism. Consider the classic Prisoners' Dilemma with two alleged criminals in which each faces a jail sentence of thirty days if both of them confess, twenty days if neither confesses, or ten days (for the confessor) and forty days (for the non-confessor) if only one confesses.[21] Assume each individual values a day in jail at one dollar; that is, each would be willing to pay one dollar to reduce jail time by one day. The two together would be willing to pay up to twenty dollars for some type of institutional arrangement that would allow them to cooperate and not confess. They might, for example, each pay a five-dollar bribe to the police officer to interrogate them in the same room at the same time. If their pleas could be entered simultaneously and in one another's presence, the incentive to defect would be eliminated. Each prisoner would be better off by five dollars, and the police officer would be better off by the amount of the bribe ($10) (ignoring any societal costs of releasing the individuals and the officer's risk that the bribe might be discovered).[22] The prisoners value cooperation; the police officer facilitates the cooperation by changing the rules of the game; and all are better (or, at least, no worse) off.[23] Is the officer self-interested, altruistic, benevolent, or exploitative? Each term has an element of truth; the important point is that all parties gain. Similarly, a hegemon—able to alter the nature of the game facing participants in the international trading system—can set an environment for mutually beneficial cooperation.

However, the payoffs in international trade and, therefore, the role of a hegemon, depend on the character of investment undertaken for trade-related purposes. This causes the implications of the strategic organizational version of hegemonic cooperation to differ from those of the traditional hegemonic stability hypothesis. That hypothesis implies a hegemonic state is *both necessary and sufficient* for a liberal trading system.[24] The hegemonic-cooperation view, on the other hand, implies that the presence of a hegemon is one possible way of supporting cooperation

[21] Elliott, Ackerman, and Millian (1985, p. 325) discuss the fundamental source of the dilemma in the Prisoners' Dilemma.

[22] This example provides a reminder that cooperation is not always desirable and that the "efficiency" of any cooperative arrangement is sensitive to the definition of the group; see the discussion of efficiency in Chapter Six.

[23] The outcome of the bargain depends on the distribution of information concerning preferences as well as parties' alternatives.

[24] Keohane (1984, pp. 31, 78) dissents from this view.

in trade—a means of governance that can support liberalization in the presence of substantial relation-specific investments. Therefore, according to the strategic organizational view of hegemonic cooperation, the presence of a hegemonic state is *neither necessary nor sufficient* for a liberal trading system.

In addition, the strategic organizational approach suggests a second proposition not implied by hegemonic stability theory: Presence of a hegemon is consistent with two quite distinct forms of trade liberalization—unilateral and multilateral.[25] The first occurs when the dominance of the hegemon and the nature of trade leave the hegemon relatively invulnerable to the trade policies of other countries. In this case, the hegemon pursues open trade to the extent consistent with domestic politics, but takes little active role in persuading or pushing other countries to adopt similarly liberal policies. We call this trade policy *unilateralism*. The second, quite distinct form of trade liberalization occurs when the nature of trade makes countries, including the hegemon, vulnerable to one another's trade policy choices. Then the value of open trade to the hegemon hinges critically on the policies followed by others. In this instance, the hegemon actively attempts to influence those policies and to establish general rules or norms to govern trade policy choices, an example of *multilateralism*.

Many authors have noted the contrasts between the actions of Britain and the United States during their respective periods of hegemony. Ikenberry and Kupchan assert that fundamental norms differed in the two cases, since British hegemony was based on "free trade" and U.S. hegemony on "liberal multilateralism."[26] Similarly, Stein notes that, "[Britain] adopted a largely free trade commercial policy *unilaterally* once the government found alternate sources of revenue. The United States was a more *activist promoter* of trade liberalization, yet it was not willing to lower tariffs except through *reciprocal arrangement*."[27] Thus, the historical evidence suggests a rough correspondence between British and U.S. trade policies during their periods of hegemony and the unilateral and multilateral forms of liberalization, respectively.[28] This correspondence will be explored in detail below.

[25] This argument was first presented in Yarbrough and Yarbrough (1985b, 1987a).

[26] Ikenberry and Kupchan (1990, p. 285n4).

[27] Stein (1984, p. 380, emphasis added). Keohane (1984, pp. 142–143) refers to the United States as an "active" and "relatively openhanded" hegemon.

[28] Neither unilateral nor multilateral trade policy is linked, by definition, to hegemony. Unilateral trade policy is undertaken by a single country autonomously—not as part of agreements with trading partners. Multilateral trade policy is undertaken by large groups of countries through agreements that subject their policies to common rules. The strategic organizational approach seeks to explain why Britain, as a hegemon, chose to pursue unilateral liberalization and the United States, as a hegemon, chose to pursue multilateral liberalization.

Classic works in the hegemonic stability tradition are usually silent on the precise form of hegemonic leadership and associated institutions. The lack of explicit treatment of these issues has led to diverse interpretations by later writers. Haggard and Simmons conclude that Kindleberger's *The World in Depression*, "links the 'stability' of the world economy to *unilateral* leadership by a dominant power; no formal international commitments or institutional machinery would be required."[29] Stein, on the other hand, interprets differently and argues that Britain's unilateral trade liberalization was not a case of hegemonic support for a free-trade regime but of Britain's inability to convince other countries to negotiate reductions in their trade barriers. This view seems to imply that Britain was less than hegemonic during the unilateral policy period (approximately 1840–1860) and acted as a hegemon only after 1860, when it formed bilateral trade treaties such as the famous Cobden-Chevalier Treaty with France.[30] We now turn to an examination of unilateral and multilateral liberalization in the British and American cases, respectively, from the strategic organizational perspective.

UNILATERAL TRADE LIBERALIZATION

Unilateral trade policies are those adopted by a single country without negotiations or agreements with others. The strategic organizational perspective developed in Chapter Two would lead us to expect unilateral liberalization only by countries with good alternatives to their current trade arrangements, that is, by countries facing little or no threat of opportunism by trading partners. This is the case whenever the country has little investment in relation-specific assets for trade that can be held up by an opportunistic trading partner. Without such assets, transactional insecurity is low, and the availability of alternate trading partners in world markets provides an adequate governance structure for trade. The ability of a country to withdraw unilaterally from trade with an opportunistic partner means that simple self-help is effective. The cell on the left-hand side of Figure 3.1 illustrates this outcome. International trade within this context approximates the arm's-length market transactions of orthodox economic theory, where a party's alternatives provide the primary safe-

---

[29] Haggard and Simmons (1987, p. 500n30, emphasis in original). James and Lake (1989, p. 3) also interpret Britain's role as unilateral.

[30] Stein (1984). The quarter-century beginning in 1842 was the heyday of Britain's unilateral liberalization (Irwin [1988, p. 1142]). Tariff revenue as a fraction of dutiable imports fell from about thirty-five percent in 1841 to about five percent in 1875 (Irwin [1988, p. 1155n11]; data from Imlah [1958, p. 159]).

		Specific Trade-Related Investment?	
		No	Yes
Effective 3rd-Party Enforcement?	No	**UNILATERAL trade policy (e.g., 19th-century Britain)**	BILATERAL trade policy (e.g., 1970-90)
	Yes		MULTILATERAL trade policy (e.g., 1945-65) OR MINILATERAL trade policy (e.g., Europe 1992)

Figure 3.1: Conditions supporting unilateral trade policy include an absence of relation-specific investment for trade, despite the presence or absence of effective third-party enforcement.

guards.[31] A complex governance structure that places a high priority on the preservation of a particular trading relationship is unnecessary due to the non-relation-specific nature of investment.

Mid-Nineteenth-Century Britain

The most commonly cited example of extensive unilateral trade liberalization is the case of mid-nineteenth-century Britain.[32] This is usually advanced as the outstanding instance of the hegemonic stability hypothesis at work. Under that interpretation, Britain's status as a hegemonic power caused it to pursue free trade and to support a generally open trading system. However, though Britain was (at least according to most analysts)[33] a hegemonic power, this alone cannot explain the unilateral nature of British policy because the later hegemon, the United States, did

[31] The section of Chapter Two on empirical evidence outlines why non-arm's-length transactions tend to involve relation-specific investment and, therefore, a hazard of opportunism against which withdrawal as self-help is an inadequate safeguard.

[32] See Cuddington and McKinnon (1979); McKeown (1983); Stein (1984); Haggard and Simmons (1987, p. 500n30); Irwin (1988, p. 1149); James and Lake (1989, p. 3); and Evans (1989, pp. 211, 221).

[33] Russett (1985, pp. 211–214) questions the hegemony of nineteenth-century Britain based on measures such as GNP and military expenditures. Others, for example, McKeown (1983) and Keohane (1984, pp. 34–39), question whether Britain's actions were consistent with or can be explained by its hegemony.

not pursue unilateral liberalization. So, while its hegemonic status almost certainly was a factor in Britain's move away from protectionism, other considerations must explain why that move took a unilateral character.[34]

Further, McKeown and Stein, among others, have argued that the actions of nineteenth-century Britain provide evidence *against* the traditional version of hegemonic stability theory.[35] That theory, according to McKeown, predicts that Britain would conduct an active, persuasive policy for lowering tariffs and successfully use its bargaining strength in other areas to coerce others into lowering tariffs.[36] The empirical evidence supports none of these predictions. Both France and the Zollverein, the other major industrialized areas of the period, followed relatively liberal policies despite a general lack of pressure to do so from Britain.[37] In addition, Britain maintained a few restrictive measures dictated by domestic interests.[38] Significantly, the smaller powers maintained trade barriers in the face of substantial unilateral reductions by Britain.

All these observations are consistent with the view that Britain pursued liberalization unilaterally because such a policy allowed her both gains from trade and low negotiation and enforcement costs. This, in turn, was feasible only because Britain faced little or no threat of opportunism by trading partners. Under these conditions, we would expect Britain to follow a unilateral trade policy—basically liberal but maintaining barriers where demanded by domestic interest groups—and not actively press for system-wide liberalization.

Unilateral liberalization was feasible for Britain because of her industrial strength, high rate of capacity utilization, and need for raw material and export markets. Purchasers of British manufactured goods faced limited alternate suppliers in the mid-nineteenth century, while most export markets and raw material sources were highly substitutable. Britain's in-

---

[34] Lipson (1985, pp. xiv–xvi) argues similarly concerning the weakness of hegemonic explanations for the security of foreign investments.

[35] McKeown (1983); and Stein (1984).

[36] The European powers, especially Britain, did play a role in spreading Western rules of private property to Asia, Africa, and Latin America to protect their investments there. Even in this role, however, Britain's actions were more circumscribed than many treatments of hegemony would lead one to expect (Lipson [1985, Chapters One and Two]).

[37] Irwin (1988, pp. 1158–1159).

[38] Irwin (1988, p. 1155). Stein (1984, pp. 360–363) covers Britain's continuing use of trade barriers. Lake (1983) focuses on a later period of British policy (1870–1938) and argues that "[h]egemonic leaders forsake protectionism at home in order to lead the international economy as a whole toward greater openness. . . . Even the most productive countries possess internationally uncompetitive industries. If a hegemonic leader were to protect such industries, it would undercut its ability to lead the international economy. Indeed, some measure of self-sacrifice in the short run may be necessary for a hegemonic leader to achieve its goal of constructing a liberal international economy" (Lake [1983, pp. 517–543]). Lake's argument addresses the free trade versus protection issue, but not the form of trade policy.

dustrial facilities were not specialized locationally for trade with any particular partner. Specific international vertical production linkages were minimal.[39] Export capacity was significant, but not dedicated to trade with any particular country. Britain would have been vulnerable, of course, to a simultaneous stoppage of trade by a sizable group of her trading partners; but the successful coalescing of such a group was unlikely, because defection and continued trade with Britain would have been beneficial for each individual country. Those British investments highly vulnerable to opportunism were protected through links of empire and extraterritorial application of British law regarding private property and the sanctity of contracts.[40] Surplus capacity was not a problem for Britain; and the industrializing British labor force was becoming mobile by the standard of the times.[41] Most smaller countries maintained trade barriers; but Britain liberalized unilaterally, capturing gains from trade and incurring low transaction costs. Britain was a hegemon as defined by most measures of status, but hegemony alone cannot be the explanation for the unilateral form of her trade liberalization.[42]

The viability of unilateral trade policies requires the presence of good alternatives. With no durable investment in unique trading relationships, changes in unilaterally chosen policies impose no significant losses on trading partners. A country gains little from threatening to close its market to imports because suppliers servicing that market can sell their wares elsewhere. Should an exporter threaten to cut off the supply of a product, alternate suppliers can be located easily, limiting the current supplier's incentive to act opportunistically.

THE BREAKDOWN OF UNILATERALISM

Britain's policies became less unilateral by the 1870s. The spread of industrialization increased competition facing British industries. Foreign investment, which until approximately 1870 had taken the relatively

[39] International vertical production linkages are user-supplier relations across national boundaries, for example, the component-assembly relationships across the U.S.-Canada border in the automobile industry. Reich (1991) provides other examples. Such linkages often involve vulnerable relation-specific assets, as indicated in Chapter Two.

[40] Doran (1971, p. 16) distinguishes between empire and hegemony by limiting empire to cases of "direct institutional control." Such an interpretation is consistent with a strategic organizational perspective: transactions that are particularly vulnerable to opportunism require direct institutional control as a governance structure.

[41] Cuddington and McKinnon (1979, p. 12).

[42] James and Lake (1989) argue that even though the repeal of the Corn Laws was unilateral (that is, not the outcome of international negotiation, agreement, or commitment), it was consciously designed to have an effect on U.S. trade policy by facilitating a pro-trade U.S. domestic political alliance between the South and West against the pro-protection North. Irwin (1988) emphasizes that British policy, although unilateral, was followed by tariff reductions by other countries.

safe form of portfolio investment in foreign government bonds, shifted sharply toward direct investments—railroads, ports, and public utilities—that were much more vulnerable to opportunism by host states.[43] As Britain became more vulnerable to the policies of her trading partners, domestic support for unilateral liberalization eroded.

By the end of World War II and the onset of U.S. hegemony, transportation and communication costs had declined precipitously from their levels during British hegemony. Manufacturing technology had made large-scale production efficient, and the number of industrialized economies had expanded.

Another major change in trade was a move away from intersectoral trade (for example, exchange of agricultural products for manufactured goods) to intra-industry and intra-firm trade in manufactures. As explained in Chapter Two, much of this trade, by its nature, leads to relation-specific investments and the associated vulnerability to opportunism. An industry importing a unique component for its manufacturing process may be unable to locate a ready alternate supplier; or, the producer of a unique component may be unable to sell it if the original buyer ends the relationship. Therefore, the rise of trade in manufactures and especially of intra-industry trade involves an increase in relation-specific assets. Firms can protect these assets from private opportunism through internalization in the form of intra-firm trade or through nonstandard contracting; this is the central idea of most modern economic theories of the multinational enterprise.[44] As we saw in Chapter Two, between one-third and two-thirds of U.S. merchandise trade now consists of intra-firm trade, protected from private opportunism through internalization. However, this still leaves a vulnerability to governmental opportunism that must be dealt with through a change in the form of trade liberalization agreements.[45]

Once relation-specific investments enter the picture, unilateral trade policies cease to be viable. For example, if Britain unilaterally liberalized its trade and another country invested in relation-specific assets to serve the British market, Britain could opportunistically threaten to close its market and extract an amount up to the difference between the value of

[43] Lipson (1985, Chapter Two).

[44] Rugman (1981), Caves (1982), Hennart (1982), and Casson (1987) are just a few of many possible examples. Contractor and Lorange (1988) provide a useful overview of the many contractual variations firms use in international contexts.

[45] Helleiner (1977) documents the rise of intra-industry trade and relates the trend to firms' increased interest in the specifics of trade policy. Milner (1988b) and Milner and Yoffie (1989) argue that the rise of intra-industry trade explains firms being much more concerned with the *form* of trade policy as opposed to some overall level of openness or protection.

the partner's relation-specific investment for the British market and its best alternate use.

MULTILATERAL TRADE LIBERALIZATION

Of course, when parties recognize the potential for opportunism *ex ante*, either the relation-specific investment will not be undertaken (and productive efficiency declines) or a more sophisticated governance structure will be required. The presence or absence of hegemony then becomes an important determinant of the structure of successful international trade agreements. With a hegemon as arbitrator and enforcement mechanism, liberalization can take the form of multilateral, negotiated reductions in trade barriers, such as those conducted under the auspices of the General Agreement on Tariffs and Trade (GATT). The lower right-hand cell of Figure 3.2 represents this outcome.

Postwar America and the Early GATT Years

The international negotiations during and following World War II officially inaugurated the U.S. role as hegemon of the world trading system. The GATT framework supported by U.S. hegemony appears to fit the strategic organizational model of hegemonic cooperation well. The

		Specific Trade-Related Investment?	
		No	Yes
Effective 3rd-Party Enforcement?	No	UNILATERAL trade policy (e.g., 19th-century Britain)	BILATERAL trade policy (e.g., 1970-90)
	Yes		**MULTILATERAL trade policy (e.g., 1945-65)** OR MINILATERAL trade policy (e.g., Europe 1992)

Figure 3.2: Conditions supporting multilateral trade policy include the presence of both relation-specific investment for trade and effective third-party enforcement, such as a hegemon.

GATT consists of a set of continuously negotiated multilateral rules for trade policies and a set of arbitration or dispute-settlement procedures for members. The goal of the GATT framework is an open, cooperative trading system; but emphasis always has been on negotiation and arbitration, not on free trade as a dogmatic ideology. The GATT contracting parties never committed themselves to follow free trade; rules always permitted protectionist policies to aid domestic industries.[46] The GATT framework does provide for punishment of protectionism (primarily through withdrawn concessions or countervailing duties), but *only* for protectionism that violates GATT commitments. These commitments may be quite specific, as in tariff bindings and the Tokyo Round tariff-cutting formula, or more general, as in the general GATT codes of conduct. Nevertheless, the variety of margins along which trade policy can be adjusted (for example, subtle and opaque nontariff barriers or exchange rate manipulation) create a significant scope for opportunism. In the GATT negotiations, the United States was not active in pressing for commitments to free trade, but in pressing for compliance with the commitments made. The understanding was that the United States would not retaliate against countries imposing trade restrictions but would retaliate against cheating or violations of trade agreements.

The GATT rules, which consist primarily of tariff bindings that prevent increased tariff rates except under certain well-specified circumstances and of restrictions on many nontariff barriers, are multilateral. These rules apply to all contracting parties, with the important exceptions noted below. The two fundamental GATT norms of nondiscrimination and national treatment exemplify the multilateral character of the GATT-based trading system.[47]

CARROTS

In the strategic organizational view, hegemonic cooperation based on U.S. leadership implies that the United States should have actively provided "carrots" to other countries to assure their support for liberalization under the GATT. In fact, the United States not only initiated and "marketed" the entire GATT system but, in exchange for support, con-

---

[46] For example, Bhagwati (1990, p. 28) refers to the "contractarian conception of GATT." See also Keohane (1984, pp. 88–89).

[47] Bhagwati (1990, p. 28) concludes that the United States was never a unilateral free trader. As noted earlier, Ikenberry and Kupchan (1990, pp. 285n, 299–307) characterize the fundamental norm of the period of U.S. hegemony as one of "liberal multilateralism." For a contrasting perspective that minimizes the role of multilateralism within the GATT, see Finlayson and Zacher (1981, especially pp. 585–589). Of course, postwar multilateralism included only GATT members and notably excluded the Soviet bloc. To emphasize this, we have referred elsewhere to the postwar trading system as one of *exclusionary multilateralism* (Yarbrough and Yarbrough [1991a]).

tinued to tolerate several practices it would have liked terminated.[48] These practices included preference systems such as that between Britain and the Commonwealth countries, use of quotas for balance-of-payments problems, and continuation of both tariffs and quotas by developing countries. Each of these clearly violated the central GATT norm of non-discriminatory liberalization. The United States also permitted continued discrimination against its exports during the early GATT years by not demanding reciprocity by either European or developing countries.[49] Simultaneously, the United States provided aid toward the reconstruction of Europe, primarily as grants instead of loans. Each of these "carrots," or concessions by the United States, was designed to achieve other countries' support. Developing countries have continued to be excused from reciprocity within the GATT—a side-payment that was (and is) clearly necessary to elicit even lukewarm support for the system.[50]

A more recent example of negotiation over "carrots" is the ongoing debate between the United States and developing countries over the Generalized System of Preferences (GSP) for developing-country exports to industrialized countries and graduation.[51] After years of opposition, the United States finally accepted the GSP to gain the cooperation of developing countries with the GATT regime. However, by insisting on graduation from GSP and severely limiting the products on which developing countries were given preference, the United States limited the size of the bribe or carrot. If the developing countries fail to honor their few policy commitments to the GATT, the preference system can be withdrawn or further restricted.

The United States generally pushed other countries toward liberalization in the postwar period, but only at a mutually acceptable pace. For example, the U.S. waged a long battle to gain entry for Japan into the GATT. The battle finally was won in stages spread over several years, but only after the United States made substantial side-payments to European countries. First, Japan could only send an observer to the GATT. Next, after a four-year campaign by the United States, Japan became a signatory, but other countries continued to discriminate against Japan in trade. Finally, over the next four years, the discriminatory trade practices gradually were dropped.

[48] This is one focus of Krasner (1979).

[49] Nevertheless, the policies were covered by multilateral rules and were not taken unilaterally.

[50] These carrots represent a type of linkage in which one of the linked issues is general support for the GATT system. As Hoekman (1989, p. 696) emphasizes, linkages within GATT negotiations themselves are typically more limited and occur primarily within rather than across issue areas.

[51] See Sapir and Lundberg (1984).

STICKS

The enforcement or "stick" role of U.S. trade policies also was clear during the early postwar years. The United States never threatened to retaliate against all protectionism by its trading partners; and it rarely claimed seriously to follow free-trade policies itself. As noted above, continued discrimination in several forms against U.S. exports was tolerated in the early years of the GATT. The United States also excluded several sectors from liberalization (most notably agriculture and later textiles) for its own domestic reasons. U.S. policy promoted a basically open trading system, especially in manufactures, and reserved retaliation for violations of GATT commitments. As Robert Baldwin put it, "a liberal trade policy does not mean being 'soft' on rule violations. On the contrary, it means adhering closely to agreed upon rules in an open and fair manner. If such a policy is to have a chance of succeeding, the U.S. government must actively promote it within the GATT. . . ."[52]

The fact that protectionist policies by the United States could immediately and directly impact approximately one-half of world trade backed its enforcement power; indirect and lagged effects would have been even greater.[53] Arrangements such as the escape-clause and peril-point provisions introduced directly by the United States supported the ability of the U.S. to engage in selective protectionism in specific industries, reallocating the gains from trade. These provisions allowed the United States to punish countries that failed to abide by their GATT commitments to liberal trade policies. Of course, these provisions also provided protection to U.S. domestic interest groups. However, the question we address is not free trade versus protectionism, but the form of liberalization. The question is why the postwar United States chose multilateral rules rather than unilateral ones to pursue its trade policies. U.S. trade policy was contingent on other countries' compliance; therefore, the U.S. pursuit of a liberal trading regime did not imply that it would itself follow free trade policies.[54]

The success of the GATT in its early years was crucially dependent on U.S. hegemony in the world trading system.[55] Otherwise, "the raison

[52] Robert E. Baldwin (1979, p. 8).

[53] MacBean and Snowden (1981, p. 79).

[54] On the other hand, the United States did not and does not pursue protection to the degree made permissible by its domestic law, for example, in the case of subsidies and countervailing duties (Robert E. Baldwin [1979, p. 12]). Also see Lipson (1985, p. 164) for examples of U.S. "willingness to manipulate imports and exports as policy instruments."

[55] The Cold War clearly affected U.S. preferences and policies in the postwar period. However, the Cold War cannot be the primary explanation for the GATT and the U.S. role in it because the GATT began to decline around 1965, long before the period of détente, much less the recently declared "end" of the Cold War.

d'être of GATT"—"to help nations agree to behave in a cooperative manner that ensures an outcome which is beneficial to all parties and more
acceptable than if each had acted independently"—would have remained
infeasible.[56] The enforcement powers of GATT or any other body against
a sovereign state are, in a legal sense, almost nonexistent.[57] Without legal
enforcement, a strong arbitrator is necessary for cooperation. The arbitration required for successful multilateral agreements is unlikely without
a hegemon to act as a supporter of international institutions such as the
GATT.

This role by the United States was responsible for the failure of sometimes rocky postwar trade relations to degenerate into the often predicted
full-scale trade wars. As long as the United States was willing and able to
act as the principal in enforcing trade agreements, the fact that other
countries negotiated increasing rights to engage in limited protection did
not cause more serious conflicts. Increased but limited protection did
make the world trading system less open; but as long as countries complied with negotiated agreements, full-scale trade wars were unlikely. In
recent years, however, the credibility of U.S. enforcement has declined.[58]

The costs of the GATT bureaucracy and arbitration procedures have
been high. If trade among GATT members had involved less relation-
specific investment, these costly institutions would have been unnecessary
since parties' alternatives would have limited opportunism and unilateral
liberalization would have occurred. The GATT dispute-settlement procedures and the range of punishments permitted for violations have preserved the long-term relationship of the contracting parties. GATT enforcement has been far from perfect; but the institution has preserved
trading relationships despite frequent disputes.

Note also that the multilateral character of postwar U.S. trade policy
did *not* extend to investment issues, which continued to be treated bilaterally in two-party Friendship, Commerce, and Navigation (FCN) treaties. Such treaties earlier covered both trade and investment, but the
United States' changed postwar position allowed support of the GATT
multilateral format for trade, freeing FCN treaties to handle investment
alone.[59] The FCN program met with some limited success and in the
1980s became the Bilateral Investment Treaty (BIT) program, which, as
its title suggests, reflects the continuing reliance of investment negotia-

---

[56] Quotations come from Hoekman (1989, p. 694).

[57] *Wall Street Journal* (1986a).

[58] Lipson (1984, pp. 9–10) cites a vivid example in the form of a quote by India's trade
minister, " 'Oh, you won't do anything,' India's trade minister told U.S. officials. 'I have
confidence in America, and I would be terribly disappointed if America went the protectionist route.' "

[59] Lipson (1985, p. 96).

tions on bilateral institutions and the extreme vulnerability of investment.[60]

Summary

The traditional hegemonic stability hypothesis views a liberal trading regime as a public good requiring provision by a hegemonic country. Empirical observations that the two periods of remarkably successful trade
liberalization corresponded to the periods of British and U.S. hegemony
support the hypothesis.

Economic theory poses two problems for the hegemonic stability hypothesis. Trade does not necessarily embody the non-excludability and
non-rivalry characteristics that define public goods; and standard economic theory suggests a hegemon probably would not find free trade its
first-best policy. These problems are reflected in the empirical observations that the two hegemons did not pursue free trade during their respective periods of hegemony and that Britain's liberalization was unilateral,
not multilateral.

The strategic organizational perspective on hegemonic cooperation
suggests a reconciliation of elements of the hegemonic stability hypothesis
and the criticisms of it. Individual countries often face incentives to engage in opportunistic protection by reneging on agreements to pursue liberal trade policies. The hegemon's role is to use its own trade policies to
support trade agreements by punishing countries that fail to comply with
their policy commitments.

Trade negotiations involve the design of a configuration of provisions
that elicits support for an agreement based on its acceptable allocation
of costs and benefits. Examples of provisions clearly conflicting with
the spirit of the GATT but nonetheless necessary to achieve the cooperation of certain countries are many. The list includes Britain's Imperial
Preference System and the General System of Preferences for developing
country exports, both of which violate the GATT principle of nondiscrimination. In our approach, these provisions can be viewed as carrots,
side-payments, or bribes to the beneficiary countries for support of the
GATT system. On the other hand, if countries depart from their trade
commitments, the hegemon must be in a position to apply sanctions or
sticks to discipline opportunism.

Our approach explains both the success of liberalization during periods
of hegemony and the failure of the hegemon to follow free-trade policies
and thereby avoids one criticism of the hegemonic stability hypothesis.

---

[60] Chapter Two examines the vulnerability of foreign direct investment and the tendency
of relation-specific investment to blur the distinction between trade and investment.

More importantly, it elucidates the very *different* trade policies followed by the two hegemons—unilateral by mid-nineteenth-century Britain and multilateral by the postwar United States.

The discipline of a hegemon is but one possible governance structure for trade. A hegemon can support negotiated trade agreements by using its own trade policy to threaten other countries contemplating opportunistic protectionism. The GATT's multilateral success in the presence of relation-specific investments has depended on U.S. hegemony for enforcement, because the discipline of the GATT itself has been minimal. Evidence suggests that the decline of U.S. hegemony in trade-related issue areas has reduced the GATT's efficacy as a governance institution; and an increasing share of organization in the international trade arena now takes place outside the traditional, multilateral GATT framework.[61] Nontariff barriers, which are less amenable to multilateral rules, have increased demands on governance structures for trade because of those barriers' intimate linkages to "domestic" policies.

With relation-specific investment and absence of a hegemon to support multilateral institutions such as the GATT, limiting opportunistic protection requires other arrangements.[62] Agreements must become more self-contained and rely on internal mechanisms for enforcement instead of a third party in the form of a hegemon.

[61] See, for example, Lawrence and Litan (1990, pp. 4, 11–13).

[62] Keohane (1984, p. 183) states that if cooperation is to persist, "Multilateral institutions must furnish some of the sense of certainty and confidence that a hegemon formerly provided." This seems to imply that hegemony and multilateral institutions are substitutes, with one or the other necessary for cooperation. Our examination of the postwar period, however, suggests that U.S. hegemony *worked through* multilateral institutions (the GATT). The question then becomes how likely multilateral institutions (as defined in this book) are to achieve major liberalization without a hegemon. The strategic organizational approach's answer is *not very likely*. The GATT continues to exist, but its role continues to change. It still provides a useful forum for discussion and framework for trade relations, but it is unlikely to be the center for major liberalization pushes as it was in the period of U.S. hegemony. In other words, multilateralism and hegemony are conceptually distinct, but multilateral institutions are unlikely to be primary centers for liberalization without governance such as that provided by U.S. hegemony. However, because Keohane (1990, p. 731) defines any institution involving more than two countries as multilateral, his conclusion is less at odds with ours than it might appear. Our bilateral and minilateral forms of trade, as long as they involve more than two countries, would be called multilateral by Keohane. Where he speaks of increasing multilateralism and changes in the form of multilateralism, we speak of moves toward bilateral and minilateral institutions. As we explain elsewhere, broad definitions of *multilateralism* that do not distinguish among the organizational forms of the GATT, the EC, and the potential NAFTA (North American Free-Trade Area) limit analysis of the causes of and differences among the arrangements.

Chapter Four

SELF-HELP AND PRECOMMITMENT: BILATERAL TRADE LIBERALIZATION

ACCORDING TO THE strategic organizational approach, when international trade involves relation-specific assets, the resulting vulnerability to opportunistic protectionism implies a need for safeguards to support cooperation. Unilateral liberalization is not viable under such conditions. Sometimes a hegemon can alter the rules of the game to allow cooperation by acting as a third-party enforcer. For example, we argued in Chapter Three that U.S. hegemony during the early postwar years supported the success of the General Agreement on Tariffs and Trade, a system that used norms of multilateralism, nondiscrimination, and most-favored-nation status. However, in a world trading system not dominated by a hegemonic country, such norms tend to break down. As U.S. hegemony in trade diminished, the percentage of GATT trade at most-favored-nation (MFN) tariff rates declined from ninety percent in 1955 to seventy-seven percent in 1970 and to sixty-five percent in 1980.[1] By 1988 only fifty percent of trade occurred at MFN rates.[2]

With extensive relation-specific investment and no hegemon, trade liberalization requires alternate institutional arrangements to support cooperation. There are two basic possibilities, both of which involve small groups of countries but differ in their enforcement mechanisms.[3] The first, which we call *bilateralism*, involves no third-party adjudication and relies on self-enforcement based on economic "hostages," reciprocity, and issue linkages. Bilateralism, illustrated in the upper right-hand cell of Figure 4.1, is the subject of this chapter. The second type of small-group cooperation, which we call *minilateralism*, involves formation of third-party adjudication and enforcement mechanisms like those currently being developed by the European Community. We postpone examination of minilateralism until Chapter Five.

---

[1] Finlayson and Zacher (1981, p. 569).

[2] Pomfret (1988, p. 6). Keohane (1984, p. 185) dates the decline of the GATT from the mid-1960s. Lawrence and Litan (1990, pp. 4, 7, 11–13) examine pessimism over the state of the GATT, and Hathaway and Masur (1990, p. 22) attribute part of the problem to GATT's inability to cover nontariff barriers adequately.

[3] Recall that the type of enforcement mechanism rather than the number of parties distinguishes bilateralism from multilateralism. Eden and Hampson (1991) discuss advantages of small-group trade arrangements. Keohane (1990) refers to any agreement having more than two parties as multilateral; see Chapter One, footnote 9, and Chapter Three, footnote 62.

		Specific Trade-Related Investment?	
		No	Yes
Effective 3rd-Party Enforcement?	No	UNILATERAL trade policy (e.g., 19th-century Britain)	**BILATERAL trade policy (e.g., 1970-90)**
	Yes		MULTILATERAL trade policy (e.g., 1945-1965) OR MINILATERAL trade policy (e.g., Europe 1992)

Figure 4.1: Conditions supporting bilateral trade policy include presence of relation-specific investment for trade and absence of effective third-party enforcement.

Liberalization agreements among small groups of countries (as opposed to large-scale multilateralism) are more likely to succeed with relation-specific assets and without a hegemon for two reasons. First, the benefits and costs of liberalization must be carefully allocated among participating countries to arrive at a mutually acceptable agreement. Such allocations become more difficult as the number of parties rises, so small groups enjoy an advantage at the *ex ante* bargaining or negotiation stage. Second, an agreement once reached must be enforced; and this requires efforts to overcome the difficulties of detecting opportunism. Monitoring a small group generally is less costly and more effective than a large one, so small groups also enjoy an advantage over larger ones at the *ex post* enforcement stage.

BINDING PRECOMMITMENTS: HOSTAGES TO FREE TRADE

One hope for a successful agreement to pursue liberalized trade is countries' ability to make binding precommitments to comply with negotiated agreements and abstain from opportunistic protectionism. The most common form of binding precommitment is provision of an economic hostage.[4] A hostage is something of value to the provider that is automat-

---

[4] Williamson (1983) developed the concept of economic hostages. Yarbrough and Yarbrough (1986a) applied the concept to international trade; Yarbrough and Yarbrough (1990a) provides a formal model.

ically forfeited to the recipient should the provider act opportunistically.[5] A party's voluntary provision of a hostage or bond serves two purposes. First, the hostage raises the cost of opportunism by the value (to the provider) of the hostage. Second, the willingness to provide a hostage signals to the recipient the provider's intention not to behave opportunistically.

The provision of hostages can take a variety of both obvious and subtle forms. During fifteenth-century trade wars between England and the Hanseatic League, the League required English merchants in Prussia to post direct bonds against the levying of British taxes on League traders. Unfortunately for the prospects for cooperation, this use of hostages violated a cardinal rule: punishment did not reliably target those responsible for opportunism. Since retaliation was sanctioned against any citizen of the "other side," the potential enforcement power of the hostages was lost.[6] The hostage aspect of a particular policy need not be so explicit. If both parties are aware of the potential hostage, an explicit bargaining link is unnecessary for the (implicit) threat to be effective.

In a modern context, some forms of technical trade standards such as safety, pollution, and health regulations may serve as a form of hostage-taking. Such standards are ideal for hostages because standards involve investment in nonsalvageable capital equipment or production procedures that are forfeited if the market is lost. Of course, not all technical standards are cases of economic hostages. These regulations are controversial and often suspected of thinly masking protectionism. Analysis of technical standards is difficult because they can serve three purposes: (i) promoting health, safety, etc.; (ii) restricting imports; and (iii) providing hostages. Standards may have no purpose beyond the obvious one of domestic health or safety goals, or may be primarily protectionist if the major effect is exclusion of foreign-produced goods (as alleged, for example, in Japan's exclusion of U.S. telecommunications equipment). Because the hostage-taking role of a technical standard need not be explicit to be effective, the stated goals of various standards provide a poor guide to their true purposes.[7]

The characteristics of a technical standard likely to be serving a hostage function include clarity and publicness, differential treatment of domestic

---

[5] Technically, a hostage provides deterrence against opportunism, but not compensation to the victim should opportunism occur. If the item in question takes a form of value to the recipient, a moral hazard to claim violation falsely in order to collect the item is introduced; such items represent collateral rather than hostages (Kronman [1985]). Interesting comparisons with other types of precommitments can be found in Elster (1979); Schelling (1980); Keohane (1984, especially Chapters 6 and 7); and Maoz and Felsenthal (1987).

[6] Conybeare (1986, pp. 153–157).

[7] Stated goals are equally worthless in sorting health and safety goals from protectionism; this is one reason why technical standards prove so difficult to handle in international trade negotiations.

and imported goods, and uniqueness of the imposed requirements.[8] When a standard is clearly and publicly defined as required under the GATT, the standard is unlikely to be primarily protectionist because foreign suppliers are free to meet the standard. On the other hand, vague, secretive, or poorly specified standards have large protectionist potential and little opportunity for hostage provision. A standard treating domestic and foreign suppliers differently is likely to represent either protectionism or a hostage, because health or safety functions are better served by restrictions on all sources, not merely imports. Uniqueness is important for the hostage function, because it makes investment to meet the standard nonsalvageable or of little use in serving alternate markets. If the country providing the hostage acts opportunistically and the trading partner halts trade in retaliation, the relation-specific value of the investment will be lost.

One example of a possible hostage role for a technical standard is the pollution and safety standards imposed on U.S. automobile imports. To export automobiles to the United States, a country must install specialized capital equipment for producing cars that meet U.S. pollution and safety standards.[9] Should the exporting country violate an agreement, the United States could close its automobile market to the country's exports, rendering the specialized equipment useless. Japanese and Americans presumably are aware of the magnitude of Japan's investment in the specialized capital equipment required to service the U.S. market under existing standards. The fact that the exporting country stands to lose the value of the hostage (the equipment) as punishment for opportunistic behavior enforces existing agreements.

Other examples of technical standards fitting the hostage role include Canadian container-size restrictions on canned and bottled goods, varying European electrical standards, and varying maximum speeds for tractors sold in different European countries. Meeting each of these standards involves significant relation-specific investment that could be lost if the trading relationship breaks down. None serve explicitly as hostages, but all have proven stubbornly unamenable to negotiation—despite the lack of apparent economic rationale for restrictions that raise production costs while providing little real protection to import-competing industries.[10]

[8] To the extent that differential treatment of domestic and foreign firms serves a hostage function, the push for "national treatment," a central issue in foreign direct investment negotiations, may be misplaced.

[9] Some firms have chosen to minimize this effect by shipping cars that do not meet some of the standards and having the necessary features installed once the automobiles are in the United States.

[10] If at least some standards do serve a hostage function, eliminating those standards requires devising an alternate governance structure. Chapter Five argues that the increased

In cases involving the provision of hostages, third-party adjudication of agreements becomes less necessary; and bargaining replaces noncompliance. The structure of an agreement with hostages automatically punishes a noncompliant party. The outcome with hostages is inferior to completely unrestricted trade (as possible in a world of costless negotiation and enforcement) because of the cost of providing the hostage. In the automobile example, the cost of the specialized equipment for meeting pollution and safety standards may exceed the benefits from actual pollution abatement and improved safety. However, the specialized equipment is serving two purposes: the obvious one of reducing pollution and improving safety and the less obvious one of helping support international trade agreements.[11]

A more general form of hostage is the future benefit expected from continuation of a trading relationship. When an agreement can be negotiated so that the present value of the expected future benefits of the relationship exceeds the expected benefits of an opportunistic violation to each party, the agreement becomes self-enforcing. In other words, the agreement itself becomes an effective hostage.

SELF-ENFORCING AGREEMENTS: TRADE AGREEMENTS AS HOSTAGES

A self-enforcing agreement exhibits three basic properties: (i) each party decides autonomously whether he/she is better off continuing or stopping the agreed-upon relationship; (ii) each party abides by the agreement if and only if the expected present value of the benefits from continuing exceeds the current benefit from stopping; and (iii) no third party intervenes to enforce the agreement, decide whether there has been a violation, assess damages, or impose penalties. Therefore, if one party violates the agreement, the other party's only recourse is termination.[12] The primary incentive for creation of self-enforcing agreements is the cost of third-party adjudication. In the case of recent trade policy, the problems are two-fold: lack of agreement on effective dispute-settlement procedures and difficulties involved in imposition of punitive sanctions against sovereign nations. For exactly these reasons, the early emergence of rules for foreign trade and investment among European nation-states took the form of self-enforcing agreements in which the "potential withdrawal of normal reciprocities" was the sanctioning device.[13]

---

dispute-settlement authority of supranational institutions within the European Community is helping to facilitate elimination of such standards within Europe. A similar argument applies to the Canada-United States Free-Trade Agreement, also discussed in Chapter Five.

[11] Yarbrough and Yarbrough (1990a).

[12] This discussion draws heavily on Telser (1980) for the characterization of self-enforcing agreements. Telser focuses on agreements between firms and consumers.

[13] Lipson (1985, p. 12).

The Mechanics

Suppose two countries agree to allow free trade in one another's products for a specified time. Each country knows if it violates the agreement in the last period it will bear no cost (remember, the only punishment is the other country's withdrawal; this has no effect in the agreement's last period). With zero costs of violation, each country has an incentive to defect in the last period if the benefits from doing so are positive. This implies that the value of the agreement in the last period is zero. If the agreement's last-period value is zero, the defection cost in the next-to-last period is zero; and violation will occur—making the agreement's value in the next-to-last period zero, and so on. This problem is sometimes called the *unraveling phenomenon* because the sequence of transactions unravels from the last period back to the first. To avoid unraveling, the last period must not be known in advance; that is, the termination date must be uncertain. At any time there must be a possibility that the agreement will continue or be extended. If the possibility of the agreement's continuation exists as long as there is no violation, any country contemplating violation faces the possibility of losing future benefits from the agreement. Clearly, self-enforcing agreements are of use only in continuing sequences of transactions; otherwise, the enforcement mechanism—based on the shadow of the future—ceases to exist.[14]

Assume two countries are considering entering a self-enforcing agreement to allow free trade in a given product with an uncertain termination date. The penalty for failure to abide by the agreement is termination; that is, the exploited country reverts to its autonomously chosen policy. What conditions will meet the requirements for a self-enforcing agreement? In other words, under what circumstances can the future benefits from the relationship cast a strong enough shadow to support current cooperation?

Let $E(c)$ (for *compliance*) represent the discounted present value of the expected stream of benefits to a country if both parties pursue trade policies consistent with the agreement. Similarly, let $E(n)$ (for *noncompliance*) denote the discounted present value of the expected stream of benefits to a country if the countries do *not* comply with the agreement.[15]

---

[14] For other examples of the importance of continuing sequences of transactions as enforcement or cooperation-inducing devices see Rubin (1978); Klein and Leffler (1981); Axelrod (1984); and Axelrod and Keohane (1986, pp. 232–234). The "shadow of the future" terminology comes from Axelrod.

[15] Under the definition of a self-enforcing agreement, either both parties comply or neither does. Violation by a single party lasts only one period, after which the partner violates the agreement in retaliation. Obviously, compliance/noncompliance or free trade/protection are not binary choices, but matters of degree. For simplicity, we assume that there is not a continuum of possible choices. Wagner (1983) discusses the problems associated with dichotomous-choice models. Parties may be unsure of the precise bounds of acceptable be-

Finally, let E(v) (for $v$iolation) represent the discounted present value of the amount that the country expects to gain from a sudden opportunistic violation. The expected benefits from compliance, E(c), and expected gains from violation, E(v), obviously depend on the agreement's terms.

The expected benefits from compliance, noncompliance, and opportunistic violation will differ both across goods and across countries at any point in time.[16] If one country imposes protection violating the agreement, giving it a benefit of v, the other country responds by terminating the agreement, the only possible penalty. On termination, each country receives E(n). Therefore,

$$E(c) - E(n) > E(v) \tag{1}$$

is both the necessary and the sufficient condition for a self-enforcing agreement.[17] The condition in Equation (1) is necessary because, if the expected gain from violation exceeded the expected gain from compliance, the agreement would be violated (or not initiated). The condition is also sufficient because its satisfaction implies that compliance with the agreement is more beneficial than violation. In words, Equation (1) asserts that the expected benefit from violation must not exceed the expected benefit from continued compliance. When this condition holds, a self-enforcing agreement is viable. Reciprocity, through cancellation or withdrawal from a relationship, provides an adequate defense against opportunism.[18] Third-party enforcement becomes unnecessary because the agreement not only provides each party with compliance incentives but also avoids a moral hazard to claim violation by the other party falsely.[19]

Implications for Trade Policy

Self-enforcing agreements tend to impose both reciprocity and a small-group character on trade policy. The condition for a successful self-enforcing agreement discussed above and represented by Equation (1) will have unique implications for each pair of potential trading partners.

There is no inherent requirement limiting self-enforcing agreements to

---

havior, and legal standards may be uncertain; Craswell and Calfee (1986); and Kaplow (1990) present early work on the implications, which include the need to adjust penalties if optimal deterrence is to be maintained.

[16] In the remainder of the discussion, references to "discounted present value of the expected benefits" are shortened to "expected benefits" for simplicity. It is, however, important to keep in mind the role of expectations in the viability of self-enforcing agreements.

[17] Telser (1980) presents a simple proof.

[18] Rhodes (1989) focuses on this type of benefit from reciprocity. Also see Oye (1986b, pp. 12–18).

[19] We examine this problem later in the context of alternatives to self-enforcing agreements.

two parties.[20] It is necessary, however, that Equation (1) hold for every party. This balancing of costs and benefits may be difficult to accomplish with large numbers of participants.[21] The commitment to the postwar norms of MFN and nondiscrimination is very strong, but a role for bilateralism in international trade policy is slowly coming to be recognized.[22] For years, departure from the most-favored-nation rule was seen as unconscionable abandonment of principle; multilateralism, initially a means of trade liberalization, had become an end in itself. More recently, discussion has moved from the morality of applying other rules to the practical effects of doing so.[23] The controversy over periodic accessions to the European Community illustrates the problems additional parties can cause. The additions of Spain and Portugal, for example, clearly altered the balance of costs and benefits to each of the ten existing members and required substantial changes in policies.[24]

Bilateral as opposed to multilateral agreements require negotiation of more agreements to achieve a given level of liberalization, presumably slowing the spread of the benefits. On the other hand, bilateralism also may slow the spread of trade problems in contexts where agreements must be self enforcing. Suppose, for example, 100 countries successfully negotiate a self-enforcing agreement through the GATT. Conditions then change unexpectedly, one country commits a violation, and the agreement terminates (or, at the very least, the remaining ninety-nine must renegotiate a new agreement).[25] The problem is like that in serial electrical wiring, where weakness in one area causes failure of the entire system (for example, strings of Christmas lights in which one defective bulb causes system failure). A trading system based on smaller-scale self-enforcing agreements is more like parallel electrical wiring, in which failure of one unit does limited damage (for example, strings of lights in which one defective bulb has no effect on the rest).

Reciprocity (even in the negative sense of threatened retaliation) is an

---

[20] Hence, the emphasis in our usage of *bilateralism* on the self-enforcing nature of the enforcement mechanism rather than the number of parties.

[21] Oye (1986b, pp. 18–22) provides a good discussion of the issues related to the number of parties.

[22] McKeown (1991) explores bilateralism from a different perspective. He examines actual trade patterns, not trade policies; therefore his bilateralism refers to countries' propensity to concentrate their trade with a single partner instead of spreading trade more broadly.

[23] Wolff (1983, p. 366).

[24] Taylor (1983, p. 304).

[25] By definition, the entire agreement must be voided on violation by one party; otherwise, the agreement cannot be self-enforcing since termination is the only possible penalty. Self-enforcing agreements can be renegotiated, by all or a subset of the original parties, following opportunism. However, anticipation of such renegotiation may lower the expected penalty for violations and weaken self-enforcement.

essential feature of self-enforcing agreements, because it forms the enforcement mechanism without third-party intervention.[26] Actual retaliation may be rare because, as we discuss later, self-enforcing agreements are not violated unless underlying conditions change unexpectedly; nevertheless, the *threat* of retaliation must be ever-present.[27]

The requirements for self-enforcing agreements are consistent with several observations concerning international trade. Countries negotiating the lowering of trade barriers do so in the expectation of a long series of future transactions—not on a one-transaction basis. The termination dates for most trade agreements are indefinite; when specific time periods are negotiated, renegotiation typically occurs before expiration.[28] Exogenous events likely to cause termination of an agreement interfere with the negotiation process; for example, a pending election often postpones negotiation. The theory of self-enforcing agreements explains all these observations.

PRODUCT LINKAGE IN SELF-ENFORCING AGREEMENTS

The idea of self-enforcing agreements also has interesting implications for the combinations of goods covered by various international trade agreements.[29] In trade negotiations, a single agreement often links peculiar combinations of goods that are seemingly totally unrelated. What is the reason for linking the products in a single self-enforcing agreement? Linkage may allow the conditions for a self-enforcing agreement to be met when this is impossible for a single product. Suppose free trade in one of

[26] The possibility that protection may be instituted in retaliation for violation of agreements has implications for the debate over compensation of exporters, such as that provided by certain voluntary export restraints. Arguments in favor of such compensation assume that tariffs or quotas are imposed purely for their protectionist effects, not as retaliatory enforcement mechanisms; see, for example, Jones (1984); and Hoekman and Leidy (1990, especially pp. 27–29). If protection is imposed (at least in some cases) as retaliation, compensation would be inappropriate and would reduce the magnitude of the punishment and thus its deterrent effect.

[27] As noted earlier, the incipient nature of violations and retaliation presents problems for empirical analysis of the type undertaken in Keohane (1988b) and Grieco (1990). A failure to observe frequent violations of international agreements would not necessarily provide evidence that compliance considerations are unimportant. The more compliance considerations are taken into account in determining the form of agreements, the higher will be the rate of compliance with existing agreements and the rarer will be observed instances of noncompliance and retaliation. In issue areas where potential compliance problems are so great that they cannot be successfully dealt with in any form, there will be no agreement to observe being violated, although bickering and ill will probably will continue.

[28] U.S.-Soviet grain trade agreements, for example, are usually negotiated for five-year periods subject to extension prior to expiration.

[29] Discussions of linkages include Tollison and Willett (1979); Sebenius (1983); Keohane (1984, pp. 91–92); McGinnis (1986); Axelrod and Keohane (1986, pp. 239–241); and Hoekman (1989).

m independent products does not satisfy the condition for a self-enforcing agreement, so noncompliance or protection gives the country the highest expected benefit. The country clearly would be unwilling to enter a free-trade agreement for that product. However, suppose another of the m products satisfies the condition for a self-enforcing agreement, so free trade in this product gives the highest expected benefit. By linking the two products together in a single agreement, cooperation on the two may satisfy the condition for self-enforcement. The possibility of linkage weakens the necessary and sufficient condition for a self-enforcing agreement. It is no longer necessary that the condition in Equation (1) hold for each product, only that it hold for the package of linked goods, for an agreement to prevail in all m products.[30]

The wider range of transactions that can be halted as punishment weakens the requirement for self-enforcement. If there is a violation of the agreement on one product, punishment must take the form of termination of free trade in *all* the products.[31] It is not any inherent relationship among the products themselves that promotes linkage, but the particular pattern of benefits from compliance and opportunism.[32]

Issue linkage has a long and interesting history in international trade negotiations. Linkage can occur in two forms. The first and most obvious is linkage of several goods or issues on which trade is to be liberalized in a single agreement. This explains the unusual combinations sometimes covered by an agreement—for example, leather, film, glass, aluminum, paper products, sporting goods, and silicon wafers in one U.S.-Japan agreement. In another example, one stage of the U.S.-Israel free-trade

[30] In terms of the model summarized by Equation (1), there will be one such equation (or inequality) for each of the m goods. The summation of those equations takes the same form as Equation (1) and represents the necessary and sufficient condition for a self-enforcing agreement in the m products as a group. Intuitively, a high benefit from continued compliance in one product (a high value of the left-hand side of the inequality for that product) can offset a high benefit from opportunism in another product (a high value of the right-hand side of the inequality for this second product). This is possible *only* if trade in all products is halted in retaliation for a violation in any of the products.

[31] Klein and Leffler (1981) discuss a similar phenomenon regarding quality-assurance by multiproduct firms. As long as consumers react to an unpleasant quality surprise in one of the firm's products by stopping purchases of all its products, the firm's entire stock of non-salvageable capital can serve as a quality-assurance bond for every good. This explains one role for extending brand names across a range of products.

[32] For inherently related products, linkage may be necessary for a successful self-enforcing agreement. Products can be related in several ways. The benefits from free trade in one product may depend on whether there is free trade or protection on related products. For example, if the United States and Japan were to remove trade barriers on steel, the benefits to Japan of removing barriers on automobiles would be lower than in the presence of barriers on steel. Japan's ability to utilize lower-cost steel increases the cost advantage of Japanese-made automobiles over U.S.-made automobiles, increasing the benefits to Japan of free trade in automobiles.

pact covers aluminum, gold jewelry, radio-navigational equipment, re-
frigerators, cut roses, and tomatoes; these goods, especially sensitive in
the negotiations, are included in the final 1995 stage of the pact. Linkages
also can occur across issues. For example, the Jackson-Vanik Amendment
explicitly linked U.S.-Soviet trade with Soviet emigration policies. In the
sixteenth century, the Swiss allowed free trade in Swiss mercenaries in
return for exemption from tariffs on various imports from France.[33] The
1968–71 U.S.-Japan talks implicitly linked reductions in Japanese auto
and textile protection to the return of Okinawa to Japan.[34] The 1962
Hickenlooper Amendment, designed to protect U.S. foreign investment
abroad, mandated suspension of bilateral foreign aid for countries dis-
criminating against or confiscating the property of U.S. investors.[35]

A second, more extensive means of linkage is the formation of longstanding groups, such as customs unions, in which members make a range
of decisions collectively. Linkages can be forged not only across goods,
but across issue areas at a point in time and across time as well. These
groups can take two forms. The first involves use of self-enforcing agreements, reciprocity, hostages, and issue linkages as suggested in this chapter, instead of creation of supranational institutions.[36] The second form,
the subject of separate treatment in Chapter Five, creates supranational
enforcement arrangements.

Trade negotiations along narrowly sectoral lines that eliminate many
possible linkages almost invariably result in strongly protectionist outcomes (for example, in the textile industry).[37] In recent U.S.-Canada trade
liberalization, an explicit decision dictated a comprehensive instead of a
sectoral approach. Not only does this allow for linkages, it also implies
that the only industries excluded from the pact will be those on explicitly
negotiated exceptions lists.

The linkage of a variety of goods in a trade agreement is similar to the
practice of "logrolling" or vote-trading in Congressional voting. A member of Congress may be persuaded to vote for a mildly unfavorable bill in
return for a promise of support on a highly favorable bill; each member
then gains a net advantage. A logrolling package is a linked self-enforcing
agreement; with no third-party enforcement, the primary constraint on
opportunism (that is, not delivering the promised vote) is the value of
contingent future cooperation.

[33] Conybeare (1984).

[34] Cowhey and Long (1983, p. 169).

[35] Lipson (1985, p. 202).

[36] Yarbrough and Yarbrough (1986b, 1990a).

[37] There are interesting exceptions such as the U.S.-Canada Automotive Products Trade
Act of 1965, but that agreement is supported by strong labor union links as well as corporate ties. Analyses of the pact are Rhodes (1989, pp. 290–293); and Acheson (1989).

ALTERNATIVES TO SELF-ENFORCING AGREEMENTS

For any given stream of benefits, a self-enforcing agreement may be impossible if the expected time horizon is too short or the potential benefits from opportunism are too large.[38] Agreement then requires some alternate enforcement mechanism. One possibility is third-party enforcement so that the agreement need not be self-enforcing. A hegemon may serve this purpose, as in Chapter Three; or a small group of linked countries can create such a third party, as shown in Chapter Five. Although third-party adjudication is important in nearly all strategic organizational situations, the problems involved in direct third-party imposition of sanctions against sovereign nations remain.

Other alternatives to a self-enforcing agreement involve a payment that changes hands contingent on compliance with the agreement. For example, each party may set aside a specified amount of money that either party stands to forfeit because of failure to comply.[39] Such escrow arrangements are common in real estate transactions where the one-time nature of a transaction precludes the use of self-enforcing agreements. This alternative differs from the use of hostages because the payment both compensates the victim of opportunism and provides deterrence.[40] The primary limitation on such arrangements is the implied moral hazard. To collect the forfeitable sum, each party may have an incentive to claim falsely that the other has violated the agreement. Nevertheless, there are some applications in international trade. Bonds of this type are used in the early investigation of dumping charges (for example, in recent U.S. charges against Japanese mobile telephone producers). After a complaint, but before a final and formal finding, exporters typically must post bonds to pay antidumping duties if the charges are substantiated. If the dumping allegations have no basis, the bond reverts to the exporter. We should note that antidumping policy is highly controversial, in part due to this moral hazard problem.

Another alternative to a self-enforcing agreement is use of contingent deferred payments. Again, moral hazard presents a problem because, to avoid making the agreed-upon payment, one party may claim falsely that the other party has violated the agreement. The presence of moral hazard may require a third party to intervene to decide whether a violation has occurred or been claimed falsely, so neither escrow nor a deferred-payment arrangement avoids the need for third-party adjudication.[41] A self-

[38] In terms of Equation (1), $E(c)$ may be too small if the time horizon is short, or $E(v)$ may be too large.

[39] Maoz and Felsenthal (1987) discuss the efficacy of such arrangements.

[40] Kronman (1985).

[41] Maoz and Felsenthal (1987, p. 198).

enforcing agreement circumvents these problems and avoids a moral hazard by allowing the expected future benefits from continued compliance to serve as the bond. If a violation were falsely claimed, the agreement would end and the party falsely claiming grievance would lose.[42] This arrangement may be especially appealing in international trade where direct financial payments (escrow, deferred payments, etc.) may be infeasible because sovereign nations have difficulty credibly committing themselves to future contingent payments.[43]

VIOLATIONS OF SELF-ENFORCING AGREEMENTS

Upon entering a self-enforcing agreement, each country anticipates the other country will abide by the agreement's terms.[44] Because the only penalty that can be imposed on a violator is termination, each country compares the value of the agreement with the benefit from cheating in each period. The terms must be such that, *given initial conditions*, the value of the agreement to each party exceeds the benefits from violation; otherwise, countries would not undertake it (see Equation [1]). Of course, this does not imply that self-enforcing agreements never will be violated. Violations will occur whenever post-negotiation changes in conditions sufficiently raise the benefits to opportunism $[E(v)]$ or lower the value of the agreement $[E(c) - E(n)]$ to one or more countries. Therefore, the theory predicts agreements would be broken in periods of rapid change when, for example, there are changes in relative prices, exchange rates, production and consumption patterns, or domestic political alignments that unexpectedly alter incentives for compliance or violation.

BILATERALISM: TRADE POLICY IN THE 1980s

Two aspects of recent trade policy have received particular attention as notable departures from earlier postwar trade liberalization. The first is

---

[42] The negative side is that a hostage in the form of a self-enforcing agreement provides deterrence against opportunism but no compensation to the victim if an agreement is violated.

[43] Keohane (1984, pp. 116–120) argues that regimes allow states to "tie their hands" as a means of credible commitment. On hands-tying more generally, see Kronman (1985).

[44] This does not mean that parties naively expect their partners to abide by all commitments, only that the terms of agreements are negotiated such that each party has an incentive, *given initial conditions*, to comply. Hirschman (1945) argues that one country could "set up" another by entering an agreement with the intention (unknown to the partner) of a future violation or holdup. This argument relies on a fundamental asymmetry of information, as discussed in the appendix to Chapter Two. Such a strategy, if possible, would risk a loss of reputation and imperil future cooperation.

the notion of reciprocity. Reciprocal agreements have always played a role in trade negotiations.[45] Recently, unilateral U.S. moves toward free trade have been rare, and the term *reciprocity* has come to encompass explicitly protectionist retaliation as well as reciprocal reductions in trade barriers.[46] The recent heated debate over reciprocity stems at least in part from lack of a precise and consistent meaning of the term.[47] Wolff's definition is closest to the meaning here: the fulfillment of the expectation that the agreement will be followed by other signatories.[48]

It is commonly argued that reciprocity, or a perception of it, is essential to liberalization because it soothes political constituencies and supports the (partially erroneous) view of liberalization as an "exchange of concessions."[49] The theory of self-enforcing agreements provides a stronger liberalization argument for reciprocity, a concept frequently attributed to protectionism.[50] Lacking other enforcement mechanisms, threats to impose protection by cancelling liberalization agreements in response to opportunistic violations may be one of few mechanisms available to encourage compliance.[51]

A recent dispute between France and Japan illustrates reciprocity to maintain open trade. Japan threatened to halt imports of French surfboards on the claim that the boards were dangerous because individuals could fall off. France, in response, noted that the same could be said for Japanese motorcycles and threatened to prohibit their importation. The threat served its purpose; trade in both surfboards and motorcycles continues.[52]

The pursuit of reciprocity leads directly to the second major change in trade policy—the increased emphasis on bilateral trade relationships and negotiations. Recent U.S. trade policy explicitly has used the threat of increased bilateral barriers in an effort to force reductions in tariffs and export subsidies by other countries.[53] In contrast, during the early postwar period, the GATT doctrine of unconditional most-favored-nation

[45] Cuddington and McKinnon (1979); and Hathaway and Masur (1990).

[46] Cline (1983); and Yeager and Tuerck (1983). A strong proponent of multilateralism, Bhagwati (1990, p. 28) agrees that the United States never supported unilateral free trade.

[47] Keohane (1986b).

[48] Wolff (1983, p. 365).

[49] On aspects of this perspective, see Finger (1987b); Baldwin (1987); Winters (1987); and Finger and Holmes (1987).

[50] For a summary of analogous views of reciprocal trading in industrial organization, see Williamson (1985a, pp. 191–195).

[51] Rhodes (1989) examines several cases to test the efficacy of reciprocity in supporting cooperative trade; her results are generally supportive of the view that reciprocity is useful.

[52] *Wall Street Journal* (1986b, p. 1).

[53] Lipson (1985, p. 184n) provides an interesting example from the Canadian oil industry.

status dictated a multilateral approach to trade policy by prohibiting many forms of geographic discrimination. The longer historical record suggests that bilateralism is more appropriately viewed as the rule and multilateralism as the exception, not vice versa.[54] The norm of multilateralism encounters problems with no hegemon, and agreements among smaller groups of countries are more likely to be successful.[55]

Despite widespread praise for the GATT norm of multilateralism or unconditional most-favored-nation status, recent liberalization of trade has involved bilateral agreements. Examples include free-trade pacts between the United States and Canada; Israel and the EC; Israel and the United States; Chile, Argentina, and Brazil; Bolivia, Colombia, and Ecuador; the Association of Southeast Asian Nations (ASEAN), the European Free-Trade Association, U.S.-Korea negotiations, U.S.-Taiwan talks, the Caribbean Basin Initiative, and ongoing talks between the United States and Mexico and between the United States and several other Latin American countries.[56] The U.S.-Israel agreement (although obviously supported by a special political relationship) has generated interest as a model because of its success in several previously troublesome issue areas. As the strategic organizational perspective predicts, enforcement institutions play a central role in these bilateral agreements.

Our approach also predicts that bilateralism would emerge in areas of trade where transactional insecurity is especially high, that is, in areas involving large relation-specific investments. Since 1981, the United States has used the Bilateral Investment Treaty (BIT) Program to encourage U.S. direct investment abroad. The treaties guarantee certain rights and protections to investors and cover issues such as national treatment, dispute settlement, and expropriation contingencies. Eighteen bilateral investment treaties have been completed under the program; and preliminary discussions are underway with other countries.[57]

Not only has liberalization outside the GATT involved bilateralism, but recent progress toward liberalization within the GATT, despite its commitment to multilateralism, involves agreements among small groups of signatory countries. A major part of the Tokyo Round consisted of negotiating codes covering technical standards, government procure-

[54] See, for example, Strange (1985), and discussions of GATT negotiations prior to the Kennedy Round.

[55] Again, we use *bilateralism* to denote self-enforcing agreements among small groups of countries, not necessarily two; see the discussion in footnote 14 of Chapter One. Bilateralism is contrasted with the norm of multilateralism that has played an important role in the GATT negotiations.

[56] Hathaway and Masur (1990) discuss many of these cases.

[57] The U.S. International Trade Commission's *Operation of the Trade Agreements Program*, published each July, summarizes annual developments under the Bilateral Investment Treaty Program.

ment, customs valuation, subsidies, and related issues.[58] The codes apply only to direct signatories (not all the GATT contracting parties); signatories per code range from twelve to forty.

The reaction to these policy changes has been mixed. The increased emphasis on reciprocity and bilateralism has been praised as a move toward "fair trade" by those who feel the United States has been taken advantage of in the past. However, advocates of unilateral free trade point out the danger of a return to the beggar-thy-neighbor policies that contributed to the 1930s economic disaster.[59] Stein refers to "bilateral discriminatory liberalization" as a "hallmark of mercantilism."[60] An outspoken critic of reciprocity as protectionism has puzzled over the lack of enthusiasm of the normally pro-protection AFL-CIO for reciprocity legislation.[61] The strategic organizational view suggests the AFL-CIO position is understandable to the extent that some forms of reciprocity support reduction of trade barriers. Thus, reciprocity presents a particularly difficult policy problem. On the one hand, it may be one of very few enforcement mechanisms available to support cooperative open trade. On the other hand, it contains an obvious vulnerability to "capture" by groups seeking protection for their own narrowly defined self-interests.[62]

Historical evidence suggests bilateralism, reciprocity, and threats of retaliation characterized even periods of successful trade liberalization. The 1960s and 1970s, often cited as the heyday of multilateral trade liberalization under MFN, now appear less successful than commonly believed. Although tariff reductions were substantial, the gains were largely offset by increases in nontariff barriers.[63] Given the unique nature of each country's nontariff measures, customized bilateral agreements may be better tailored for successful liberalization under such conditions.

Finally, note that the strategic organizational argument does *not* imply that the GATT no longer has a role to play in the international trading

[58] Grieco (1990) develops a "realist" interpretation of the codes negotiations. Our approach is contrasted with that of Grieco in the appendix to Chapter Two.

[59] Hanke (1983); and *Wall Street Journal* (1990b). On the endogeneity of tariffs, see Bohara and Kaempfer (1991).

[60] Stein (1984, p. 366).

[61] Cline (1983, p. 122).

[62] We refer to *capture* in the sense used by Stigler (1974), in which an industry is able to gain control of a government body created to regulate that industry. Rhodes (1989, p. 288) is sensitive to this problem in her analysis of U.S.-Japanese bargaining over trade policy in the automobile sector during the early 1980s: "While congressional speeches indicate that one of the motivations behind protectionist legislation against Japanese car imports was the enforcement of reciprocity, it is also clear that there was a good deal of pressure for protection regardless of the reciprocity issue." As in the case of technical standards discussed earlier (see footnote 7), congressional speeches offer an unreliable guide to true motivations.

[63] Ray and Marvel (1984).

system. It still provides a valuable consulting and negotiating forum. In addition, it provides an institutional structure to generate and transmit information.[64] Such a structure is important to support reputations that, in turn, ease agreements of the type examined in this chapter. Bilateral trade negotiations, especially among smaller countries, may be quite infrequent. Under such circumstances, reputations for abiding by agreements are difficult to establish and maintain without a central information transmitter such as the GATT.[65]

SUMMARY

Without a hegemon, the absence of an international authority to impose sanctions for noncompliance threatens to foreclose trade liberalization agreements. However, if an agreement can be designed to impose costs automatically on any noncomplying party, agreement may be feasible. Reciprocity can provide this automatic enforcement mechanism. By explicitly embodying a (credible) threat of retaliation or reciprocity, an agreement becomes self-enforcing and lessens the need for a third party to judge and punish noncompliance.

Almost by definition, self-enforcing agreements impose both reciprocity and a small-group approach to trade policy. The necessary and sufficient condition for a self-enforcing agreement has unique implications for each group of potential trading partners. Reciprocity, even in the sense of threatened retaliation, is essential because it is the enforcement mechanism replacing third-party adjudication. Retaliation may be rare, because the terms assure self-enforcing agreements will not be violated unless underlying conditions change unexpectedly; nevertheless, the threat of retaliation must be present.

The theory of self-enforcing agreements makes several predictions consistent with observed trade policy. First, self-enforcing agreements are useful only in a relationship with an uncertain termination date. International trade agreements typically do provide for renegotiation or extension before expiration and thereby render the termination date uncertain. Second, for any given gains from cooperation, the expected horizon must be sufficiently long to support a self-enforcing agreement. Trade relationships typically are of long duration. The longer the expected horizon, the greater the value of a trade-liberalizing agreement. Third, countries entering a self-enforcing agreement do not anticipate violations. The theory

---

[64] Keohane (1984) emphasizes this role for international regimes.

[65] See Milgrom, North, and Weingast (1990). The GATT can also make institutional adjustments. For example, a recent proposal would improve dispute settlement by eliminating the current unanimity requirement for panel reports (*San Francisco Chronicle* [1990]). However, the strategic organizational approach suggests this ability is limited.

explains violations as responses to unexpected changes in the underlying factors that determine the terms of the agreement. Again this is consistent with historical evidence, as periods of uncertainty (just before elections, for example) often generate postponement of trade negotiations. Finally, the theory of self-enforcing agreements explains the peculiar groups of goods often linked in single trade agreements.

Chapter Five

THIRD-PARTY GOVERNANCE AND GROUP
MEMBERSHIP: MINILATERAL TRADE
LIBERALIZATION

SO FAR, we have analyzed two strategic organizational responses to relation-specific contracting problems: *multilateral* liberalization under the
governance of a hegemon (Chapter Three) and *bilateral* liberalization under self-enforcing agreements (Chapter Four).[1] A third option—*minilateralism*—is the subject of this chapter. Small groups of countries may create
supranational institutions to perform a third-party governance role. Such
creations are problematic, of course, as they necessarily impinge on national sovereignty. Nonetheless, when relation-specific investments are
extensive, the benefits of minilateralism may outweigh its obvious problems.

One way of viewing preferential trade agreements, such as the European Community and the Canada-U.S. Free-Trade Agreement, is as minilateralism. Preferential trade agreements (PTAs) are a hybrid form of international organization with two sets of rules, one covering behavior
with nonmembers and another with members. By providing an organizational structure that can deter opportunistic behavior, preferential
trade agreements may produce benefits beyond those typically recognized.

Economists have had difficulty developing a consistent rationale for
PTAs. From the perspective of neoclassical trade theory, they are an economically inefficient alternative to universal free trade. The usual tack by
economists has been to view PTAs as non-economic-based entities but
conduct an economic analysis of their welfare implications.[2] This presents
a dilemma because "an incentive to form and enlarge customs unions per-

---

[1] The other option, also in Chapter Three, is *unilateral* liberalization (for example, mid-
nineteenth-century Britain). It applies in situations in which the limited scope of any relation-specific investment minimizes the hazard of opportunism, allowing countries to follow
autonomously determined (that is, unilateral) trade policies.

[2] Corden (1984, especially pp. 112–124) gives a brief but useful survey of the relevant
economic literature, including its inability to explain many observed phenomena. A subset
of the literature somewhat closer to our perspective focuses on tariff bargaining; for example, Johnson (1965), Caves (1974), Mayer (1981), and Wonnacott and Wonnacott (1981).

sists until the world becomes one big customs union, that is, until world free trade prevails."[3] Because we do not observe such expansion of PTA groups, the existing economic theory is obviously incomplete.

Political scientists' treatments of regional integration, like those of economists, are incomplete if the criterion is ability to explain when and where integration will or will not occur and succeed.[4] World events better predict theory than the other way around. As Moravcsik observes, "When the EC stagnates, as in the 1970s, scholars speak of the obsolescence of regional integration theory; when it rebounds, as in 1985, they speak of the obsolescence of the nation-state."[5]

The shortcomings of understanding in this area are especially noticeable in light of renewed interest in PTAs. The nature of these developments is a matter of controversy among international trade analysts and policymakers. Traditional economic analyses ignore relation-specific investment and associated strategic organizational problems and therefore assume technology, not organizational form, determines production costs and patterns of comparative advantage.[6] The perspective here suggests PTAs arise as a strategic organizational response when trade involves large relation-specific investments subject to opportunism, particularly opportunistic government policies.

As we argued earlier, international trade by its nature often involves relation-specific assets. Firms develop user-supplier relations that cross national boundaries. Specialization according to comparative advantage necessarily involves expansion of productive capacity to serve export markets; and, sometimes, these markets are such that the associated investment consists of dedicated assets whose value would be lost if a particular market were closed. Transactions involving such assets are vulnerable to opportunistic holdups. Without institutions and techniques for handling opportunism, international relation-specific investments will be avoided. Specialization will be curtailed, and general-purpose production techniques will be used even where more specific ones would result in lower production costs. Therefore, the absence of governance structures sufficient to support relation-specific investment can reduce the produc-

---

[3] Kemp and Wan (1972), cited by Corden (1984, p. 122).

[4] Keohane and Nye (1975) provide a useful survey.

[5] Moravcsik (1991, p. 56).

[6] Nonetheless, contracting problems have been shown to be important in the determination of both size and internal structure for a number of types of organizations; see, for example, Yarbrough and Yarbrough (1988) on the firm; Rugman (1981) and Caves (1982) on multinational firms; and Sandler and Cauley (1977) and Conybeare (1980) on international organizations.

tive efficiency of the world economy.[7] Organizational form then becomes a major determinant of costs.[8]

PREFERENTIAL TRADE AGREEMENTS AS GOVERNANCE STRUCTURES

We have argued that opportunism can arise from two sources: from the *firms* involved in a particular transaction or from *government* trade policies. If a Country Two firm undertakes relation-specific investment to service Country One's automobile market, the relationship can be threatened by opportunistic price decreases by importers in One, price increases by the firm in Two, import restrictions by the government of One, or export restrictions by the government of Two. For opportunism by the firm, private contractual arrangements can reduce the hazard; these include long-term contracts, entry fees as bonds, marketing restrictions, and vertical integration.[9]

Private contractual arrangements between firms are inadequate, however, to prevent possible opportunistic changes in government policies. To provide safeguards against opportunism by governments, the governments themselves must make credible commitments to abide by their promises.[10] Preferential trade agreements are, in this sense, a public-sector analogue of vertical integration.

This implies it may be impossible to have both cost-reducing relation-specific investment *and* universal, nonpreferential trade liberalization; strategic organizational problems may introduce a trade-off between the two. The efficiency loss from a preferential trade agreement (compared with universal free trade) may be more than offset by productive efficiency gains from relation-specific investment—investment that would not be undertaken without the PTA's governance structure.

If formation of preferential trade arrangements has as a primary goal the safeguarding of transactions involving vulnerable relation-specific as-

[7] The appendix to this chapter presents a hypothetical numerical example, drawn from Yarbrough and Yarbrough (1990a). In the example, the governance provided by a PTA allows a country to undertake specific investment that makes it the low-cost producer of a good. When this effect of PTAs in altering the pattern of comparative advantage is taken into account, groups that appear to be trade diverting may in fact be trade creating.

[8] Portions of the strategic trade policy literature emphasize the ability of government policies (for example, industrial policies) to affect patterns of comparative advantage; one example is Tyson and Zysman (1983). This differs from our argument that the degree of effectiveness of governance structures in international trade affects costs.

[9] This argument is outlined in Klein, Crawford, and Alchian (1978); Klein (1980); and Williamson (1983). On the effects of the Single Europe Act (SEA) and liberalization of the internal market on merger activity in Europe, see Sandholtz and Zysman (1989, pp. 118–120). Rugman (1981); Caves (1982); and Casson (1987) treat multinational firms.

[10] This process is particularly complex for nontariff barriers since they lack transparency and are entangled with domestic policies.

sets, there should be identifiable governance-oriented elements within PTAs. As we have seen, these elements can take two basic forms.[11] First, arrangements can be self-enforcing as discussed in Chapter Four. Bilateralism, issue linkages, and economic hostages then support Tit-for-Tat and *quid pro quo* self-help strategies. Second, arrangements can be hierarchical—where a third party (for example, a hegemon or a supranational organization) enforces commitments and punishes opportunism. Even as trade arrangements move toward institutions that depend less on third-party enforcement with the decline of U.S. hegemony, there are regional groups attempting to build supranational institutions as third-party governance mechanisms. We refer to such arrangements as *minilateralism* (represented in the lower right-hand corner of Figure 5.1).[12] Examples include the European movement toward economic integration in 1992 under the Single Europe Act and the Canada-U.S. Free-Trade Agreement. The EC is particularly interesting because it provides a single case that embodies examples of both bilateral and minilateral institutions as well as the "substitutability" of the two.

The European Community

Changes in the European Community between its 1957 formation and the push toward 1992 reveal a gradual shift from bilateral, self-enforcing trade arrangements of the type discussed in Chapter Four toward more third-party enforcement by supranational institutions.[13] Bilateralism uses linkages and hostages to support reciprocity as self-help with no third-

---

[11] Keohane (1990, p. 731), by defining *multilateralism* as any coordination of policy by three or more states, subsumes both bilateralism and minilateralism by our definitions. In his usage, the GATT, the European Community, and the free-trade agreement among Chile, Argentina, and Brazil are all examples of multilateralism. Our usage endeavors to introduce distinctions among what seem very different arrangements. See Chapter One, footnotes 9 and 14, and Chapter Three, footnote 62.

[12] The distinctions between bilateralism and multilateralism are closely related to those between confederations and federations, respectively. Three key features of federalism are (i) constitutional prohibition against members' secession, (ii) an independent central authority, and (iii) possible constitutional amendment with less than unanimous consent of members (Taylor [1983, p. 270]). All three items are central to the issues raised in this chapter. On the historical connections between free trade and federation, see Dorfman (1991, pp. 578–579). Dorfman traces confederation (for example, the Zollverein which became Germany) to Frederick List's adoption of Alexander Hamilton's ideas on an internally open but protected home market for development of manufacturing industries.

[13] The concrete dating of the switch from bilateralism to minilateralism is obviously an oversimplification. The key element, as argued below, is the Single Europe Act and its implications for weighted-majority rather than unanimity voting on some Community decisions. Sandholtz and Zysman (1989, p. 95) characterize the SEA as a "disjunction" in the history of European integration, not a "culmination" of the pattern begun in the 1950s.

		Specific Trade-Related Investment?	
		No	Yes
Effective 3rd-Party Enforcement?	No		BILATERAL trade policy (e.g., 1970-90)
		UNILATERAL trade policy (e.g., 19th-century Britain)	
	Yes		MULTILATERAL trade policy (e.g., 1945-65) OR **MINILATERAL trade policy (e.g., Europe 1992)**

Figure 5.1: Conditions supporting minilateral trade policy include presence of specific trade-related investment and creation of effective third-party enforcement.

party enforcement. *This suggests that use of linkages and hostages should decline with creation of more efficacious supranational governance institutions.* We now turn to a brief examination of the experience of the European Community to see how the manifestations of minilateralism supplant bilateralism.[14]

Bilateralism in the "First" EC: 1957–1985

At the time of the formation of the EC in 1957, the countries of Western Europe needed to build closer economic relations. The GATT covered a circumscribed range of trade issues, primarily trade in manufactures, and limited liberalization to the lowest common denominator. Europe needed more—liberalization in a broader class of goods and elimination rather than reduction of tariffs. Acting outside the GATT required providing one's own governance structure; the U.S. hegemony that bolstered enforcement within the GATT would be of little use. The United States en-

[14] Sandholtz and Zysman (1989) and Moravcsik (1991) provide very different interpretations of changes in the European Community, especially the 1986 passage of the Single Europe Act. Sandholtz and Zysman emphasize the changes as part of a bargain by elites and the product of entrepreneurship by the EC Commission. Moravcsik, in contrast, interprets the SEA as an interstate or intergovernmental bargain among France, Britain, and Germany. Moravcsik (1991, pp. 21–27) compares the two perspectives. Garrett (1990, p. 41n27) discusses side-payments involved in passage of the SEA.

couraged Europe to form a customs union after World War II, but Europeans resisted a supranational authority to enforce liberalization.[15]

During the early period of European integration, supranational institutions were few, powerless, and constrained by unanimity voting. The major exception was the European Coal and Steel Community (ECSC) formed by the Treaty of Paris, which created a supranational executive with substantial powers in the coal and steel sectors. Even here, however, the Treaty required declaration of a "manifest crisis" for supranational control to be made nonvoluntary for member states; and German opposition typically blocked the needed declaration.[16]

Outside the coal and steel sectors, the characteristics outlined in Chapter Four as typical of bilateral liberalization—small group size, linkages, hostages, and reciprocity—were apparent in European integration. Instead of one large European customs union, there were three small ones—Benelux, the European Free-Trade Association (EFTA), and the European Community. Expansion of EC membership did not happen until the 1970s, with a renewed push toward efficacious supranational institutions.

During the early years, the EC was almost purely intergovernmental. There was no effective third party to enforce agreements or, as Moravcsik notes, no "European hegemon."[17] Linkages and hostages were essential to intra-group cooperation. The original Treaty of Rome that formed the EC was a clear example of linkage or a "package deal."[18] France got a highly advantageous Common Agricultural Policy (CAP).[19] Germany won a market for industrial goods and a postwar return to international respectability. Italy obtained development aid for the underdeveloped southern region that threatened Italian political stability. Belgium, the Netherlands, and Luxembourg received access to a much larger market and a bigger voice in European affairs.[20]

---

[15] Milward (1984); and Strange (1987, p. 561). Despite the apparent lack of consistency between these negotiations and the underlying postwar norm of nondiscriminatory multilateral liberalization, the negotiations are consistent with other moves taken by the United States to reconstruct and strengthen postwar Europe.

[16] The ECSC policed members' compliance with agreements in the coal and steel sectors. For example, Italian firms were taken to the European Court of Justice for violation of ECSC minimum-price rules. The firms allegedly accepted twenty-percent penalties for late delivery in their contracts and then specified delivery dates that were impossible to meet, allowing the firms to sell at prices twenty percent below the ECSC minimum (Tsoukalis and da Silva Ferreira [1980, p. 361]).

[17] Moravcsik (1991, p. 25).

[18] Taylor (1982, p. 759); Moravcsik (1991, pp. 54–55).

[19] Sebenius (1983, p. 292); Vernon (1982, p. 495); and Taylor (1983, p. 299). Britain's entry and dispute over the Common Agricultural Policy threatened this part of the bargain in 1982–1984 (Moravcsik [1991, p. 32]).

[20] The voting-power analysis of Brams, et al. (1991, pp. 4–15) suggests that effective voice (that is, voting power) and number of votes are less than perfectly correlated.

Even beyond the formative Treaty of Rome, the typical pattern in the early years of the Community involved package deals negotiated by member governments.[21] Ralf Dahrendorf christened this intergovernmental approach to integration the "Second Europe," whereas the more idealized "First Europe" referred to creation of centralized European institutions above the member governments.[22] Taylor argues the "package deal" or linkage approach would not have evolved had the Community moved sooner to weighted-majority voting, as originally scheduled under the Treaty of Rome.[23]

Use of economic hostages to support trade also was evident in the early days of European integration. Health, safety, pollution, and other technical standards within Europe provided many opportunities for provision of hostages. One example, the variation in European electric plugs, is famous worldwide.[24] This remarkable variation typically is viewed as a reflection of protectionism; but there may be hostage-taking involved as well. Once the Dutch electronics firm, Philips, invests in the specific capital equipment necessary to produce each country's variation, it has provided a hostage in its trade with that country. A cutoff of trade would make the special equipment useless, or nearly so. Other examples of technical standards that may serve a hostage role include different automobile and truck equipment and safety standards and varying tractor speed capabilities for different European countries. Meeting each of these standards involves significant specific investment that could be lost should the trading relationship break down. The result is a complex web of mutual hostages, with each country's firms providing vulnerable capital that could be devalued by a breakdown of trade. The amounts involved are not trivial; for example, Philips estimates that reworking computerized telecommunications exchange equipment for each European country requires an average of fifty to one-hundred man-*years* of software engineering because of differing technical standards.[25]

Bilateralism, linkages, and hostages enhance cooperation by supporting Tit-for-Tat and *quid pro quo* self-help strategies. They help make agreements self-enforcing, but they also impose substantial efficiency costs on the European economies. These costs fall into two major cate-

[21] Sandholtz and Zysman (1989, pp. 102, 115).

[22] Taylor (1982, p. 743).

[23] Taylor (1983, pp. 95–96).

[24] Some plugs have three prongs; others have two. Some prongs are straight, others angled; some are round, others rectangular. And some are thin, fat, or sheathed. The plug faces are circles, squares, pentagons, and hexagons. Some have perforations where others have notches. Some French plugs look like keyholes; and plugs in Britain contain fuses.

[25] *Wall Street Journal* (1985, p. 32). Mr. Wisse Dekker of Philips was a leader of business support for European market liberalization (Sandholtz and Zysman [1989, pp. 116–117], and Moravcsik [1991, pp. 22–23]).

gories. The first, highlighted by the Philips case mentioned above, is the obvious economic efficiency costs of complicated and inconsistent technical standards and the bureaucratic costs of administering them. Community documents announcing the 1992 target for removal of all internal barriers focused on these costs and their implications for declining European competitiveness.[26] The EC's Cecchini Report estimated the gains from reducing approximately 100,000 technical standards and border formalities at thirty billion ECU.[27] For example, if the proposed changes take full effect, the average 80-minute delay for commercial vehicles at border crossings will be eliminated.

The second category of costs stems from the fact that enforcement under self-enforcing agreements, based as it is on reciprocity and retaliation, is inherently a "disintegrative" process. For example, if one member breaches, others may be authorized to take countermeasures, such as offsetting the effect of an exchange rate alteration or imposing countervailing duties in response to an illegal subsidy.[28]

Attention within the EC during the 1970s centered on these problems and on alternate approaches to integration that might help alleviate them. An early 1980s proposal called *Europe à la carte*, highlights the strategic organizational nature of problems facing the Community and the governance-based nature of proposed solutions.[29] Under the proposal, EC agreements would have required several signatories, but less than unanimity, to become effective. Non-signatory Community members would have the option of acceding to the agreements later.[30] A variant would have permitted subsets of EC members to progress at faster or slower paces toward integration.[31] Either approach would have amounted to eliminating the veto power of member states, a result much like the move to weighted-majority voting effected in 1986.

During the early 1980s, there were many proposals for a two-tier Eu-

---

[26] One example is the Commission of the European Communities (1985). Grieco (1990, pp. 203–206) discusses European perceptions of the importance of the technical-standards issue. Sandholtz and Zysman (1989) argue that Europeans' perceptions of their declining competitiveness relative to that of the United States and especially Japan provide the key to answering the "Why now?" question concerning the EC events of 1985.

[27] Emerson, et al. (1988, p. 56).

[28] See Taylor (1983, p. 291).

[29] Taylor (1983, pp. 304–306).

[30] Note the resemblance to the "codes" approach of the Tokyo GATT Round; see Stern and Hoekman (1987).

[31] Even now, within the negotiations surrounding 1992, a subgroup of EC members (France, Germany, Belgium, the Netherlands, and Luxembourg) is removing their own internal barriers ahead of the overall EC schedule. The move, under the Schengen Agreement, encountered temporary problems over French fears of immigration from (then, East) Germany. Those problems now solved, Italy, Spain, and Portugal are likely to join the group.

rope (*Europe à deux vitesses*).[32] By threatening to proceed without countries that were unwilling to refrain from vetoing action in various issue areas, proponents hoped to discipline members to go along. Scholars writing about the EC as well as policymakers and participants voiced the threats.[33] The biggest effect of the two-tier threat was on Britain which, before 1985, was most vocal in its reservations about Community moves that impinged on or threatened to impinge on national sovereignty.[34] Exclusion would have entailed major costs for Britain: loss of both direct Community benefits and a voice in shaping the future of Europe.[35] Britain was sensitive to both categories of costs, since it had been a late entrant into the EC and spent much energy trying to undo Community decisions made before its accession, particularly those related to the Common Agricultural Policy.

Minilateralism in the "Second" EC: 1986–1992

In the late 1970s and early 1980s, the Community experienced many examples of countries defying Community rules and using reciprocity or retaliation as self-help. This is precisely what the strategic organizational perspective would suggest, since bilateral institutions would be the only alternative in the face of the *liberum veto*. There are many examples. The French defied an injunction of the Community Court by forbidding imports of British lamb. The British and West German governments threatened to withhold their legally required financial contributions to the Community in response to a budget increase. The British refused to comply with their Community obligations without a reduction in their budgetary contribution. French subsidies to turkey farmers, alleged by Britain to be illegal under Community policy, caused Britain to suspend vaccinating birds against pests—to justify a policy of keeping out French turkeys to protect the newly disease-vulnerable British birds.[36]

The strategic organizational approach suggests that eliminating bilateralism, self-enforcement, linkages, and hostages requires replacement with effective third-party enforcement mechanisms.[37] The Single Europe

[32] Moravcsik's discussion (1991, pp. 33, 36) captures the flavor of the proposals.

[33] For example, prior to the Single Europe Act, Taylor (1983, pp. 306, 310) tentatively recommended expulsion of Britain as a way of preventing Britain from blocking movement toward further integration; the legal status of such a move is not clear. Wallace and Ridley (1985, Chapter Five) has a good discussion of the two-tier proposals.

[34] Moravcsik (1991, p. 21) concludes that the two-tier threat against Britain was "essential" to passage of the Single Europe Act. See also Lodge (1990, pp. 6, 12); and Garrett (1990, p. 16).

[35] Moravcsik (1991, p. 26).

[36] Taylor (1982, p. 755).

[37] Garrett (1990, pp. 5, 28–31) contains a good discussion of enforcement in the EC.

Act (the basis for 1992) accomplished this by a limited move toward majority voting rather than unanimity in EC policymaking.[38] This is crucial, because unanimity requirements automatically eliminate effective supranational enforcement; a single country can always veto.[39] This is a subset of the more general observation that requiring unanimity tends to "bring decision-making to a standstill."[40] The ability of one party to block enforcement of group rules is the element of most direct relevance here.

Although majority voting took *de jure* effect in the Treaty of Rome, an unwritten agreement called the Luxembourg Compromise limited its use.[41] In 1974, Community members agreed majority voting should take effect on some issues; but the impact was minimal since designating the issues to be subject to majority voting required unanimity.[42] The Stuttgart Declaration in 1983 attempted to limit the use of the veto, but its results disappointed. The Declaration suggested (but did not require) that members voluntarily abstain in votes, not invoke their veto. France, Britain, Denmark, Greece, and Ireland made clear their continuing support for the Luxembourg Compromise and ignored the Stuttgart Declaration.[43] Taylor agrees unanimity requirements (still in practice at the time of his writing) limited Community action to the "lowest common denominator."[44] Cooper concurs: majority voting "committed all member countries to the 1992 program and altered substantially the bargaining environment by preventing single countries from holding up the Community for special privileges or compensation."[45]

The strategic organizational approach suggests that the pairing in the Single Europe Act (SEA) of (i) a move to qualified majority voting, and (ii) liberalization of the internal market was hardly a coincidence.[46] The

[38] Grilli (1989, p. 311); Cooper (1989, p. 326); and Lodge (1990, p. 3). On the veto, see Garrett (1990, p. 19); and Brams, et al. (1991, pp. 2–3). Also see footnote 13 above.

[39] A more familiar arena exhibiting the same phenomenon is the United Nations Security Council. Following the move by the EC, other international groups also have tried to limit the veto. Examples include the Conference on Security and Cooperation in Europe (*USA Today* [1991]) and the GATT (*San Francisco Chronicle* [1990]).

[40] Patterson (1983, p. 225); Young (1989, p. 360); Sandholtz and Zysman (1989, pp. 115–116); and Lodge (1990, p. 3).

[41] On the Luxembourg Compromise and its lack of legal standing, see Moravcsik (1991, p. 20).

[42] Taylor (1982, p. 762). There was some steady increase in use of majority voting between 1966 and 1984; ten decisions were so taken between 1966 and 1974, thirty-five between 1974 and 1979, and more than ninety between 1979 and 1984 (Moravcsik [1991, p. 51]).

[43] Moravcsik (1991, p. 34).

[44] Taylor (1983, p. 305).

[45] Cooper (1989, pp. 325–326).

[46] On the aims of the SEA, see Lodge (1990, p. 3).

second was not possible without the organizational reform represented by the first. A tight link between the two is common to analysts of different persuasions and to key participants, but the reasons are rarely explicit.[47] Moravcsik notes that, "The SEA links liberalization of the European market with procedural reform [majority voting]."[48] Public speeches by Helmut Kohl and Jacques Delors linked the two issues.[49] The link is also apparent from its negative image—majority voting is applicable only to matters related to the liberalization of the internal market.[50]

Under the weighted-majority voting now in effect, two large members and a small one are necessary to prevent Community action; so effective supranational action and enforcement become possible.[51] Sandholtz and Zysman characterize the move to majority voting as having "cleared the way politically for progress toward unifying the internal market."[52] One way to view 1992 is as a move to reduce costs associated with self-enforcing agreements based on linkages and hostages by replacing bilateralism with an alternate governance structure: minilateralism.[53]

If this view is correct, progress toward 1992 should be concentrated in issue areas requiring only weighted-majority voting, that is, in industrial standards, capital liberalization, and air and sea transport policy. These are, in fact, the areas of progress. These issues dominate the 282 White Paper Directives that are the bureaucratic basis of 1992; and progress on the Directives is most advanced in these areas. By January 1990, 159 proposals had been formally adopted, of which over two-thirds concerned technical standards, plant and animal hygiene, and border administration.[54] Other areas of EC policy lack the potential for supranational en-

---

[47] See Garrett (1990, p. 3).

[48] Moravcsik (1991, p. 19). See also Sandholtz and Zysman (1989, p. 116).

[49] Moravcsik (1991, pp. 36, 40).

[50] Moravcsik (1991, pp. 42, 49). There remains the possibility of a veto even in matters pertaining to the internal market, but that option is now much more circumscribed than under the Luxembourg Compromise; Moravcsik (1991, pp. 43–44) describes the conditions.

[51] See Garrett (1990, pp. 19–20); and Brams, et al. (1991) which also discusses the implications of a hypothesized veto by France and Germany.

[52] Sandholtz and Zysman (1989, p. 100). They also state that "the fundamental bargain is expressed by the end of the single-nation veto system, which changed the logic of Community decision making" (p. 127). Brams, et al. (1991, pp. 13–14) use a voting-power analysis to suggest that the SEA increased the power of the Commission to act by 300 to 400 times.

[53] Garrett (1990, p. 5, 28–31) covers enforcement within the EC, including the requirement that member states make EC rules into domestic laws (more on this later). Note that Garrett (for example, pp. 1, 9) refers to the EC as multilateral. As we noted earlier, this usage, while technically correct, carries the disadvantage of lumping an arrangement like the EC into the same category with the GATT or the United Nations; see Chapter One, footnotes 9 and 14, and Chapter Three, footnote 62.

[54] Cooper (1989, p. 334).

forcement because they still require unanimous decisions. These include agricultural reform, taxes and other fiscal matters, movement of people, rights of workers, environmental policy, and moves toward a common currency or central bank.[55]

Also consistent with the strategic organizational approach is the fact that attention within the EC is turning increasingly toward enforcement.[56] Of the eighty-eight measures due for complete implementation by all twelve members by January 1990, only fourteen had actually reached that status. In 1989, the European Commission received 1,391 complaints of member countries ignoring regulations. Most were settled informally, with only six finally referred to the European Court for formal adjudication. As of June 1991, eighty-nine of the 282 directives remained to be passed and implemented; and the Commission had passed only eleven in the preceding six months. However, passage of approved directives into national law has speeded up, with about seventy-two percent of adopted proposals implemented. The Commission relies largely on bad publicity (that is, reputation effects) to encourage members' compliance.[57] As the December 31, 1992, deadline nears, most noncontroversial items have been passed and only the more difficult items remain.[58]

The strategic organizational perspective suggests that other potential problems for the EC center on entrance to and exit from membership. Accession will become more difficult as the scope of Community activity expands. A new member must revamp broad ranges of its economic, political, and social policies; no longer will it be a matter of removing tariffs toward members and agreeing to the Common External Tariff. Members must renounce their right to make trade agreements with nonmember states; they may enter only those agreements negotiated by the Community.

The possibility of exiting the Community also raises interesting questions. A period of membership alters a nation's economy—and those of the other members. The relationship between international political and economic linkages, on the one hand, and formal political and economic integration, on the other, is a two-way street. Countries with extensive existing ties are more likely to find formal integration worthwhile; and formal integration biases further political and economic ties inward toward the group.[59] Two fundamental views of integration reflect this two-way effect.[60] One suggests that formal integration should occur gradually as nations' natural dealings bring them into closer association and make

---

[55] Moravcsik (1991, pp. 20, 42).
[56] See the discussion in Garrett (1990, pp. 5, 28–31).
[57] The Economist (1990, pp. 69–70).
[58] Wall Street Journal (1991a).
[59] Eden and Molot (1991, pp. 1, 9).
[60] A good survey is Keohane and Nye (1975).

ex post formal ties more attractive. The other suggests that formal integrative institutions can be imposed *ex ante* and allowed to encourage the later development of more extensive patterns of interaction.

What happens if a party wishes to sever ties developed over a period of Community membership? Thus far, only Greenland (a part of Denmark) has withdrawn from the Community after joining. In the "divorce," Greenland received duty-free access for exports to the EC in return for Community access to fishing grounds. But what if a full member decided to withdraw from the EC?[61] Firms and other member countries would stand to lose their specific investments, undertaken on the assumption of continued access to the country's market.[62]

The other side of the exit issue is the possibility of expulsion from the Community. One thing that all members have in common is democratic governments. The three newest members—Greece, Portugal, and Spain—all joined shortly after the demise of dictatorships. EC members pledge democracy, and any member installing a "non-democratic" government can be expelled. Such an act could impose enormous costs on everyone, since the web of industrial cooperation the Community fosters would be severed.

Although its scope and history make it unique, the European Commu-

---

[61] A related case is the Soviet republics' relationship to the Soviet Union before and after the August, 1991 "breakup." The Soviet constitution was one of very few "federal" constitutions that permitted secession (Taylor [1983, p. 271]); see footnote 12 above. The quarrel between the central government and the secession-oriented republics prior to the breakup revolved around the legal procedure required for secession, especially a five-year waiting period. The centrally planned Soviet system produced an extremely regionalized economy. For example, a Lithuanian nuclear power station and major oil refinery are permanently knitted into the Soviet energy system; and factories in Lithuania are the *only* suppliers of key parts for every television set, car, and tractor produced in the Soviet Union (*San Francisco Examiner* [1990]). Similarly, a single Armenian producer is the only source of a filter used in all Soviet power stations. Even for standard components that would present little opportunism hazard in a market economy, ruble inconvertibility and a "hard" currency shortage limit the short-run availability of alternate suppliers. Because of the large scale and highly regionalized nature of Soviet manufacturing, the breakup risks separating suppliers from markets and components from assembly. Republics accuse one another of opportunistically withholding key supplies and components to affect the terms of any new bargain. Attempts to reach economic agreements to support continued trade among the republics dominate the post-breakup agenda. The breakup also raises strategic organizational questions between the Soviet Union and other countries. With no central government in control, western countries hesitate to provide aid and investment; and creditors worry about repayment responsibility for debts of the earlier regime. Foreign firms considering investment cite as a reason for delay the lack of clarity in who has authority to sign binding contracts.

[62] See footnotes 32 through 33 above. Scholars disagree on the legal status of secession within the European Community (Taylor [1983, pp. 275–277]). For evidence that firms undertake international investments with the intention of a long-term relationship, see Gatignon and Anderson (1988).

nity is not the only current case of steps toward minilateral trade policy. The Canada-U.S. Free-Trade Agreement is particularly interesting because the governance issues that are our primary focus are its whole raison d'être.

THE CANADA-U.S. FREE-TRADE AGREEMENT

The issue of trade liberalization between Canada and the United States has a long and politically volatile history.[63] The extensive economic ties between the two create pressure for closer consolidation, while issues of political and cultural autonomy push against existing and incipient economic ties, especially for Canadians. The United States and Canada have long been one another's primary trading partner. Even before the 1988 Free-Trade Agreement, the bulk of trade passed duty free. As negotiations began in 1985, approximately eighty percent of Canadian exports to the United States and sixty-five percent of U.S. exports to Canada were duty free; so trade liberalization in the narrow sense of tariff reduction was not the major issue, although the final agreement eliminated most remaining tariffs.[64] Each country's interest centered on governance issues: for Canada, secured access to the U.S. market and assurances against contingent protectionism and, for the United States, a more stable and reliable Canadian investment environment.

Canadian Concerns

The initiative to begin negotiations came from Canada. The primary concern was the nature of access for exports to the U.S. market.[65] Although relatively open, the market seemed unpredictable and access less than assured.[66] The source of the problem from the Canadian perspective was the unpredictable, contingent, or opportunistic application of U.S. trade-remedy laws. Those laws include escape-clause actions, antidumping duties, and countervailing duties.[67]

---

[63] Wonnacott (1987, pp. 11–19) provides a brief history.

[64] See Wonnacott (1987, p. 69). At the time of negotiations, remaining U.S. tariffs against Canadian exports averaged about five percent; the analogous figure for Canada was about ten percent.

[65] See, for example, United States International Trade Commission (1985, pp. 31–34, 36–37).

[66] Harris (1989) provides the most thorough discussion of the issues related to market access; he discusses the Canadian-U.S. case on page 264.

[67] United States International Trade Commission (1987, chap. 1, p. 6). Escape-clause actions permit protection against imports injuring or threatening to injure a domestic industry. Antidumping duties offset the effects of "dumped" foreign exports on domestic producers. Countervailing duties compensate producers for the effects of foreign subsidies.

The major benefit to Canada of access to the U.S. market is to allow large-scale production and achievement of economies of scale.[68] Investment in such facilities creates relation-specific assets since those assets often are dedicated to serve a certain market.[69] Should that market be closed by an unpredictable or opportunistic application of U.S. trade-remedy law, Canada could suffer substantial losses. As former Canadian trade negotiator Rodney Grey put it:

> Industries in small countries, if they are to compete on world markets, must produce in plants of optimum size, . . . [exporting] perhaps three quarters of the output of their plants. An antidumping or a countervailing duty action against exports of an optimum-sized plant in a small country can be particularly damaging, simply because it affects such a large portion of the plant's output.[70]

The size of the U.S. market, combined with its low tariffs and proximity to Canada, "enticed" Canadian producers, but the market seemed unreliable.[71] Trade-remedy laws provided a threat that discouraged specialization and trade, as well as a means of harassment to extract concessions from Canadian firms or policymakers.[72] Canada viewed the solution as a more binding set of rules to cover Canada-U.S. trade. According to Canadian Prime Minister Mulroney, "The answer to this problem lies in sound agreements, legally binding, between trading partners, to secure and remove barriers to their mutual trade."[73] Similarly, Canada's Minister of International Trade, James Kelleher, described Canada's objective in the negotiations as "to secure and enhance our access to the U.S. market by enshrining a better set of rules whereby our trade is conducted," and "to develop a more predictable environment for trade and investment."[74] Those new rules were to provide security of market access, eliminate the continual threat of one-sided changes in the rules of the game, and strengthen dispute-settlement mechanisms.[75]

U.S. Concerns

Most analysts agree that the U.S. stake in the Canada-U.S. negotiations was much smaller than that of Canada.[76] This is consistent with neoclas-

---

[68] Wonnacott (1987, p. 7).

[69] Wonnacott (1987, pp. 66, 70).

[70] Grey (1983, pp. 248–249); and Harris (1989, p. 264).

[71] Wonnacott (1987, p. 66).

[72] Wonnacott (1987, p. 67).

[73] Quoted in United States International Trade Commission (1986, chap. 1, p. 12).

[74] Quoted in United States International Trade Commission (1986, chap. 1, p. 12).

[75] United States International Trade Commission (1986, chap. 1, p. 12).

[76] The empirical estimates of the gains from trade liberalization differ widely depending on how many countries are assumed to liberalize; see Wonnacott (1987, pp. 24–32). Al-

sical trade theory which implies that gains from trade accrue dispropor-
tionately to small countries.[77] It is also consistent with the strategic organizational approach because, while Canada is the United States' largest
single trading partner, U.S. trade is much less dedicated toward Canada
than vice versa. Therefore, it is not surprising that the free-trade initiative
came from Canada; but the United States was not without parallel concerns and interests. From the U.S. perspective, the key problem in recent
economic relations with Canada had been in the area of investment policy.[78] A series of disputes plus the volatile nature of Canadian policy toward foreign investment caused considerable uncertainty on the U.S. side
of the border.

In 1973, Canada instituted the Foreign Investment Review Agency
(FIRA) that screened and restricted foreign investment in Canada, particularly that originating in the United States. Although FIRA could and did
prohibit certain investments, it more commonly negotiated legally binding agreements with investors to require them to satisfy export targets or
Canadian-content quotas. Throughout the next decade, the United States
disputed the FIRA restrictions, culminating in the 1983 GATT finding
that FIRA's Canadian-content quotas for foreign investors violated
GATT Article III. In 1985, the Investment Canada Act, which reduced
the number of investments reviewed by ninety percent and provided an
environment generally more conducive to inward foreign investment, replaced the FIRA.[79] Despite the switch from FIRA to the Investment Canada Act, perceptions in the United States were that the winds of change
can blow in many directions; investors still perceived Canada as insecure.

The United States also expressed concern about the Canadian federal
government's ability to make policy commitments binding on provincial
governments, which remain more autonomous than U.S. states. Under
Canadian law, for example, provincial governments retain control over
all natural resources in their territories.[80]

The Agreement

Although the two parties' concerns on entering the negotiations differed,
both sets of concerns revolved around governance-related issues into
which the strategic organizational approach provides insight. The Agree-

---

though this empirical literature makes a distinction among unilateral, bilateral, and multilateral tariff reductions, the distinction is the non-organizational one dealing with the number of countries lowering tariffs, not the strategic organizational distinction. In other words,
if ten countries lowered tariffs, each independently, the result would be multilateral in the
terminology of the empirical literature, not unilateral as in our usage.

[77] United States International Trade Commission (1987, chap. 1, p. 12).

[78] United States International Trade Commission (1985, pp. 40–41).

[79] United States International Trade Commission (1985, p. 136).

[80] United States International Trade Commission (1985, p. 42).

ment eliminated tariffs and outlined rules covering new trade measures in services; but major developments were in market access, governance, dispute settlement, and enforcement.[81]

The Agreement partially exempts each country from the other's escape-clause actions to deal with surges in imports that cause or threaten to cause serious injury to domestic producers.[82] During a ten-year transition period (1988–1998), either country can take escape-clause actions by reinstating the industry's pre-agreement or most-favored-nation tariff rate for up to three years, but only once for any given product. In global Canadian or U.S. escape-clause actions under GATT Article XIX, the other country's exports are exempted unless they are substantial and contribute importantly to injury. In sum, the agreement provides the countries with preferential treatment in one another's escape-clause actions; each can be "punished" only for the effects of its *own* exports, not for those of third countries.

A new Canada-U.S. Trade Commission oversees the implementation of the Agreement and resolves disputes arising over escape-clause actions.[83] The Commission consists of equal numbers of Canadian and U.S. representatives. In a dispute, the specified procedure involves the following: (i) consultation; (ii) if consultation is unsuccessful within thirty days, a meeting of the Commission with technical advisors or a mutually accepted mediator; and (iii) after thirty more days without success, referral to binding arbitration by a panel of five, two chosen by each country from a roster maintained by the Commission and the fifth chosen by the Commission or the four chosen arbiters.

The most controversial area is dispute settlement in cases of antidumping (AD) and countervailing duties (CVD). The Agreement takes a two-track approach: (i) establishment of a five- to seven-year "working group" to develop new rules covering subsidies and unfair pricing, and (ii) a new interim review procedure for AD/CVD cases.[84] Until the countries determine a new set of rules, each will continue to apply its own AD and CVD laws to imports from the trading partner. But a country's final case determination will be reviewed by a *binational* panel employing the standards and legal principles of the country in which the case is brought—not by the national courts. The binational review panels are to be composed of five members, two chosen by each country from a roster and one chosen by consensus. Even the binational review panel's deci-

---

[81] The U.S.-Canada agreement was aided by similarities in the two nations' legal systems (Eden and Molot [1991, p. 19]).

[82] United States International Trade Commission (1987, chap. 1, p. 7).

[83] United States International Trade Commission (1987, chap. 1, p. 11).

[84] United States International Trade Commission (1987, chap. 1, p. 11).

sions can be challenged and reviewed by a panel of three judges or former judges under an "Extraordinary Challenge Procedure."[85]

The Canada-United States Free-Trade Agreement represents a tentative step toward minilateral trade policy. The countries have been careful to make clear their continuing support of the GATT and multilateral approaches. They chose a comprehensive agreement over a sectoral one in part so that the requirements for legality under the GATT would be satisfied. The extent to which the Agreement's new governance institutions represent a supranational or minilateral approach will be determined only as the procedures and outcomes from particular disputes can be analyzed.

CAN MINILATERALISM BECOME MULTILATERAL?

Our analysis of preferential trade agreements brings us full circle, back to the starting point of our argument. Is there a role for preferential trade agreements? Are they an apologia for protectionism, a stepping stone to future multilateral agreements, or one of several alternate governance structures for strategic organizational issues?

The strategic organizational approach implies minilateralism can enhance trade liberalization by alleviating contracting and enforcement problems. Therefore, arrangements such as the "new" European Community and the Canada-United States Free-Trade Agreement are unlikely to be mere fronts for protection.[86] The extent to which minilateral groups are potential "building blocs" for some future large-scale multilateral trading system is more questionable. There are at least four possible ways of interpreting the question, "Can minilateralism become multilateral?" Not surprisingly, the answer to the question is sensitive to the definition one has in mind.[87]

The first interpretation uses the narrow definitions of *minilateralism* and *multilateralism* used throughout the book. The question then asks whether a trading system based on creation of supranational enforcement institutions by small groups of countries (minilateralism) is likely to evolve into a system where a single set of multilateral rules governs the trade policies of many countries. Once phrased this way, the question's

[85] The first extraordinary challenge decision was handed down, in favor of Canada, in June 1991. The case ruled on U.S. countervailing duties on Canadian pork exports (*Wall Street Journal* [1991b]).

[86] This does not imply that a "fortress" outcome is impossible, only that minilateralism in itself does not necessarily reflect a move toward protectionism. Jacquemin and Sapir (1991, p. 167, emphasis added) conclude that to avoid this result, "EC authorities must then ensure implementation of *credible rules* that are directly applicable to all. . . ."

[87] Jacquemin and Sapir (1991, p. 16) note the desirability of "making compatible regionalism and multilateralism." Also see Martin (1991).

obvious answer is *no*, at least in the current context where emergence of a hegemon of stature roughly equivalent to that of the postwar United States appears unlikely.[88]

The other three interpretations of the "Can minilateralism become multilateral?" question use looser definitions of the two key words. This allows the question to take on a different focus: Is trade liberalization, undertaken minilaterally, likely to spread? For example, are the liberalization efforts within the EC, between Canada and the United States, or among the United States, Canada, and Mexico, likely to lead more countries to liberalize? There are at least three channels through which such an effect might operate.

The first is the direct or "building bloc" idea. As David Richardson asks, "What is the likelihood that recent 'minilateral' agreements between Canada and the United States, and within Europe will lead to a strategic multilateral agreement among regional blocs that negotiate on behalf of their constituent governments?"[89] As we noted earlier, to the extent EC members liberalize their future trade vis-à-vis nonmembers, this will be the approach because the EC prohibits members from pursuing agreements with nonmembers individually. The fundamental advantage of the building bloc idea is its mitigating effect on transaction costs by limiting the number of parties involved in negotiations.[90] Within each bloc, members can negotiate the side-payments necessary to reach a unified negotiating position. Inter-bloc negotiations then proceed as a second stage, enjoying the advantages associated with smaller numbers.[91] The strategic organizational approach implies minilateral agreements among countries with the most intense and vulnerable trade, so the second level of negoti-

---

[88] We argued in Chapter Three that multilateralism, while conceptually distinct from hegemony, is more likely to be successful with a hegemon willing and able to provide sufficient sticks and carrots in terms of its own trade policy.

[89] Richardson (1990, p. 132). Note that Richardson's definition of *minilateralism* is much broader than ours; he simply refers to agreements among small groups of like-minded countries without regard to the organizational structure of the agreements.

[90] An analogy can be drawn with labor negotiations in which a union negotiates with a management group instead of each employee negotiating individually with his or her supervisor.

[91] Of course, the two levels or stages of negotiations would not be truly separable. This point is made with increasing frequency about domestic politics and international trade policy (see, for example, Putnam [1988]; Milner [1988b,c]; and Cohen [1990, especially pp. 268–270]). The most interesting current case is the talks between the EC and the European Free-Trade Association (EFTA) aimed at creation of a European Economic Space (EES). EFTA took a much different approach to trade liberalization than the EC and deliberately avoided creation of any supranational institutions. Now, EFTA fears losing access to EC markets. The relevant question is how much say EFTA members will be given in an EES if they refuse to take the further steps toward integration taken by members of the EC.

ations—between blocs—typically would involve less demanding governance issues.[92]

How would we characterize an agreement between two minilateral blocs (for example, between the EC and a North America Free-Trade Area [NAFTA])?[93] The most likely case is a bilateral agreement, one that has no supra-bloc enforcement institution and is reliant on reciprocity, hostages, and issue linkages (as in Chapter Four). The alternative would be a minilateral agreement between minilateral groups, creating a supra-bloc institution (above the EC Commission and its NAFTA equivalent); but such a course is unlikely.

There are two additional channels through which minilateral trade policy could spread: imitation of technique and imitation of results. Successful international agreements, such as those underlying the new European Community and the Canada-U.S. Free-Trade Agreement, are extensively studied and analyzed. Innovative bargaining strategies, side-payments, or other techniques become available for imitation or copying by other groups. Through this demonstration effect, minilateral agreements can "spread."[94]

Similarly, the results of minilateral trade policy may lead to demonstration effects. If the European Community in the mid-to-late 1990s enjoys the growth rates some analysts have predicted as a result of the Single Europe Act, one would certainly expect other countries, especially small ones, to pursue similar policies.[95] Also, fear of being "left out" creates

[92] Buzan (1984) suggests a combination of liberal trade within blocs and welfare-based protection between blocs.

[93] The NAFTA currently under negotiation consists of Canada, Mexico, and the United States. It is not yet clear to what extent a NAFTA would be truly minilateral; for example, who would negotiate on its behalf? The EC is clearly minilateral in this respect; final judgement on the minilateral character of the Canada-U.S. Free-Trade Agreement awaits its implementation, particularly in the case of disputes.

[94] See Lawrence and Litan (1990). Note also that the GATT, endeavoring to improve its record in dispute settlement, has proposed using panels of outside experts with a one-year maximum on the ruling and appeal process. Under current GATT procedures, panel reports must be accepted unanimously, and the losing party typically vetoes (San Francisco Chronicle [1990]).

[95] It is important to note that the strategic organizational approach implies that the benefits and costs of minilateral trade policy are very sensitive to the particular economic interactions among the countries involved; this suggests caution for countries considering imitation. In other words, imitation of technique does not assure imitation of result. Geography, for example, may play an important role in the gains from integration. The original International Trade Organization (the precursor and supposed successor to the GATT) restricted customs unions to contiguous countries or regional groups. The GATT provision for customs unions contains no such restrictions (Jacquemin and Sapir [1991, pp. 168–169]). The strategic organizational approach implies that minilateral arrangements will arise when countries have extensive relation-specific trade ties, so that the high efficiency costs of self enforcement outweigh the costs of negotiating minilateral trade institutions.

incentives for countries to pursue PTAs; for example, Mexico and several other Latin American countries pursued PTA talks with the United States following the Canada-U.S. Agreement. Again, minilateral agreements "spread."

SUMMARY

The assumptions of neoclassical economics imply that preferential trade agreements are an inefficient alternative to universal nondiscriminatory free trade. Yet such agreements persist and are becoming more prevalent. A satisfactory theory of PTAs must explain both why they exist and what limits their size and growth. The strategic organizational perspective suggests that relation-specific investments and contracting problems are key elements in explaining the different institutional arrangements that perform a governance role in international trade. With these elements, PTAs emerge as an institution that uses minilateralism, or small-group third-party enforcement, for a particular organizational problem: opportunistic policies in the presence of large and recurrent relation-specific investments.

CHAPTER FIVE APPENDIX

THIS APPENDIX provides a simple hypothetical numerical example of one type of gain the governance structure implicit in a preferential trade agreement may be able to provide.

TRADE CREATION AND TRADE DIVERSION

The static economic effects of preferential trade agreements include trade creation and trade diversion.[1] Trade creation refers to the increased efficiency of intragroup trade that results from the removal of intragroup trade barriers. Trade diversion, on the other hand, is the reduction in the gains from trade when a PTA diverts trade from low-cost nonmember suppliers to higher-cost member suppliers.[2] The dynamic economic effects of preferential trade agreements include increased intragroup competition, economies of scale of producing for a larger market, terms-of-trade effects, and increased bargaining strength vis-à-vis nonmembers. For simplicity, we refer to all the standard efficiency-enhancing effects of PTAs (both static and dynamic) as trade creation and all efficiency-reducing effects as trade diversion.

Table 5.1 illustrates simple static examples of trade creation and trade diversion by a PTA. The (constant) costs of production for a single good, an automobile, in Countries One, Two, and Three are $3500, $3000, and $2000 respectively. With no tariff, Country One would import automobiles from Three, the low-cost producer; the first line of Table 5.1 illustrates this outcome by boldface characters.[3] The second line of Table 5.1 summarizes the situation if Country One imposes a one hundred percent nonpreferential tariff on imports of automobiles. The tariff causes One to become self-sufficient in automobiles; that is, the one hundred percent nonpreferential tariff is prohibitive. But if Country One forms a PTA with Country Two while Three remains a nonmember subject to a one hundred percent preferential tariff, Two satisfies One's demand for automobiles (see the middle row of Table 5.1). The transfer of automobile production from One (under a one hundred percent nonpreferential tariff) to Two (under a PTA between One and Two) represents trade *creation* because Two is a lower-cost producer of automobiles than One ($3000 <

---

[1] See Lipsey (1960); Krauss (1972), and the literature cited there.

[2] No trade diversion occurs if member suppliers are low-cost producers relative to nonmember suppliers; see Yarbrough and Yarbrough (1991b, Chapter Eleven).

[3] As noted earlier, the governance issues we raise are even more troublesome in nontariff barriers; we use the tariff example for simplicity.

$3500). The last two lines of Table 5.1 illustrate a similar situation but with the one hundred percent tariff replaced by a sixty percent tariff on imported automobiles. A nonpreferential sixty percent tariff by One does not shift production away from Country Three (the free-trade producer). The formation of a preferential trade agreement by One and Two, however, moves automobile production to Two. This move represents trade *diversion* by the PTA because Country Two is a high-cost producer relative to Three ($3000 > $2000), whose exports are eliminated by the preferential nature of the tariff.

Effect of Cost-Reducing Relation-Specific Investment

With consideration of the governance role for preferential trade agreements, changes in trade patterns that appear to be trade diverting may be trade creating. Table 5.2 provides a simple numerical illustration of this point. The data in Table 5.2 are identical to those in Table 5.1 except for one change in assumption: *Country Two now has the option of profitable cost-reducing relation-specific investment to serve Country One's market.*[4]

Tariff by 1	Country 1	Country 2	Country 3
No tariff	$3500	$3000	**$2000**
100% nonpreferential tariff	**$3500**	$6000	$4000
100% preferential tariff on Country 3 (PTA with Country 2)	$3500	**$3000**	$4000
60% nonpreferential tariff	$3500	$4800	**$3200**
60% preferential tariff on Country 3 (PTA with Country 2)	$3500	**$3000**	$3200

Table 5.1: Price in Country One of Automobiles Produced in Countries One, Two, and Three. *Source*: Yarbrough and Yarbrough (1986b, 1990a).

---

[4] Baumgartner and Burns (1975, p. 128) distinguish between "process-level" exchange where institutions are taken as given (as in Table 5.1) and "structure-level" exchange, which determines the institutions and incentives under which process-level exchange will proceed (as in Table 5.2).

If this investment occurs, Country Two's production costs fall from $3000 to $1500. However, if Two makes the relation-specific investment and One closes its borders to imports, Two would lose part or all of its investment. Because of this opportunism potential, Two would undertake the investment *only* with institutional arrangements for limiting opportunism, that is, under a PTA. Otherwise, Two would continue to use general-purpose techniques with production costs of $3000. General-purpose techniques, less specifically suited to the task at hand, typically involve higher production cost; however, the techniques avoid the holdup problem because they are invulnerable to opportunism. In other words, unlike Table 5.1, Table 5.2 allows production costs to depend on organizational form. A "dynamic" effect occurs because the governance role of the PTA encourages investment that changes the pattern of comparative advantage.

The first line of Table 5.2 reproduces the free-trade result in which Country Three, the low-cost producer without cost-reducing investment by Two, serves One's automobile market. In the second row of Table 5.2, a one hundred percent nonpreferential tariff causes One to become inefficiently self-sufficient in automobiles as in Table 5.1. The important difference from Table 5.1 is reported in the middle row of Table 5.2. The one hundred percent preferential tariff shifts automobile production to Two, the same type of trade *creation* that occurred in Table 5.1. Moreover, the static trade-creation effect is enhanced by a dynamic one be-

Tariff by 1	Country 1	Country 2	Country 3
No tariff	$3500	$3000	**$2000**
100% nonpreferential tariff	**$3500**	$6000	$4000
100% preferential tariff on Country 3 (PTA with Country 2)	$3500	**$1500**	$4000
60% nonpreferential tariff	$3500	$4800	**$3200**
60% preferential tariff on Country 3 (PTA with Country 2)	$3500	**$1500**	$3200

Table 5.2: Price in Country One of Automobiles Produced in Countries One, Two, and Three. *Source*: Yarbrough and Yarbrough (1986b, 1990a).

cause the PTA now permits Country Two to undertake relation-specific investment that lowers production costs to $1500 from $3000. Two is now the low-cost producer not only relative to One (as in Table 5.1) but, in the presence of the PTA, relative to Three as well ($1500 < $2000).

The change is even more dramatic with the sixty percent tariff (see the bottom two rows of Table 5.2). In Table 5.1, the formation of a PTA between Countries One and Two in the sixty percent tariff case was trade diverting. In Table 5.2, a nonpreferential sixty percent tariff places automobile production in Country Three, the low-cost producer *given* the absence of investment by Two. The formation of the PTA along with the cost-reducing investment it encourages makes Two the low-cost supplier ($1500 < $2000). Table 5.1 reported a similar shift of production from Three to Two, but there the effect was trade *diverting* because Two was a high-cost producer relative to Three ($3000 > $2000). When the PTA induces Two to undertake investment that makes it the low-cost producer relative to Three, the PTA's effect in moving production from Three to Two becomes trade *creating*. Therefore, once we appreciate the governance role of preferential trade agreements, changes in trade patterns that appear trade diverting may in fact be trade creating.

Chapter Six

THE STRATEGIC ORGANIZATIONAL APPROACH TO INTERNATIONAL INSTITUTIONS AND THE NEW ECONOMICS OF ORGANIZATION

THE FUNDAMENTAL TRADE POLICY CHOICE—between open trade and protectionism—varies across at least three dimensions: time, country, and sector or industry. For example, trade was relatively open in the 1860s but closed in the 1930s; Hong Kong's trade policies generally are more open than India's; and textile and apparel trade is subject to more restrictions than most other manufacturing sectors. Each of these dimensions of trade policy has received considerable attention from both economists and political scientists, although definitive answers still are lacking in several areas. The business-cycle, political power/voting, and hegemony-based trade theories outlined in Chapter One provide just a few examples of the extensive work done.

However, another aspect of trade policy has received considerably less scrutiny. That aspect is the institutional or organizational form of trade policy. How is trade policy managed or organized; in particular, is policy unilateral, bilateral, multilateral, or minilateral? In one sense, the comparative neglect of this issue is surprising. After all, policymakers must choose the format or forum in which to pursue policy as surely as they must choose a position on the free trade-to-protectionism continuum. Canada, for example, made a deliberate policy decision to approach the United States about a free-trade agreement, and the United States faced a policy choice in reacting to the extra-GATT initiative.

The literature addressing the issue of the institutional form of trade policy tends to be highly prescriptive, arguing for one "correct" form (in recent years, most often nondiscriminatory multilateralism) and condemning all others as wrongheaded, noncooperative, or worse. However, history clearly provides examples of unilateral, bilateral, multilateral, and minilateral trade policy. Each has its supporters and critics.

What has been lacking is neither awareness of different forms of trade policy nor opinions concerning the pros and cons of each. The key missing element in the literature has been an analysis of the conditions under which we might expect to see the different forms of trade policy emerge. This is the void that our strategic organizational approach attempts to fill. In developing that approach, we have drawn on a body of literature known as the new economics of organization (NEO). The purposes of this chapter are to outline the key characteristics and insights of NEO, to bring those insights to bear on the firm and the state as central institutions of international political economy, and to assess NEO's potential contributions to the study of international institutions, especially those related to the strategic organization of international trade policy.[1]

THE CONCERNS OF NEO

The institutional and organizational questions that once defined political economy are now widely perceived as belonging to social sciences other than economics, but the centuries-long movement of economics away from institutional concerns has recently been interrupted by the emergence of the new economics of organization.[2] NEO, although most highly developed in its analysis of the firm, is notable for its range and scope, encompassing literature on the family, the state, and international relations.[3] The contributions, diverse in perspective, share a goal of a theoretical foundation for understanding key institutions, avoiding the "black

---

[1] The "unidirectional" approach of this chapter should not be construed to imply that the new economics of organization could not be strengthened by drawing on the insights of international relations theorists; in fact, our strategic organizational approach to international trade policy attempts to do just that, instead of merely "applying" NEO to trade.

[2] There are at least four literatures that examine institutional variety and institutional change: (i) the tradition of economic historians, such as Douglass North (1981, 1990), who focus more on the path-dependent historical process of institutional change and less on institutional variety resulting from relation-specific investment; (ii) the law and economics and industrial organization tradition, exemplified by the work of Oliver Williamson (1985a), that concentrates on institutional or organizational variety, with institutional change being defined more implicitly; (iii) the more diverse game-theoretic literatures that emphasize the composition and dynamics of cooperative and noncooperative social organization (for example, economists Holmstrom [1982], Telser [1980], and Yarbrough and Yarbrough [1987c]; political scientists Axelrod [1984, 1986], and Brams, et al. [1991]; and social philosopher Ullman-Margalit [1977]); and (iv) the law-oriented literature associated with Llewellyn (1931), Benson (1989), Jackson (1990), and Ellickson (1991). The strategic organizational approach taken in this book draws elements from all of these traditions, in addition to the international trade literature, each of which has contributions to make to our understanding of complex empirical phenomena in international trade.

[3] Subsets of, and alternative names for, the new economics of organization include the new institutional economics, transaction-cost economics, and the economics of property rights. Examples of NEO treatments of various institutions include Ben-Porath (1980); Pollak (1985); Putterman (1986); Leibenstein (1987); Yoshino and Lifson (1986); North (1981, 1990); Winship and Rosen (1988); and Yarbrough and Yarbrough (1985a,b; 1986a,b,c; 1987a,b; 1988; 1990a; 1991a). A useful collection can be found in four special issues of the *Journal of Institutional and Theoretical Economics* (1984, 1985, 1986, 1987).

box" approach.[4] While grounded firmly in economics, NEO is an explicitly interdisciplinary approach to social institutions and incorporates contributions from law, organization theory, and the other social sciences.

Although the origins of NEO clearly lie in the study of the firm, the central *problématiques* of NEO are precisely those of political economy, as defined by Susan Strange:

> The study of international political economy . . . concerns the social, political and economic arrangements affecting the global systems of production, exchange and distribution, and the mix of values reflected therein. Those arrangements are not divinely ordained, nor are they the fortuitous outcome of blind chance. Rather they are the result of human decisions taken in the context of man-made institutions and sets of self-set rules and customs. . . .
>
> The ways things are managed, how they got to be managed in that particular way, and what choices this leaves realistically open for the future, these three aspects or *problématiques* of political economy are implicit in the semantic origins of the word 'economics.' It derives from the Greek *oikonomia*, which meant a household—typically in the ancient world, not a small nuclear family but rather a patriarchal settlement of an extended family and its slaves, living off the crops and flocks of the surrounding land. The management of the *oikonomia* thus included the choices made in cropping and in breeding, in the provision of security from attack or robbery, in the customary relations between men and women, old and young, the teaching of children and the administration of justice in disputed matters. In other words, it was far more about politics than about economics.[5]

Before the arrival of work in NEO, these concerns—"the ways things are managed, how they got to be managed in that particular way, and what choices this leaves realistically open for the future"—had been largely dormant within economics since the decline of American institutionalism.

NEO ORIGINS AND GOALS

The "old" institutionalism of Thorstein Veblen, John Commons, Wesley Mitchell, and Clarence Ayres had limited impact on mainstream econom-

---

[4] The "black box" terminology symbolizes (among both economists and political scientists) acknowledgement of the limitations of traditional noninstitutional approaches; see, for example, Aoki (1984, pp. 4, 10, 52); Williamson (1985a, p. 15); Haggard and Simmons (1987, pp. 497, 513); Alchian and Woodward (1988, p. 65); Ikenberry (1988, p. 242); Ikenberry, et al. (1988, p. 3); and Langlois (1988, p. 30).

[5] Strange (1988, pp. 18–19).

ics.[6] Until recently, economics took a quite different path, since neither legal formalism, with its focus on state enforcement of formal rules, nor strict behavioralism, with its direct link between opportunities and behavior, left much role for institutions. The old institutionalists focused on methodological criticism more than development of an alternate research program.[7] Their criticisms centered on mainstream economics' search for abstract universal laws and theoretical generalizations, its methodological individualism, and its narrow focus on the efficiency of anonymous, price-mediated markets. Their emphasis on methodological criticism led the institutionalist writers to take positions similarly subject to criticism.[8] This, combined with the failure to set out a viable alternate research agenda, foreclosed a major role for institutionalist views in a crucial period in the development of economics. As a result, economics lost valuable insights into the importance of institutions and the nature of process.

NEO represents a broad attempt to recapture those insights and incorporate them into a research program aimed at observed "problems and puzzles," not methodology.[9] NEO writers' criticism of much of standard economic theory remains blunt, but aims less at methodology than at the focus on artificial or "toy" problems existing in a social and institutional vacuum. Yoram Barzel's comments are typical:

> Virtually no features of Walrasian economics qualifies it as a social science. People interact only in the market, where cheating will not occur since it can be costlessly detected, and the identity of transactors is of no significance. The auctioneer, the only social functionary, plays a strictly mechanical role and provides his service free of charge. Individuals' maximizing behavior leads automatically to Pareto optimum. Moreover, since property rights are well defined and contracts are costless to enforce, even a legal system is not needed. . . . [In reality] people trade with each other because they expect to gain, but when transacting is costly, each person spends resources in attempting to capture a greater share of the gain. Traders are not anonymous; their

---

[6] Langlois (1988) traces the relationship between the "old" institutionalists and more modern work in NEO. Two special issues of the *Journal of Economic Issues* (September and December 1987) contain a useful collection of recent papers in the institutionalist tradition. Continuing work by economists in this tradition often is referred to as "neoinstitutionalism" to distinguish it from the "new institutionalism" associated with the work of Williamson and other related approaches. Adams (1990) explores the relationship between institutionalism and social-choice theory. Ramstad (1989) argues that new work along institutionalist lines tends to ignore the contributions of the "old" institutionalists, especially John Commons.

[7] This point, as made by Coase (1984, pp. 229–230) is virtually identical to Keohane's (1988a) admonitions to scholars of the "reflective school" of international relations. On the shortcomings of the "old" institutionalism, see also Hodgson (1988, pp. 21–24).

[8] Langlois (1988).

[9] Williamson (1985b, p. 188).

names—their identities—serve to lower the costs of exchange. Thus the social aspect of trade is of fundamental importance. Social institutions are erected to aid in further facilitating the exchange.[10]

Thus, NEO writers' criticisms of neoclassical (or Walrasian) economics echo many concerns or criticisms typically expressed toward the application of economics to the study of international relations.

The broad goal of NEO is to understand social institutions, seen as facilitating cooperation in situations where autonomous action produces inferior outcomes, implying existence of potential gains from effective mutual agreements.[11] As Harvey Leibenstein notes, social organization faces two simultaneous problems: the "size of the pie" and the "division of the pie."[12] Common interests in expanding the size of the pie can be obscured by conflictual interests in dividing it, leading to mutual defection.

However, most NEO work does not focus on the mutual defection outcome. Instead, it focuses on the potential for a noncooperative outcome to create an incentive for actors to establish institutions to prevent that outcome. As Oliver Williamson argues,

> The benefits from cooperation notwithstanding, the achievement of cooperation is widely thought to be frustrated by the relentless logic of the prisoners' dilemma. To be sure, it has always been evident that defection can be deterred if payoffs are appropriately altered. But that strategem is held to be infeasible or is otherwise dismissed, on which account the dilemma persists or appeal is made to "exogenous norms of cooperative behavior [that are] adhered to by the actors." I submit that the feasibility of crafting superior *ex ante* incentive structures warrants more attention. A leading reason for its neglect is that the study of the institutions of contract has occupied such a low place on the research agenda. Subtle incentive features incorporated in nonstandard contracting practices have gone undetected as a consequence of this nonchalance—hence the practical significance of the prisoners' dilemma to the study of exchange has been vastly exaggerated.[13]

In other words, observed situations represent a combination of underlying circumstances and institutional responses.[14] This theme—the poten-

[10] Barzel (1985, p. 15). Hodgson (1988, Chapter Eight) uses the Walrasian auctioneer to demonstrate that even markets are "social institutions."

[11] NEO cannot itself delimit the range of social relations that fit this description; see the discussion below, especially footnote 89.

[12] Leibenstein (1987, p. viii).

[13] Williamson (1985a, pp. 204–205).

[14] Gowa (1986) makes a related argument about the relevance of Prisoners' Dilemma for international relations. Keohane (1990, p. 738) notes the lack of a "hypothetical institution-free baseline from which to measure the impact of actual institutions on state capabilities."

tial for cooperation supported by contract-like institutions even in situations characterized by a prisoners' dilemma or similar problem—is consistent with pluralist, institutionalist, or liberal views in international relations.[15]

DISTINGUISHING CHARACTERISTICS OF NEO

Beyond its institutional focus and interdisciplinary character, two other features distinguish most NEO work from more traditional economic approaches. The first deals with the nature of the relevant environment, and the second concerns the interaction of agent and structure.

The Relevant Environment

Unlike the textbook neoclassical world of *homo oeconomicus*, the NEO world is an institutional setting in which uncertainty prevails, individuals are only boundedly rational, legal enforcement of agreements is costly and imperfect, and opportunistic acts cannot be ruled out. In such a world, even potentially mutually beneficial relationships may require complex institutional structures to support cooperation.

The NEO world is populated by individuals who are "*intendedly* rational, but only *limitedly* so."[16] Both parts of the definition of bounded rationality matter: individuals pursue goals to the best of their abilities, but abilities are constrained by imperfect information, complexity of problems confronted, and limits on computational competence and foresight.[17] Bounded rationality effectively eliminates the possibility of comprehensive long-term agreements defining precisely every contingency, since not all contingencies can be foreseen. As a result, agreements must maintain flexibility; to use Williamson's metaphor, bridges must be crossed as reached, not in advance.[18]

Individuals are also potentially opportunistic. They can and sometimes do take advantage of others' bounded rationality, particularly when the inevitable incompleteness of agreements creates a gap between compliance in letter and spirit. As Williamson points out, opportunism is "self-interest seeking with guile" or "the incomplete or distorted disclosure of information, especially . . . calculated efforts to mislead, distort, disguise, obfuscate, or otherwise confuse."[19]

---

[15] See Keohane (1984), Oye (1986a), and the comparison with realism in Grieco (1990).

[16] Simon (1961 [1947], p. xxiv). See Langlois (1986).

[17] Williamson (1985a, pp. 30–32, 44–47); and Hodgson (1988, Chapters Five and Six). Also see Keohane (1984, pp. 111–116).

[18] Williamson (1985a, p. 57).

[19] Williamson (1985a, p. 47; also pp. 30–32; 47–52; 64–67).

Bounded rationality and opportunism, resulting in incompletely specified and imperfectly obeyed agreements, increase the scope of uncertainty. In addition to uncertainty arising from different states of the world, behavioral uncertainty can arise from an actor's lack of information about other actors' preferences or actions. This makes coordination difficult even when all parties act in good faith. It creates a demand for norms to enhance predictability and social institutions to support exchange and other forms of cooperation.[20] Uncertainty also can arise if actors can conceal or disguise their preferences or behavior deliberately, to take advantage of other parties. This behavioral uncertainty makes some institutions and norms (such as the strategy to "always cooperate" in Prisoners' Dilemma) not viable as means of supporting cooperation.[21] The nature of the issues raised by the NEO environment, like those raised by international relations, focuses attention squarely on the relationship between agent and structure.

Interaction of Agent and Structure

NEO is sensitive to the problems arising in trying to define even a single observed institution. Most analysts agree, for example, the state is an institution, but there is no consensus about its major attributes: Is it the current government officials, the constitution with its bureaucracy and administrative apparatus, the ruling class, or the legal order emanating from recognition of sovereignty?[22] In what sense can the state act; and to what extent does legal sovereignty translate into autonomy of state action or insulation from pressures emanating from the domestic society or the international system?[23] NEO arose from analogous questions about the firm: Is it current owners or employees, the legal entity created by documents of incorporation, or management? In what sense does the firm act, and to what extent is the firm's behavior autonomous from internal and external pressures? Dealing with these questions for the case of either the state or the firm hinges on recognition of the interactive relationship between the individual and the group. More is involved than a choice between individualism and holism; presence of a multilevel hierarchy, in

[20] This is the emphasis of Keohane (1984).

[21] Williamson (1985a, pp. 56–59).

[22] This is, of course, one of the central groups of questions in the ongoing debate between proponents of realist and pluralist or institutionalist schools of international relations theory; see Benjamin and Duvall (1985); and Ikenberry (1986, especially pp. 54–55). Field (1981) makes a similar point about institutions more generally.

[23] Robert H. Jackson (1987, p. 529) distinguishes between juridical statehood based on "negative" sovereignty, or the *right* of self-determination, and empirical statehood based on "positive" sovereignty, or a *capacity* for effective and civil government.

which parts are also wholes and wholes also parts, characterizes the agent-structure problem.[24]

While textbook neoclassical economics' unit of analysis is the autonomous individual, household, or firm, and that of realist political analysis is the state, the unit of NEO analysis is the transaction.[25] The transaction is viewed as a relationship or contract, not an instantaneous exchange in a world of perfectly specified property rights and perfectly enforced contracts. It is a relationship in which parties' performance typically is non-simultaneous, and nonperformance can leave an aggrieved party with little recourse. Given these elements of anarchy, cooperation requires an institutional structure consistent with self-enforcement or self-help. Institutional economists, like international relations theorists, have noted that conflict is a relational phenomenon.[26]

Although the emphasis of NEO analysis is on individual action, the relational focus implies careful attention to compositional principles through which individual actions produce collective action or social outcomes.[27] Individuals, not organizations or groups, have objectives; social wholes do not act based on aims and interests distinct from those of the constitutive individuals.[28] However, social wholes are more than the simple sum of their parts; society may affect individual objectives, and social institutions both constrain and enable individual behavior. In acknowledging the importance of both structure and process and both individual and group, NEO walks the thin line between reductionism, on the one hand, and methodological holism or reification, on the other.[29] As Hodgson argues,

[24] Wendt (1987); and Dessler (1989) provide useful guides to these issues; see also Hodgson (1988, p. 70). In the study of international relations, Singer (1961) emphasizes that the choice of level of analysis determines what will and will not be "seen" by the analyst.

[25] A notable exception is North (1990), whose primary units of analysis include organizations and institutions. Viewed metaphorically, North's descriptions of the interactions of organizations and institutions in a path-dependent historical context often take on a biological or even anthropomorphic character where organizations are like bodies (organisms) and institutions are like minds (formal and informal constraints) involved in complex mind-body interactions.

[26] Rummel (1966); and Commons (1934, p. 4). Functionalist and neofunctionalist integration theory (for example, Mitrany [1948, 1966]; and Haas [1958, 1964, 1975]) also emphasizes transactions.

[27] Langlois (1988, p. 20) defines a compositional principle as a proposition "about how the individual behavior links up or ties together to form the aggregate result."

[28] Langlois (1988, especially pp. 25–30); and Seyfert (1985, especially pp. 171–173).

[29] Reductionism is explanation of the whole based solely on behavior of the parts. Methodological holism claims distinct aims and interests for social wholes and suggests that they are sufficient levels of analysis. Structure refers to the distribution of capabilities among units, and process to the ways in which the units relate to each other (Keohane and Nye [1987, p. 745]). Although neoclassical economics is strongly identified with methodological

For too long economists have considered households or firms simply as uni-
tary elements, making decisions as if they were single actors, and disregard-
ing the real individuals involved. . . . At the level of abstraction of the theory
of the firm or the household it is a positive step to attempt to explain their
nature and dynamics partly in terms of the structured groups and individuals
within them. This breaks the widespread habit of treating these institutions
as if they were purposeful units in themselves. . . .

   What is left out of this approach is the continuous influence of social institutions, such as the family or the firm itself, and the social culture and roles,
on the preferences and purposes of individuals involved. Whilst the aims and
character of individuals help to explain the behaviour of social structures,
also roles, culture and institutions have a partial effect on the goals and behaviour of individuals.[30]

Joint maximization requires an institutional structure or a set of incentives and constraints (not necessarily pecuniary) that influences individual
behavior in a manner consistent with joint maximization. An example is
provided by Adam Smith, who described a mechanism in which the individual is "led by an invisible hand to promote an end which is no part of
his intention."[31] In Smith's view, the coincidence of individual and social
interests was not automatic; it was the outcome of certain social institutions, primarily well-defined and enforced property rights and open domestic and international competition. Within that institutional context,
the aggregate outcome (for Smith, maximization of national wealth) mir-
rored the individual pursuit of self-interest (individual wealth). Smith's
work was, after all, a critique of the mercantilist system—an institutional
context in which, he argued, the pursuit of individual wealth reduced aggregate wealth. In today's international relations terminology, Smith's
work was a call for a change in regime, a redefinition of "basic property
rights" and "acceptable patterns of behavior," or a change in institutions.[32] His treatise was a comparative-institutional exercise, since he
placed individuals in two alternate social contexts (laissez-faire and mer-

individualism, the standard economic treatment of the firm as a monolithic profit-maximiz-
ing entity is vulnerable to charges of methodological holism or reification, as are many economic treatments of the household or family. For discussions of these issues and their relationship to the study of international relations, see Wendt (1987); and Dessler (1989). A
related debate concerns voluntarism (that is, human volition and action) versus determinism
in the structure and outcomes of international relations. Yarbrough and Yarbrough (1991a)
highlights the issue of voluntarism in the choice among the "lateralisms" in trade policy and
"polarities" in security.

[30] Hodgson (1988, p. 68). The same points could be (and have been) made about much
of political scientists' work on the state (see Krasner [1984]).

[31] Smith (1937 [1776], p. 423).

[32] Quotes come from Krasner's (1982b, p. 5) definitional work on regimes.

cantilism) and, using theory and historical evidence, compared the aggregate outcomes reflecting the interaction of individual behavior in those contexts.

The choice of the transaction as the basic unit of analysis reflects NEO's focus on the interaction between individual preferences and behavior on the one hand and group outcomes on the other. Institutionalist John Commons argued the transaction captured the essential elements of analysis—conflict, dependence, and order[33]—by focusing on situations in which an agreement could be mutually valuable but difficult to reach. Social institutions are viewed as various forms of contract—not an unyielding, written, and legally enforceable document but, instead, a framework of working rules. As Karl Llewellyn observes, a contract can provide "a framework for well-nigh every type of group organization and for well-nigh every type of passing or permanent relation between individuals and groups;" this "highly adjustable" framework "almost never accurately indicates real working relations, but . . . affords a rough indication around which such relations vary [and serves as] an occasional guide in cases of doubt."[34]

The law associated with contracts differs in an important respect from many other aspects of law, as Bruce Benson notes: " 'contract law' refers to the 'law' parties in exchange bring into existence by their contractual agreement rather than to the law of or about contract."[35] In other words, contract law is the law of custom and usage, the law that actors find useful in supporting their cooperation. When an unforeseen circumstance generates a dispute within a contractual relationship, the goal of dispute-settlement is to maintain continuity and find a solution the parties themselves might have reached had they foreseen the circumstance when contracting.[36] This strongly suggests parallels with a Grotian perspective on international law, much of which is explicitly "created" through treaties and other forms of bargaining and agreements.

NEO PERSPECTIVES ON KEY INSTITUTIONS: THE FIRM AND THE STATE

The Governing Firm

The nature of the firm is the question that has received the most attention from NEO theorists.[37] In the NEO environment—characterized by

---

[33] Commons (1934, p. 4). Yarbrough and Yarbrough (1988) trace the importance of Commons' insights in NEO.

[34] Llewellyn (1931, pp. 736–737). This view has obvious commonalities with Durkheim (1933 [1893]); and Parsons (1937).

[35] Benson (1989, p. 649). Also see Ellickson (1991).

[36] Williamson (1985a, pp. 68–84).

[37] The characterization here draws heavily on Oliver Williamson's work, which repre-

bounded rationality, uncertainty, imperfect legal enforcement, and opportunism—transactions are differentially vulnerable to breakdown and therefore require support from institutions of varying complexity. Williamson's key dimension in explaining assignment of certain transactions to certain types of organization is asset specificity.[38] An asset is specific if it is durable and designed for a particular use with a particular partner; the asset's value is greatly reduced in another use or with another partner.[39] When a relationship involves few specific assets, availability of alternate partners safeguards the parties; if the current partner attempts to behave opportunistically, replacements are available at low cost. The primary task of institutions in such transactions is to support flexibility and autonomy. The "market" as an institution provides alternate partners and standardized norms of exchange (for example, price), and these suffice when continuity in any particular relationship is not highly valued.

On the other hand, when a relationship involves significant investment in specific assets, the relationship is more vulnerable. A breakdown can cause irreparable damage because the value of the specific asset (which, by definition, is useful only in the specific relationship) will be lost. All parties therefore value continuity; but if conditions change, requiring adaptation, each party also faces an incentive to hold out for more favorable terms—an attempt to capture the full value of the relationship over the partner's best alternative.

In this type of relationship, alternate partners no longer suffice; the anonymous trading world of neoclassical markets, in which the identity of a party is unimportant, disappears. Self-help through unilateral withdrawal no longer provides adequate safeguards. The relationship undergoes what Williamson calls the "fundamental transformation," reminiscent of Karl Polanyi's "great transformation," which referred to market society's displacement of traditional society, the movement of the livelihood of man from a position embedded in the noneconomic institutions of society to a separate price-mediated sphere.[40] For Williamson, the fundamental transformation works in the opposite direction; a relationship moves out of the autonomy and anonymity of the market into a more

---

sents the single most fully developed NEO argument. Not only has Williamson been a central contributor to NEO, but his framework has spawned a growing body of empirical work. Joskow (1988) surveys some of that empirical literature. Shugart (1990, Chapter Three) contains an introductory presentation of "modern" theories of the firm, including that of Williamson. Other treatments include Yarbrough and Yarbrough (1988); and Tirole (1988).

[38] Uncertainty and frequency of transacting are the other dimensions of transactions that play important roles.

[39] Chapter Two discusses numerous examples of relation-specificity with relevance to international trade.

[40] Williamson (1985a, pp. 61–63); and Polanyi (1944).

socially embedded sphere, supported by relation-specific incentive structures or safeguards. Investment in such a relationship forecloses alternatives, imputing a branchlike or history-dependent structure to the choices facing the parties.[41] The primary task of institutions then becomes one of supporting and signalling the parties' continuing commitment to the ongoing relationship. These institutions are by necessity unique, based in identity, loyalty, and reciprocity. The result is a special relationship, with incentives, dispute-settlement procedures, and regularities or norms of behavior that may differ significantly from those of the autonomous, impersonal, standardized world of market exchange. Therefore, transactions that are vulnerable because of highly specific assets tend to be integrated or organized uniquely, while the availability of alternate partners in the "market" adequately safeguards less vulnerable transactions.[42]

The firm, from this perspective, is a mini-society with its own incentives, dispute-settlement procedures, and norms. Transactions brought under the internal control of the firm are those that require a more extensive governance structure to support cooperation than can be provided by the market. The firm, therefore, is an institution of governance, one in which commitment replaces (at least partially) autonomy and flexibility.[43] The NEO governance-oriented view of the firm represents a significant departure from the textbook neoclassical view. There, the firm is a technologically-determined production function, a black box turning inputs into outputs, with all exchange occurring in anonymous, price-mediated markets.

The Trading State

According to one dictionary, a state is an organized community under a system of authority. This broad, inclusive definition implies that the NEO's governing firm could be considered a state, since the governing firm is a mini-society with its own system of authority, dispute-settlement procedures, and norms of behavior.[44] Defining the state more narrowly

---

[41] Arguments along this line in international relations include Krasner (1984), and Gowa (1989a). Wagner (1988, pp. 479–480) points out "important differences . . . between negotiating a new aid or trade relationship and renegotiating an existing one," but seemingly fails to account for the possibility of a "fundamental transformation" within a relationship. Hodgson (1988, p. 301) makes the more general point that the relative costs of various forms of organization depend in part on the *status quo*.

[42] This finding, strongly supported by the existing empirical evidence (Joskow [1988]), provides the link between intra-firm trade and relation-specific investment outlined in Chapter Two.

[43] Eden and Hampson (1991) analyze firms and states as governance structures.

[44] Conversely, Robert H. Jackson (1987) argues that such definitions of states imply that many third-world "quasi-states," particularly many African governments, fail to qualify.

and focusing on its territorial dimension limits these complications. Rejai and Enloe, for example, define the state as "an independent and autonomous political structure over a specific territory, with a comprehensive legal system and a sufficient concentration of power to maintain law and order."[45] Recent theorists, both political scientists and economists, add that the state has the power to tax and to specify and enforce property rights—both powers supported by a comparative advantage in violence.[46] This portrays the state as inherently a *trading* institution, not in the sense of international trade, but of trading enforcement of property rights for revenue.[47]

As the definer and enforcer of property rights, the state controls access and exclusion, both domestically and internationally. The state trades this access and exclusion on at least three levels. First, on the domestic level, the state trades "protection and justice" to its citizens in return for revenue. Second, on the transnational level, the state trades access to its territory to foreign firms in return for revenue (for example, the relationship between multinational enterprises and host states). Third, on the international level, the state trades access to its territory to other states in return for reciprocal access or another favor, as occurs, for example, in the multilateral tariff reductions negotiated through the General Agreement on Tariffs and Trade.

The three levels are, of course, not independent.[48] This point is vividly illustrated by seventeenth- and eighteen-century mercantilism in which trading companies received domestic monopolies in exchange for revenues for the Crown. This domestic contract required a policy of exclusion in international trade, just as an earlier contract between local guilds and feudal lords had dictated exclusion. In England, the policy of international exclusion (mercantilism) changed to one of access (liberal trade) only after alterations in the balance of power between Parliament and the Crown broke down the trading companies' monopoly-for-revenue contract.[49]

The extent of trade in access and the resulting scope and density of activity across national borders are important elements in modern views of the state.[50] Although states are territorially organized, a characteristic used to contrast them with markets, the control over access and exclusion

[45] Rejai and Enloe (1969).
[46] North (1981); Levi (1988); and Strange (1988, pp. 39–42).
[47] North (1981) speaks of the state exchanging "protection and justice" for revenue.
[48] This point is emphasized by Strange (1988, p. 40).
[49] Ekelund and Tollison (1981) provide an extensive analysis along this line.
[50] See, for example, Keohane and Nye (1970); David Baldwin (1985); Rosecrance (1986); 1988 special issue of *International Organization*, "The State and American Foreign Economic Policy;" and Strange (1988).

exercised by states makes territoriality a flexible constraint. Of course, a few states now, as throughout history, choose to make their borders a hard-and-fast constraint by pursuing autarky as a policy goal. Ness and Brechin characterize differential "permeability" of boundaries as an aspect of "varying sovereignty" since "[s]ome states effectively control their boundaries, others have little control."[51] If, however, permeability of boundaries is a choice variable, then permeability would not necessarily reflect weak sovereignty. Many key areas of current controversy in international trade relations (for example, immigration, capital and technology flows, national treatment, and trade in electronic-media sectors) revolve around changing capacities for access and exclusion.

Even countries actively engaged in foreign trade differ considerably in the directness of state involvement in trade. The traditional neoclassical economic theory of trade largely ignores the state; in that view, trade is an activity in which individual consumers and firms engage. The irony of the state's absence in something called "international trade theory" struck neoclassical economist Francis Edgeworth: "International trade . . . in plain English [means] trade between nations; it is not surprising that the term should mean something else in Political Economy."[52]

Despite the absence of the state in neoclassical international trade theory, the state as the definer and enforcer of property rights maintains control over access and exclusion. But, like the environment of NEO, the environment in which the state trades access and exclusion is one of bounded rationality, uncertainty, imperfect enforcement, and opportunism. Mutually beneficial long-term cooperation requires an institutional structure to bolster that cooperation—a structure that involves both firms and states and both trading and governance across national boundaries.

NEO AND INTERNATIONAL RELATIONS

Although a recent addition to modern economic theory, the "governing firm" concept has formed the basis for a centuries-long debate concerning the interaction of firm and state. Thomas Hobbes argued corporations, which he likened to "many lesser common-wealths in the bowels of a greater, like worms in the entrails of a natural man," potentially weakened the state.[53] Adam Smith considered the two roles of trader and sovereign as inherently incompatible:

> No two characters seem more inconsistent than those of trader and sovereign. If the trading spirit of the English East India company renders them very

[51] Ness and Brechin (1988, pp. 254–255).
[52] Edgeworth (1925, p. 5); cited in Viner (1975 [1937], p. 595).
[53] Hobbes (1962 [1651], p. 245).

bad sovereigns; the spirit of sovereignty seems to have rendered them equally bad traders. While they were traders only, they managed their trade success-fully. . . . Since they became sovereigns . . . they have been obliged to beg the extraordinary assistance of government in order to avoid immediate bank-ruptcy.[54]

More recently, Susan Strange and others have implicitly used the con-cept of the governing firm to develop a "web-of-contracts" view of trans-national relations in which

trade between countries in goods and services will be, and is being, sustained by a complex network or web of transnational, bilateral bargains—bargains between corporations and other corporations, between corporations and governments, and between governments. The interest of both parties to these bilateral exchanges is (and will continue to be) a far more powerful influence on the level, the direction, and the content of international trade than the puny efforts of states to interfere with market forces.[55]

Whether we agree with Hobbes' metaphor of firms as parasites, Smith's fundamental incompatibility of governing and trading, or Strange's "puny" efforts of states to interfere with market forces, two points seem clear. First, international relations reflect the interaction of strategies fol-lowed not only by states but also by firms.[56] Second, the traditional view of states as governance structures (the narrow province of political sci-ence) and firms as traders (the narrow province of economics) provides inadequate perspective on both institutions. As noted by earlier institu-tionalist writers (particularly John Commons) and retained by NEO an-alysts, a focus on the transaction, relation, or contract captures the inex-tricable linkage of governing and trading.

The concept of contract has a long history in political and social theory, notably in the work of Thomas Hobbes and John Locke and more re-cently in that of Douglass North, Margaret Levi, and Geoffrey Brennan and James Buchanan.[57] In each case, the idea of contract is a key element in explaining the state, which is viewed as trading the definition and en-forcement of property rights for revenue. Thus far, however, in interna-tional political economy, contracts have been notable primarily for their *absence*—a central element in the "anarchy" typically used to describe the international arena.[58] According to the anarchy-based view, even mu-tually beneficial transactions may fail without a central authority to en-

[54] Smith (1937 [1776], p. 771).
[55] Strange (1985, p. 234); also see Keohane and Nye (1970).
[56] Eden (1991).
[57] North (1981); Brennan and Buchanan (1985); and Levi (1988).
[58] Oye (1986a); Milner (1988a); and Grieco (1990).

force contracts, because no party can rely on others not to behave opportunistically. The absence of enforcement power, leaving states no recourse to higher authority in their dealings with one another, renders international economic relations less secure and more discordant than domestic ones.[59]

NEO, however, suggests that the dichotomous view of the domestic arena as law-ordered and the international arena as anarchic is potentially misleading. As argued by Hedley Bull, anarchy (i.e., the absence of formal supranational government) does not rule out cooperation, coordination, and informal forms of governance.[60] If firms are hierarchical governance structures that arise to facilitate cooperative production when law-based, anonymous, price-mediated market exchange provides inadequate safeguards to support cooperation, then the domestic and international arenas differ in degree, not kind, along the law-to-anarchy continuum. If so, NEO's progress in understanding the institutions that individuals and firms devise under uncertainty, bounded rationality, opportunism, and imperfect enforcement may prove helpful in analyzing international institutions. Williamson, whose work has focused on the firm (broadly defined), is cautiously optimistic about the approach's relevance for "noncommercial enterprise;" other writers, such as Leibenstein, explicitly claim applicability to noneconomic organizations.[61]

Despite striking parallels between the central questions of NEO and those of international relations, applicability of NEO to international questions encounters several difficulties. Some are inherent in NEO itself, at least in its current state; others relate specifically to extending NEO to international relations.

Criticisms of NEO for the Study of International Institutions

FUNCTIONALISM AND EFFICIENCY

The most widely heard criticism of NEO centers on its functional approach to institutions. Mark Granovetter's statement is representative:

> The general story told by this school [NEO] is that social institutions and arrangements previously thought to be the adventitious result of legal, historical, social, or political forces are better viewed as the efficient solution to certain economic problems. The tone is similar to that of structural-func-

---

[59] Oye (1986a).

[60] Bull (1977). See also Ostrom (1990), and Ellickson (1991).

[61] Williamson (1981, pp. 573–574); and Leibenstein (1987, p. 1). Moe (1984) critically evaluates the usefulness of NEO for the study of public bureaucracy. Grieco (1990) dismisses, in our view prematurely, the promise of NEO applications in international relations; see the discussion in the appendix to Chapter Two.

tional sociology of the 1940s to the 1960s, and much of the argumentation fails the elementary tests of a sound functional explanation. . . .[62]

This disagreement can be traced, at least in part, to a difference in usage of the word *functional*. Functional explanations dominated mid-twentieth-century sociology and anthropology, but tightening of requirements for a valid functional theory led many to conclude that those requirements were rarely if ever satisfied in the social sciences.[63] For example, Jon Elster argues that a valid functional explanation requires that the institution both serve an unintended and unrecognized function for a group and provide feedback to maintain or reproduce the institution.[64] The latter requirement, the survivability or natural-selection element, seems especially weak in explanations of international institutions. Axelrod develops one possible "evolutionary" approach based on the "principle that what works well for a player is more likely to be used again while what turns out poorly is more likely to be discarded."[65] Based on his insistence on a comparative-institutional perspective, Williamson subscribes to what he calls "weak-form selection," in which *fitter* institutions survive although they may not be the *fittest* in an absolute sense.[66] " 'Flawed' modes of economic organization for which no superior feasible mode can be described are, until something better comes along, winners nonetheless."[67]

Consistent with Axelrod's and Williamson's usages, a less stringent definition comes from Herbert Simon: "Institutions are functional if reasonable men might create and maintain them in order to meet social needs or achieve social goals."[68] Functional explanations under the Simon definition lose much (although not all) of their vulnerability to the teleological and compositional fallacies that plague functional explanations under the

[62] Granovetter (1985, p. 488).

[63] The most influential functionalist works include Radcliffe-Brown (1935); Malinowski (1944); and Goldschmidt (1966). Important criticisms of functionalism in the social sciences include Merton (1947); Turner and Maryanski (1979); Elster (1983); and Dow (1987, especially section 4).

[64] Elster (1983); and Williamson (1988). See also Dessler's (1989) discussion of Waltz's narrow focus on unintended rules as opposed to intended ones.

[65] Axelrod (1986).

[66] Williamson (1985a, p. 23). Also see Keohane (1984, p. 81). Evolutionary themes in economics predate those in biology. Evidence suggests the classical economists, including Smith and Malthus, provided inspiration for Darwin's theory (Jones [1986]). Hodgson (1991) criticizes the evolutionary implications of Alchian (1950) and Williamson. However, Williamson's focus on a fitter surviving institutional *variety* as a response to the transacting environment is distinct from the Alchian approach where only similarly fit firms survive in a competitive environment.

[67] Williamson (1985a, p. 408).

[68] Simon (1978, p. 3). Haas (1990) uses a similar definition.

more stringent definition.[69] Under the Simon definition, a functional explanation does not require that the function served be either unintentional or unrecognized, and success in solving a problem can support an institution's survival. This looser definition of social institutions as functional corresponds closely to what institutionalists call a purposive, intentional, or instrumental explanation—that is, one based in the idea of problem solving.[70] It is also consistent with the organizational perspective on political economy offered by Susan Strange and quoted early in this chapter.[71]

However, as noted by Haggard and Simmons, a key weakness of functional explanations is a failure to explain when and in what issue-areas creation of a problem-solving institution works.[72] Some evidence suggests human volition plays an episodic role, which is important when change exceeds the capacity of current institutions to cope or when there is what Leibenstein calls "a shock to the culture."[73] This view provides one explanation for a common pattern of institutional change during and after wars, including creation of major international organizations (the United Nations, International Monetary Fund, GATT, and World Bank) following World War II. Varying potential for collective action explains differential efficacy of human volition across issue areas, but more work is needed to understand the role of collective action (involving both state and nonstate actors) in international relations.[74] These issues present a significant challenge to analysts working in NEO, both in its traditional area of application and in potential new areas such as international relations. This points again to the importance of microanalytic research that focuses on periods of institutional change and on comparisons of the efficacy of problem-solving institutions across issue areas.[75]

[69] On the teleological and compositional fallacies, see Turner and Maryanski (1979); and Langlois (1988).

[70] Schotter (1986); Neale (1987); and Dow (1987, especially pp. 27–28). Among the "old" institutionalists, Commons believed that Veblen seriously underestimated the volitional or purposive component of institutions and therefore overemphasized the extent that institutions merely bound society to the past. In international relations theory, the debate over voluntarism versus determinism reflects this.

[71] See footnote 5 above; and Keohane (1984, especially pp. 80–83; 1990, p. 759).

[72] Haggard and Simmons (1987, pp. 507–509).

[73] Leibenstein (1987, p. 131); see also Gordon (1967); Krasner (1984, especially pp. 240–243); Ikenberry (1988); and Goldstein (1989).

[74] Olson (1965); Dow (1987, pp. 32–33); Gowa (1988, 1989b); and Young (1989).

[75] For example, in its study of the firm, NEO has yet to answer definitively why firms within some cultures are able to handle transactions through the market (for example, by subcontracting) that would, in other cultures, require vertical integration; see Williamson (1985a, pp. 120–130); Yarbrough and Yarbrough (1986c); and Hamilton and Biggart (1988). The presence or absence of cooperation in various issue areas raises similar ques-

International relations theorists and NEO analysts share a tendency to regard the presence or onset of cooperation (along with accompanying rules or norms) as desirable, and the absence or breakdown as undesirable.[76] Given the problem-solving approach to institutions offered by NEO, this conclusion is not surprising, though it obviously hinges on adopting the perspective of a certain group.[77] Consider a paradigmatic case from the traditional domain of NEO: the merger between General Motors and Fisher Body. From the perspective of the two firms, the merger represented an "efficient" adaptation to the increasingly specific and therefore vulnerable nature of the transactions between them.[78] Competitors would have, no doubt, preferred decades of continued contractual bickering between the two, since this would have resulted in less effective competition.[79] Consider a parallel case in the international arena: the actions of the Organization of Petroleum Exporting Countries (OPEC) during the 1970s. What OPEC regarded as a success was hardly interpreted by oil-importing economies as an example of desirable cooperation. Evaluation of the erosion or breakdown of existing systems of cooperation is similarly sensitive to the perspective or definition of the relevant group.[80]

Once we establish the desirability of any cooperation-supporting institution as dependent on group perspective, the NEO concept of opportunism becomes subject to two-way interpretation. Opportunism involves failure to abide by the spirit if not the letter of an agreement; and it is, by definition, negatively evaluated by the parties to the agreement. Outsiders, on the other hand, might evaluate opportunism positively, as in the pre-merger holdup of General Motors by Fisher Body or price-cutting and quota-cheating by OPEC members.

---

tions for international relations, as in Lipson (1984); Ness and Brechin (1988, p. 271); and Young (1989).

[76] Haggard and Simmons (1987, pp. 508–509); Keohane (1988a); and Ness and Brechin (1988, p. 248).

[77] To further complicate matters, an institution may cease to serve the original beneficiary group and begin to serve another. "Capture" theories of economic regulation (Stigler [1971]), for example, suggest that agencies designed to regulate industries in pursuit of social goals often are captured by those very industries; but these theories are largely devoid of institutional considerations, as noted by Kalt and Zupan (1984).

[78] See the citations in Chapter Two, footnote 25. Note that the "small" party in a transaction may be able to hold up the large, as acknowledged by Keohane (1984, p. 198) and exemplified in the General Motors-Fisher Body case.

[79] Williamson explicitly recognizes the possibility of undesirable social outcomes (such as the exploitation of monopoly power) from "efficient" governance structures (for example, [1985a, p. 17]), although he considers monopoly power an inadequate and overemphasized explanation for observed governance structures.

[80] Other discussions of this issue are Strange (1982); Keohane (1984, especially p. 93); and Eden and Hampson (1991).

This does not, however, eliminate the usefulness of opportunism as a concept in the study of institutions. The fundamental strength of NEO is its emphasis on the role of potential *ex post* opportunism in the *ex ante* choice among alternate governance structures. It is opportunism from the viewpoint of the acting group that molds this institutional choice and affects the outcome.[81] Evaluation of that outcome from the perspective of the larger society is a related but conceptually distinct question. The two often merge in NEO's efficiency-based terminology, in which "efficiency" has meaning only in reference to a specified group, defined in most NEO work as the group involved in creating a problem-solving institution.

PRIVATE ORDERING AND THE LAW

NEO draws on empirical evidence and growing sentiment among legal scholars and practitioners that legal centralism places too much emphasis on formal written contracts and their legal adjudication.[82] As a result, the focus of NEO is on "private ordering" and the concept of "contract as framework."[83] Nonetheless, Williamson notes, in the domestic firm-centered arena, courts do provide "ultimate recourse" for "protection against egregious abuses of which 'might is right' is an elementary example."[84] Hodgson argues that this recourse is essential to support exchange and is given insufficient attention in Williamson's work:

> Of course, most contractual disputes are resolved without direct recourse to the courts; but this does not mean that the state has no place in the everyday process of contract. After all, the mere possibility of access to the courts is sufficient for the legal system to bear upon contractual agreements. It is not necessary that people actually appear in court for the state to have such a function. Whilst both formal and informal norms and rules play an important part in a system of exchange, in a modern society these rules are buttressed and sometimes created by law and the state.[85]

The efficacy of legal recourse as opposed to private ordering, both domestically and internationally, ultimately is an empirical question—one raised but not answered by NEO in its current state. The question is the crux of debates over international law, the appropriateness of the anarchy formulation of international relations, and the nature and role of inter-

---

[81] Hodgson (1988, p. 205) argues that, given the possibility that private and social valuations of opportunism differ, the key in Williamson's work is not opportunism *per se*, but simply uncertainty as to whether or not a contract will be fulfilled.

[82] Llewellyn (1931); Macaulay (1963); MacNeil (1974, 1978); Galanter (1981); Kronman (1985); Benson (1989); and Ellickson (1991).

[83] Williamson (1985a, Chapters Seven and Eight). See also Ostrom (1990).

[84] Williamson (1985a, p. 203).

[85] Hodgson (1988, p. 154).

national regimes. Again, however, it is easy to overemphasize the domestic-international dichotomy.

Strengths of NEO for the Study of International Institutions

BEYOND FORMAL LEGALISM

Formal legalism, which assumes a central role for formal rules enacted and effectively enforced by a hierarchical authority such as the state, dominated late nineteenth- and early twentieth-century political science and economics.[86] In contrast, NEO recognizes the importance of informal institutions and does not posit a direct link between behavior and formalized rules.[87] Institutional approaches such as NEO suggest that formal structures represent only one part of the web of interactions that comprise political and economic behavior. The United Nations system, for example, exists as a single element of the more complex state system. Similarly, the formal structure of the GATT is relevant to, but not determinative of, behavior in trade. Concentration on formal legal structures may prove not only incomplete but misleading, since effective enforcement of rules often is attenuated, particularly in international relations.

This insight extends beyond the obvious point that attention must be paid to informal institutions and norms (such as reciprocity, loyalty, identity, and ideas) as well as more formalized and visible forms (such as treaties, legal contracts, and formal market exchange). Institutions may be so pervasive that the underlying ("institution-less") structure of a situation can be difficult or impossible to discern.[88] As noted in the earlier Williamson quote, Prisoners' Dilemma situations do *not* necessarily lead to a noncooperative outcome, since its mutually unsatisfactory nature creates an incentive for parties to avoid it. The underlying structures of international relations in the economic, political, and security spheres have been the basis of an enduring debate.[89] While NEO, as an approach or perspective rather than a theory, cannot delimit the range of relations appropriately

---

[86] Benson (1989) argues that this view, in which the state is essential even for effective formal law, is mistaken and uses the medieval *lex mercatoria* as evidence. Milgrom, North, and Weingast (1990) provide further evidence. See also Ostrom (1990), and Ellickson (1991).

[87] See Krasner (1984, especially pp. 229–230); and Williamson (1985a, pp. 20–21, 164–166).

[88] For example, "old" institutionalist Walton Hamilton (1932) characterized the "world of use and wont" as a "tangled and unbroken web of institutions." A similar perspective on institutions is explored in Krasner (1982a,b); Puchala and Hopkins (1982); Young (1982); and Nye (1988). See also Keohane (1990, p. 738).

[89] Just a few of many possible examples are Jervis (1982); Lipson (1984); Nye (1988); Keohane (1988a, p. 386); Gowa (1989a); Grieco (1990); and Snidal (1991).

conceptualized as having a particular structure, it can serve as a useful reminder of the ambiguity caused by the web of existing institutions.

FLEXIBILITY AND COMMITMENT

The NEO approach stresses that flexibility and commitment are not equally valued in all relationships.[90] In transactions involving no "fundamental transformation," flexibility safeguards the relationship, and standardized "market-like" institutions support that flexibility. In such situations, autonomy and flexibility are key elements of power. This is Hall and Ikenberry's focus when they argue: "the power of the state is greatest when the state is able to maximize options at subsequent moments of decision. The ability to act flexibly—to intervene, withdraw, reform or abstain—is at the heart of state capacity."[91] However, in transactions involving a fundamental transformation, commitment provides the safeguards, and the role of institutions becomes one of supporting that commitment. As summarized by Keohane, "To pursue self-interest does not require maximizing freedom of action. On the contrary, intelligent and farsighted leaders understand that attainment of their objectives may depend on their commitment to the institutions that make cooperation possible."[92] In such a situation, autonomous flexibility (in particular, maintaining future options) may hinder, not buttress, the desired cooperation. Flexibility, the capacity to commit oneself credibly, and the ability to recognize whether flexibility or commitment is needed in a particular situation are *all* essential elements of state capacity.

SUMMARY

The last few years have been a period of great progress by political scientists and by economists in their understanding of the firm, the market, and the state. Although the corners of the black boxes remain dark, we now see that much more than anonymous, price-mediated exchange occurs within the firm and that states are much more than sovereign peaks of territorially defined hierarchies. Trading and governing are inextricably linked aspects of long-term cooperation, and international political economy is not a realm of anarchy any more than domestic exchange is a

[90] This point is obvious in individual relationships, which also embody different degrees of relation-specific investment. Moving along a continuum from grocer to physician to employer to spouse, for example, relationships involve progressively more specific investment and require a greater emphasis on commitment and less on flexibility. The existing NEO literature suggests that movement along the continuum is associated with a shift from reliance on formal law to an emphasis on private ordering.

[91] Hall and Ikenberry (1989, p. 97).

[92] Keohane (1984, p. 259).

world of comprehensive, perfectly enforced law. Firms and states, both domestically and internationally, face common tasks of reaching and enforcing cooperative agreements under conditions of uncertainty, bounded rationality, imperfect legal enforcement, and opportunism, while various transactions differ along these margins. The result is an array of observed institutions.

Political scientists and economic historians generally concern themselves more than economists with explaining these international institutions. The study of institutions must be microanalytic and sensitive to historical and political context, since general patterns may lie hidden under particularistic layers. Nevertheless, the traditional focus on specific historical episodes has hindered development of a unified framework capable of explaining the variety of existing and past institutions.

The strategic organizational approach to international trade institutions, outlined in the first five chapters, draws on NEO and its recognition of private ordering, economic historians' insights into path dependence, game theorists' perspectives on cooperation and related institutions, legal scholars' appreciation of the strengths and weaknesses of law, and international relations scholars' understandings of the world political economy. The result is an approach that stresses institutional variety and change and is skeptical of arguments that one institutional form is "correct" to the exclusion of others. In other words, the strategic organizational approach suggests that particularistic layers of observed international trade institutions reflect alternate governance structures, or "the way things are managed."

Chapter Seven

THE STRATEGIC ORGANIZATIONAL APPROACH: AN ASSESSMENT

ALTHOUGH modern international trade policy provides many fascinating episodes, observations, and issues, most work by economists and political scientists explores the choice between free trade and protectionism. We have chosen instead to focus our examination of international trade policy on the three central *problématiques* of political economy as articulated by Susan Strange: "the ways things are managed, how they got to be managed in that particular way, and what choices this leaves realistically open for the future."[1] In particular, why has trade policy, whatever its fluctuating balance between free-trade and protectionist elements, taken such strikingly different organizational or institutional forms?

THE WAYS THINGS ARE MANAGED

Peacetime income taxes relieved trade policy of its major fiscal or revenue responsibilities between the mid-nineteenth and early twentieth centuries in most major economies. Since then, the balance between the free-trade and protectionist elements of trade policy has differed widely across time, countries, and sectors.[2] We have seen, for example, the protectionism of the Smoot-Hawley bill, which raised the average U.S. tariff level to over fifty percent, and then, only five years later, the liberalization of the Reciprocal Trade Agreements Act, which laid the groundwork for fifty years of tariff reductions.

However, the wide swings in policy along the free-trade-to-protectionism continuum comprise only one of many patterns to be explained. Because of the complexity of international trade policy, it is hazardous to characterize the policies of a historical period with a single adjective. Nonetheless, craftsmen of all trades—including political economists—must make a rough first cut, one that always is imperfect but focuses the perspective of the analysis. Our strategic organizational approach to international trade policy takes as its first cut the various governance structures that support trade agreements. We have characterized those gover-

---

[1] Strange (1988, p. 18).

[2] Chapter One outlines the major literatures addressing the choice between free trade and protectionism. Figure 1.2 summarizes the main implication of each.

nance structures as unilateral, multilateral, bilateral, and minilateral. Although the names of the "lateralisms" suggest that the number of parties is the defining attribute, we have in mind a set of subtler and richer distinctions. Although the four governance structures exhibit differences in typical group size, they are, in our view, derivative differences, ones that follow from the key attribute: the enforcement mechanism used to support trade agreements.[3] Two of the governance structures (unilateralism and bilateralism) use self-help, while the other two (multilateralism and minilateralism) rely on third-party enforcement. Based on the stylized facts of modern trade history, we identify four episodes corresponding to the four governance structures.[4]

Mid-nineteenth-century Britain lowered trade barriers unilaterally. Though hegemonic by most definitions, Britain did remarkably little to force or persuade other countries to open their trade. Her dominance in key markets influenced Britain's decision to move toward free trade; so, in one sense, hegemony provides an easy and not unreasonable explanation for observed policy. However, the explanation is not complete. Existing hegemony-based explanations, in particular the hegemonic stability hypothesis, imply that Britain would have actively cajoled, bribed, or railroaded other countries into liberalization. Such was not the case. Britain made the move to free trade autonomously or unilaterally, not based on agreements with trading partners.

The post-World War II United States liberalized trade on a scale to match the earlier British move, but in a very different way. The United States engineered creation of the General Agreement on Tariffs and Trade that promoted nondiscriminatory multilateral liberalization. GATT contracting parties took on mutual obligations to bind tariffs at negotiated rates, refrain from proscribed protectionist practices, and provide most-favored-nation status to other contracting parties. The GATT involved little free-trade rhetoric, and provisions supported punishment for protectionist actions that violated countries' commitments. U.S. trade policy often was not autonomous, but a response to others' policies and a tool of enforcement for GATT commitments. As in earlier nineteenth-century Britain, U.S. postwar dominance of key technologies and market sectors

[3] We define *multilateralism* differently from Keohane (1990), who uses the word for any arrangement involving more than two countries. For our purposes, such a definition is not useful because it does not distinguish, for example, between a U.S.-Canada-Mexico free-trade agreement and the GATT; both are multilateral in Keohane's usage. See Chapter One, footnotes 9 and 14, and Chapter Three, footnote 62.

[4] What follows is a brief summary of each episode; details can be found in Chapter Three (unilateral liberalization by mid-nineteenth-century Britain and multilateral liberalization by the post-World War II United States), Chapter Four (bilateral liberalization since U.S. hegemony and the dominance of the GATT have declined), and Chapter Five (recent minilateral liberalization by the United States and Canada and by the European Community).

contributed to her free-trade orientation. Therefore, hegemony again provides an obvious explanation; but it is incomplete since it cannot explain why U.S. policy was so different from Britain's, that is, multilateral rather than unilateral.

In the mid-1960s, the dominant role of the United States and the GATT in world trade policy began a noticeable decline. Scholars and policymakers expressed (and continue to express) concern over a possible shift toward protectionism and dramatized this concern by making comparisons with the protectionism of the 1930s.[5] Although protectionist pressures clearly became more prevalent, the lack of measurable moves to close the trading system surprised many analysts. Trade continued to grow at a respectable rate, despite an apparently more discordant and acrimonious international trading system.

In terms of our central concern—the organizational form of trade policy—two trends emerged with the decline of the United States and the GATT. The first, which we call *bilateralism*, consists of self-enforcing liberalizing agreements among small groups of countries, but not necessarily only two.[6] Examples include the U.S.-Israel, EC-Israel, ASEAN, and European Free-Trade Association agreements. Reliance on self-help to enforce agreements characterizes the groups. Reciprocity, economic hostages, and issue linkages support cooperation; and the primary discipline is the threat of withdrawal, because there is no third-party or supranational dispute-settlement to transcend national sovereignty.

The second trend, which we call *minilateralism*, also involves small groups of countries. Here, groups create supranational enforcement institutions to support cooperation. Examples include the Canada-U.S. Free-Trade Agreement and, most notably, the European Community drive toward 1992 under the Single Europe Act. In both cases, agreements link countries with extremely close economic ties, for whom the pace of progress in the GATT was insufficient. Both agreements contain pathbreaking dispute settlement, a fundamental characteristic of the strategic organizational approach.

All the episodes mentioned involve trade liberalization.[7] Thus, the normative view in which one "correct" organizational approach to trade policy is consistent with liberalization while all others lead inexorably to protectionism seems inconsistent with the historical record. Things have been organized in several different ways, each with some success (and some

[5] Unlike many casual comparisons, Milner (1988c) provides a careful study of trade policy similarities and differences between the 1930s and the 1970s.

[6] See footnote 3 which distinguishes our usage from that of Keohane (1990).

[7] Of course, pure liberalization is rare. All episodes have had some elements of protectionism. For example, Britain continued tariffs on a few goods, and the GATT continues to sanction many protectionist policies.

failure). Why the different forms? Our chosen task is to align the organizational forms of trade policy with other characteristics of trade.[8] We want to know what circumstances tend to produce unilateral, multilateral, bilateral, or minilateral trade liberalization. In other words, how did trade get to be managed in the particular way we observe for each episode?

HOW THINGS GOT TO BE MANAGED IN THAT PARTICULAR WAY

Specialization and trade according to comparative advantage increase the size of the available "pie."[9] However, specialization and trade also cause redistributions of income, both domestically and internationally. The interdependence inherent in trade can generate conflict, and those harmed often turn to the state for aid and protection. Therefore, trade policy is subject to substantial degrees of uncertainty stemming from the interaction of domestic politics and international trade.

Trade liberalization hinges on specialization of production according to comparative advantage. Thus, liberalization alters the pattern of production. A firm or a country altering its production patterns to take advantage of international trade must be cognizant of the possibility of increased protectionism by the trading partner.[10] Each party's alternatives—that is, the opportunities available should the current trading relationship break down—are a key element in willingness to engage in trade. If alternatives are good because of the availability of many potential trading partners on roughly the same terms, trade can proceed with little attention to the hazards of breakdown. But, if the nature of trade is such that one or both parties faces poor alternatives, the hazard of breakdown must be reckoned with if trade is to develop.

The degree of relation-specific investment involved in trade determines the quality of parties' alternatives. Relation-specific investment is expenditure that increases the benefits of the existing relationship, but would

[8] Williamson (1985a), in his work on the firm and corporate governance, refers to this process as "dimensionalizing." In our case, dimensionalization involves explicating the connections among a small number of key characteristics of international trade (that is, [i] relation-specific investment and [ii] third-party governance) and unilateral, multilateral, bilateral, or minilateral forms of trade policy.

[9] The demonstration of this result is the fundamental contribution of neoclassical trade theory. Although questioned in recent years by economists emphasizing imperfect competition and economies of scale, it emerges largely intact, if somewhat reoriented (see Richardson [1990]).

[10] Although the strategic organizational approach emphasizes international or systemic elements in its explanations, the importance of domestic political pressure in affecting the likelihood of opportunism in trade agreements introduces what has been called the "tangle" of domestic politics and international relations (Putnam [1988, p. 427]).

be worth less in any other relationship and therefore would be lost if the current relationship ended. A party making relation-specific investment becomes vulnerable to opportunism by the trading partner, who can threaten to leave unless the terms of the relationship are made more favorable.

The clearest trade-related examples of relation-specific investment are infrastructure facilities developed especially for trade between two distinct parties. The European-Soviet gas pipeline, examined in Chapter Two, is one case. Europeans have provided technology and construction aid in return for future Soviet exports of natural gas. Once in place, the pipeline would be worth much less to both parties if the Soviet-European trade in gas ended; neither party faces good alternatives for the asset. Thus, the Soviet Union could opportunistically reduce natural gas exports; or, Europeans could refuse to maintain the pipeline unless the Soviets increased gas exports. In other words, each party is vulnerable to an attempted holdup or forced renegotiation by the other party. If such vulnerable transactions are to be consummated, they must be supported by governance structures that safeguard the parties from one another's opportunism.

Although less obvious than infrastructure examples, dedicated assets are probably the most common form of trade-related specific investment.[11] Dedicated assets are put in place to service a particular market; therefore, loss of that market would impose large-scale excess or redundant capacity on the investor. One of many possible examples is the Japanese automobile capacity designed for servicing the U.S. market.

Any relationship involving relation-specific investment is subject to opportunistic behavior. By threatening to withdraw, one party can take advantage of the other's poor alternatives and force a renegotiation of terms. Empirical evidence outlined in Chapter Two suggests that relation-specific investment is quantitatively important in trade. Using intra-firm trade as a conservative proxy, between one-third and two-thirds of all U.S. merchandise trade is affected.[12]

In international trade, participants face two distinct sources of opportunism: firms and states. A firm in Country A undertaking relation-specific investment for trade with a firm in Country B can be held up either by the Country B firm or by the government of A or B. Firms protect themselves from opportunism by other firms through long-term con-

---

[11] Williamson (1985a, especially pp. 194–195) explains the concept of dedicated assets.

[12] Chapter Two presents the empirical evidence. For more on why intra-firm trade proxies for relation-specific investment, see Chapter Six. On the conservatism of the proxy, see footnote 13 below.

tracts, licensing, multinationalism, or vertical integration.[13] However, for trade involving relation-specific investment to succeed, governments also must commit themselves not to act opportunistically. In a world of sovereign states, this raises the classic problem of cooperation under "anarchy" and provides the basis for the strategic organizational approach to international trade institutions.

Despite gains from specialization and trade, parties hesitate to make themselves vulnerable by undertaking relation-specific investment for trade without a governance structure to discipline opportunism. When opportunistic behavior is a threat, there are two possible approaches to governance: self-help and third-party enforcement.[14] Thus, we can dimensionalize the problem along two margins as in Figure 7.1.

The first margin of our dimensionalization asks, "To what extent does trade involve relation-specific assets?" This defines the extent of the hazard of opportunism and, therefore, the strength of the demands placed on the governance structure. The left-hand cell of Figure 7.1 represents cases with relatively little relation-specific investment and, therefore, little threat from opportunism. Parties can rely on self-help, and simple gov-

| | | Specific Trade-Related Investment? | |
		No	Yes
Effective 3rd-Party Enforcement?	No		Opportunism problem; Internal safeguards
		No opportunism; Few safeguards	
	Yes		Opportunism problem; External safeguards

Figure 7.1: Determinants of international opportunism and safeguards.

[13] This is the central point of much of the modern literature on multinational corporations, such as Rugman (1981); Caves (1982); and Casson (1987). Only the most vulnerable transactions are integrated within the firm; those with intermediate levels of vulnerability use long-term or nonstandard contracts as hybrid organizational forms; see Williamson (1985a), and Contractor and Lorange (1988). This implies that use of intra-firm trade as a proxy for trade involving relation-specific investment is conservative, since it captures only transactions with the very highest levels of vulnerability. A better proxy, intra-firm trade plus trade subject to long-term or nonstandard contracts, would show much larger percentages of trade as relation-specific.

[14] A third possibility, of course, is to avoid transactions embodying a hazard of opportunism. Since many such transactions are potentially mutually beneficial, this is a costly option.

ernance structures embodying few or weak safeguards against opportunism suffice. The right-hand cells in Figure 7.1 represent the opposite case, the one in which trade involves relation-specific investments.[15] As a result, opportunism presents a serious problem, and governance structures must contain safeguards adequate to assure parties they will not be held up by trading partners.

Here, the second facet of our dimensionalization comes into play: Is there a third-party enforcement mechanism available to enforce agreements and punish attempts at opportunism? If the answer is *no* (in the top right-hand cell of Figure 7.1), parties must deal with the hazard through self-help. The absence of external governance by a third party requires safeguards internal to the relationship. Agreements will be self-enforcing, using hostages, reciprocity, and issue linkages to assure compliance. If the answer is *yes* (corresponding to the lower right-hand cell of Figure 7.1), third-party enforcement can substitute for self-help. Safeguards can be external to the relationship itself, as in day-to-day economic transactions in which the domestic legal system protects parties.

The next step in the strategic organizational approach to international trade institutions relates the dimensionalization in Figure 7.1 to the observed organizational forms of trade policy. Figure 7.2 illustrates this step.

As described briefly earlier in this chapter and in more detail in Chapter Three, mid-nineteenth-century Britain followed a policy of unilateral trade liberalization. Britain enacted few explicit trade agreements with partner countries and did remarkably little, given its dominant status, to bribe or force other countries to liberalize. Trade liberalization clearly altered Britain's production pattern as industries grew to service worldwide markets, but this involved few relation-specific assets. Britain needed raw material and export markets, but these were largely substitutable. With little to fear from opportunistic trading partners, Britain captured the gains from trade and incurred few bargaining or negotiation costs by pursuing unilateral liberalization (see the left-hand cell of Figure 7.2). Hegemony provides one piece of the puzzle why Britain did what it did in trade policy. A second piece—lack of vulnerability to holdup by trading partners—is necessary to understand why Britain's policy differed so markedly from that of the next hegemon, the postwar United States.

By the time the United States established undeniably its hegemony during World War II, the nature of the world economy had changed considerably from the period of British hegemony. The number of industrialized

---

[15] The extent of relation-specific investment would be characterized more accurately as a continuum, not a dichotomy. As a rough first cut, it seems useful to contrast transactions with no relation-specific investment to those characterized by large amounts to tie opportunism hazard to the type of governance structure.

		Specific Trade-Related Investment?	
		No	YES
Effective 3rd-Party Enforcement?	No	UNILATERAL trade policy (e.g., 19th-century Britain)	BILATERAL trade policy (e.g., 1970-90)
	YES		MULTILATERAL trade policy (e.g., 1945-65) OR MINILATERAL trade policy (e.g., Europe 1992)

Figure 7.2: Organizational variety in international trade.

economies had grown. Technology had changed and with it the scale of efficient production. Capital-intensive industries commonly invested in assets designed for use in trade with particular partners. Tight vertical production linkages grew across national boundaries. Most importantly, foreign investment had shifted from portfolio to direct investment. As a result, firms gained operating control of foreign operations, and intersectoral trade gave way to intra-industry and intra-firm trade. All these trends contributed to an increase in trade-oriented relation-specific investment.

In such circumstances, unilateral liberalization, with its reliance on self-help and lack of safeguards against opportunism, ceases to be viable. The United States, like Britain before, needed raw material and export markets. It got them by supporting a multilateral, nondiscriminatory system of liberal trade based on the apparently weak organizational structure of the GATT.[16] During the twenty years following World War II, what GATT lacked in enforcement will and ability, the United States possessed. The multilateral GATT-based system was an array of sticks and carrots wielded and promised by the United States with the goal of supporting a relatively open trading system. Free trade was not the goal, but negotiation of attainable degrees of openness with punishment for acts of protection that reneged on international promises. Quite different from earlier Britain, the United States (because of the vulnerability of its trade-related specific investments) did not use hegemony to go its own way and liber-

[16] Chapter Three discusses the U.S.-GATT case at length.

alize unilaterally. Instead it used its own trade policy as an enforcement mechanism for a multilateral system of trade agreements. As long as the United States was willing and able to perform this role, the answer to our second dimensionalizing question (Is there a third-party governance mechanism to enforce agreements and punish opportunism?) was *yes*, as in the lower right-hand corner of Figure 7.2. The decline of U.S. hegemony shifted the answer to *no*.

By the mid-1960s, large amounts of relation-specific investment undertaken for international trade characterized the world economy. With the United States no longer able and willing to enforce multilateral agreements through the GATT, trade discord accelerated, and concerns about lost momentum in liberalization and increased protectionist pressures grew. There were two choices: (i) recognize the fading influence of U.S. hegemony and create self-enforcing agreements that relied on self-help, or (ii) create new third-party governance mechanisms among like-minded countries. The right-hand side of Figure 7.2 notes both possibilities.

The first of the two possibilities is represented by most of the growing number of small trade groups such as the U.S.-Israel and EC-Israel trade agreements, the Association of Southeast Asian Nations, several trade groups in the Middle East and Mediterranean, and the European Community in its early years before passage of the Single Europe Act. These reflect bilateralism (upper right-hand corner in Figure 7.2), agreements among small groups of countries based in self-help that use reciprocity, economic hostages, and issue linkages to assure compliance and deter opportunism.[17] Such agreements are the only option when (i) trade involves relation-specific assets, (ii) no hegemon is willing to enforce multilateral agreements, and (iii) countries are unwilling to create supranational institutions to enforce agreements and mediate disputes. As in other self-help systems, relations in these groups often are rocky. Groups come and go as members exercise their right to self-help by withdrawing from membership.

The second possibility, minilateralism (lower right-hand corner of Figure 7.2), involves small groups of countries creating their own governance mechanisms or supranational institutions to enforce agreements and settle disputes.[18] Two examples are the Canada-U.S. Free-Trade Agreement and the recent evolution of the European Community under the Single Europe Act. In both cases, the countries involved have unusually intensive and intimate economic ties, and the pervasive relation-specific investment places great demands on the governance structure.

---

[17] Chapter Four explains the mechanics of how these elements combine to comprise a governance structure.

[18] Chapter Five contains a detailed treatment.

The Canada-U.S. agreement grew out of the two parties' concerns over security of access to the other market. Canada's worries centered on their perception of opportunistic use of U.S. countervailing and antidumping policies. The United States experienced similar worries about the erratic character of Canadian policy toward inward foreign direct investment. The agreement, besides eliminating tariffs on most items, addressed both parties' concerns by enhancing dispute-settlement procedures. In the case of the EC, a single country's ability to veto Community action, thereby eliminating reliable punishment of opportunism within the group, hindered internal enforcement of promises. The Single Europe Act, by limiting the veto, eased further elimination of trade barriers in goods, services, and factor movements; in other words, the procedural changes in the Single Europe Act allowed a different type of governance structure that, in turn, made possible completion of the internal market. Of course, judgement of the success of both the U.S.-Canada and EC examples awaits cases that fully stress the new procedures.[19]

Thus, the strategic organizational approach dimensionalizes historical periods of trade based on the presence or absence of relation-specific investment and the presence or absence of third-party enforcement.[20] The confluence of these two factors affects the viability of different governance structures. Pursuit of trade policy through different observed institutional or organizational forms reflects those governance structures, summarized in Figure 7.3. In other words, the dimensionalization explains how trade policy got to be managed in the particular ways observed historically, bringing us to the third and final *problématique*.

WHAT CHOICES THIS LEAVES REALISTICALLY OPEN FOR THE FUTURE

The growth of economies of scale, intra-industry trade, and intra-firm trade suggests increasing relation-specific trade-oriented investment.[21] Thus, opportunism in agreements will continue to be a hazard. The growth of trade will require that adequate governance structures secure transactions. Unilateral trade liberalization is unlikely to be viable on a significant scale. Most scholars of international relations agree that no new hegemon is on the horizon. Consequently, the likelihood of significant pushes toward liberalization in a large-scale multilateral format is

[19] The first dispute between the United States and Canada over trade in pork just completed the final stages of the new multistep dispute settlement process outlined in Chapter Five (*Wall Street Journal* [1991b]).

[20] The choice of only two key margins obviously paints history with a very broad brush. Below we suggest several avenues for future research based on finer distinctions.

[21] Economies of scale accentuate the pattern of sectoral specialization in trade; see Richardson (1990, p. 115).

Institutional form	Relation-specific investment?	Enforcement	Example	Enforcement in example
Unilateral	No	Self-help	Mid-nineteenth-century Britain	Withdrawal
Bilateral	Yes	Self-help	U.S.-Israel Free-Trade Area Agreement	Self-enforcing agreement with linkages, hostages, reciprocity
Minilateral	Yes	Third-party	Post-1985 European Community	Supra-national EC institutions
Multilateral	Yes	Third-party	Postwar GATT	U.S. hegemony

Figure 7.3: Alternate governance structures for international trade.

reduced. From the alternatives in Figure 7.3, bilateralism and minilateralism are more likely to play important future roles as governance structures in the international trading system.

In some circles, particularly among economists, both bilateralism and minilateralism are often portrayed as sure roads to protectionism, because of the emergence of conflictual blocs or fortresses. Others have noted that "when we think about cooperation after hegemony, we need to think about institutions" that help governments pursue their interests through cooperation, and such institutions need not centralize authority or be universal to be effective.[22] The strategic organizational approach lends support to the second position. Several different institutional structures have had some historical success in trade liberalization, and none has proven to be perfect or infinitely lived. There is little evidence that any one of the governance structures—unilateralism, multilateralism, bilateralism, or minilateralism—is a sure road to trade warfare. Likewise, there is little evidence that any one is the road to trade nirvana, even if all were to agree on the characteristics of such a place. Instead, the strategic organizational approach highlights the advantages and disadvantages of different organizational forms and aligns them with circumstances in which we might expect each to be used.

Just how persuasive is the strategic organizational argument? Readers

[22] Quote from Keohane (1984, p. 246).

will, of course, have to judge; but we can offer a few guidelines. First, a final reminder of the task that we set for ourselves. The question has not been why the free trade and protectionist elements of trade policy fluctuate across time, countries, and industry sectors. That is an important and interesting question; but it has been addressed frequently, if not completely satisfactorily. Instead, the perhaps more difficult but nonetheless central question is this: *Why, despite the fluctuating balance between free trade and protectionism, does trade policy take such different organizational forms?* Thus, we have tackled a more comprehensive set of observations than that typically addressed.

We have argued that the perspective of the strategic organizational approach is consistent with the "stylized facts" of modern trade history. Mid-nineteenth-century Britain followed a unilateral trade policy despite its likely ability to force or persuade other countries to liberalize reciprocally. The postwar United States, hegemonic like Britain, took a very different path and never followed unilateral trade policies. Instead, it liberalized multilaterally by using trade policy to support the General Agreement on Tariffs and Trade as a multilateral forum for negotiation of trade rules. Since the decline of U.S. hegemony and the GATT, some countries have liberalized bilaterally through self-enforcing agreements, while other groups have created supranational institutions to permit minilateral liberalization.

Other existing theories can explain one or two episodes, but none is broad enough to encompass all. Those theories address why free trade or protectionism seems to have dominated particular periods, not why trade policy took the *form* it did. Of course, designing a perspective consistent with the past is only part of the problem. To be both robust and nontautological, the strategic organizational approach must be consistent with some but not all possible future events.[23] In other words, actual events must be consistent with the framework, and realized future outcomes must be a subset of all possible outcomes, some of which would be inconsistent with it.[24]

What future developments would call the strategic organizational approach seriously into question? For one, a substantial return to unilateral trade liberalization in a world now characterized by high and rising levels of relation-specific investment. The strategic organizational approach implies that, in such a world, self-help or retaliatory withdrawal (the only enforcement mechanism of unilateralism) will prove an inadequate gov-

---

[23] On the current verification-falsification methodological debate, see Caldwell (1991).

[24] In fact, the theoretical framework of what we call *the strategic organizational approach* was developed in 1985, well before events in the European Community related in Chapter Five. To our delight, those events unfolded as the final piece of the strategic organizational approach—a small but reassuring piece of supporting evidence.

ernance structure. For another, a return to an international trading system strongly dominated by large-scale multilateralism without a hegemon.[25] Multilateralism, while conceptually distinct from hegemony, requires a mechanism for enforcement of its rules. The outstanding modern example of multilateralism, the GATT during the early postwar years, was crucially dependent on the support of the United States. Both developments, a return to unilateralism or to multilateralism, would be supported by many scholars and policymakers in the trade-policy community.[26] Despite widespread support, our analysis suggests that both are unlikely for strategic-organizational or governance-based reasons.

What future developments would provide further support for the strategic organizational approach? The key prediction is for further minilateral agreements between or among countries whose close economic ties lead to significant mutual benefits from trade-oriented relation-specific investment. The active example is Mexico's free-trade talks with the United States and Canada. Ironically, a spring 1991 Congressional vote coupled extension of the "fast-track" authority for negotiations in the GATT Uruguay Round with provision of presidential authority to proceed with the U.S.-Mexico-Canada talks.[27] The debate surrounding the votes was either/or, as if support for minilateral initiatives necessarily doomed the GATT to irrelevance and sentenced the trading system to a future of fortress arrangements. The strategic organizational approach implies such an emphasis is misplaced. Although the decline of U.S. hegemony means the GATT cannot play the dominant role it once did in the world trading system, there are still useful roles for it. Among those roles are provision and transmission of information, maintenance of a format for international discussions and negotiations, and a repository of trade history, precedent, and country reputations.[28]

The other major world development whose future will be helpful in evaluating the strategic organizational approach is the integration of former Eastern bloc countries into the world economy. Many of these coun-

---

[25] As noted earlier, this does not imply that we expect GATT to cease to exist or to become unimportant. See the comments at the end of Chapter Four.

[26] For an argument favoring a return to unilateralism, see *Wall Street Journal* (1990b), quoted in Chapter One. Cline (1983) is just one of many examples of calls for a return to multilateralism. See also Bhagwati (1990). On the importance of definitions of the "lateralisms" in comparing predictions, see Chapter One, footnote 9 and Chapter Three, footnote 62.

[27] Fast-track authority gives the president the right to present results of GATT talks to Congress for a vote of approval or disapproval, with no amendments or alterations allowed. Most trade-policy observers view the fast-track procedure as essential to passage, since amendments open the debate to too many pressures from narrow special-interest lobbies.

[28] See Keohane (1984, p. 245); Milgrom, North, and Weingast (1990); and the discussion at the end of Chapter Four.

tries are trying to attract foreign investment and trade, although currency inconvertibility and political instability slow the attempts. The new governments have little in the way of reputations and thus find it even more difficult to commit themselves credibly in a way that would ease rapid transitions. The strategic organization approach implies that such a situation would lead to new organizational forms using hostages and bonds to alleviate the governments' inabilities to commit themselves. Trade with Eastern bloc countries was a fertile source for organizational innovation even before the opening of 1989; but the extensive changes since 1989 provide a rare opportunity to observe trade institutions' responses to alterations in the political-economic environment.[29]

The "tests" of the strategic organizational approach suggested thus far require that we wait for the future to provide additional data. There are, however, many avenues for research using existing information. As noted at several points, our approach has been to paint with a very broad brush. This seems appropriate for the initial task, but must eventually lead to more detailed examinations of historical periods, countries, and sectors.[30]

Along these lines, many interesting questions suggest themselves. How well can the strategic organizational approach, with its augmentations and alterations of the hegemonic stability hypothesis, explain the breakdown of world trade in the 1930s? To what extent can the approach explain where the Soviet Union attempted to "draw the line" in permitting exit from the Eastern bloc, for example, allowing (East) Germany and Poland to exit, but taking a harder line against the Baltic republics?[31] Do industries never covered under the GATT (for example, agriculture) or industries whose treatment departed early from the GATT framework (for example, textiles or steel) have special characteristics that we can understand from a strategic organizational perspective? What about aspects of trade policy, such as countervailing and antidumping duties, that can potentially be used both offensively (as an opportunistic holdup of trading partners) and defensively (to deter opportunism)? Does the "dual" character of these policies explain why they are so persistently controversial and unamenable to negotiation? A research program addressing these and related questions is essential to extend the insights of

[29] See for example, Alexandrides and Bowers (1987, especially pp. 33–38, 207–215).

[30] In Williamson's terminology, research must become more comparative and more microanalytic.

[31] Both the destructuring and the restructuring of a group such as the Soviet Union should shed light on the strategic organizational framework. The "old" Soviet Union was inordinately centralized, with extreme interdependencies (see Chapter Five, footnote 61). The new union will be less so. The old centralized structure resembled a hegemonic one. The new union should use more bilateral techniques (for example, issue linkages, hostages, and reciprocity); an alternative is a new, smaller union (excluding the most independence-minded republics) with minilateral institutions.

the strategic organizational approach, integrate those insights with other theories of international trade policy, and understand fully this vital aspect of international economic relations. This book represents a first step along that path; we hope others will find the approach sufficiently promising to join us in following it.

BIBLIOGRAPHY

Acheson, Keith, 1989. Power Steering the Canadian Automobile Industry: The 1965 Canada-USA Auto Pact and Political Exchange. *Journal of Economic Behavior and Organization* 11:237–252.

Adams, John, 1990. Institutional Economics and Social Choice Economics: Commonalities and Conflicts. *Journal of Economic Issues* 24:845–860.

Aggarwal, Vinod K., 1985. *Liberal Protectionism: The International Politics of Organized Textile Trade.* Berkeley: University of California Press.

Aggarwal, Vinod K., Robert O. Keohane, and David B. Yoffie, 1987. The Dynamics of Negotiated Protectionism. *American Political Science Review* 81:345–366.

Akerlof, George A., 1970. The Market for Lemons: Quality Uncertainty and the Market Mechanism. *Quarterly Journal of Economics* 84:488–500.

Alchian, Armen A., 1950. Uncertainty, Evolution and Economic Theory. *Journal of Political Economy* 58:211–221.

Alchian, Armen A., and Susan Woodward, 1988. The Firm is Dead; Long Live the Firm. *Journal of Economic Literature* 26:65–79.

Alexandrides, Costas G., and Barbara L. Bowers, 1987. *Countertrade: Practices, Strategies, and Tactics.* New York: John Wiley.

Anderson, Gary M., and Robert D. Tollison, 1985. Ideology, Interest Groups, and the Repeal of the Corn Laws. *Journal of Institutional and Theoretical Economics* 141:197–212.

Anderson, Erin, and David C. Schmittlein, 1984. Integration of the Sales Force: An Empirical Examination. *Rand Journal of Economics* 15:385–395.

Aoki, Masahiko, 1984. *The Co-Operative Game Theory of the Firm.* Oxford: Oxford University Press.

Axelrod, Robert, 1984. *The Evolution of Cooperation.* New York: Basic Books.

———, 1986. An Evolutionary Approach to Norms. *American Political Science Review* 80:1095–1111.

Axelrod, Robert, and Robert O. Keohane, 1986. Achieving Cooperation under Anarchy: Strategies and Institutions. In Kenneth A. Oye, ed., *Cooperation under Anarchy.* Princeton: Princeton University Press, pp. 226–254.

Baack, Bennett D., and Edward John Ray, 1983. The Political Economy of Tariff Policy: A Case Study of the United States. *Explorations in Economic History* 20:73–93.

———, 1985a. Special Interests and the Adoption of the Income Tax in the United States. *Journal of Economic History* 45:607–625.

———, 1985b. The Political Economy of the Origin and Development of the Federal Income Tax. In Robert Higgs, ed., *Emergence of the Modern Political Economy.* Greenwich, Ct.: JAI Press, pp. 121–138.

Bagwell, Kyle, and Robert W. Staiger, 1990. A Theory of Managed Trade. *American Economic Review* 80:779–795.

Baldwin, David A., 1979. Power Analysis and World Politics. *World Politics* 31:161–194.

———, 1985. *Economic Statecraft*. Princeton: Princeton University Press.

Baldwin, Robert E., 1979. *The Multilateral Trade Negotiations*. American Enterprise Institute Special Analysis No. 79–2. Washington, D.C.: American Enterprise Institute.

———, 1982. The Political Economy of Protectionism. In Jagdish Bhagwati, ed., *Import Competition and Response*. Chicago: University of Chicago Press, pp. 263–292.

———, 1984a. The Changing Nature of U.S. Trade Policy Since World War II. In Robert E. Baldwin and Anne O. Krueger, eds., *The Structure and Evolution of Recent U.S. Trade Policy*. Chicago: University of Chicago Press, pp. 5–27.

———, 1984b. Trade Policies in Developed Countries. In Ronald W. Jones and Peter B. Kenen, eds., *Handbook of International Economics*, vol. 1. Amsterdam: North-Holland, pp. 571–619.

———, 1985. *The Political Economy of U.S. Import Policy*. Cambridge, Mass.: MIT Press.

———, 1987. Multilateral Liberalization. In J. Michael Finger and Andrzej Olechowski, eds., *The Uruguay Round: A Handbook on the Multilateral Trade Negotiations*. Washington, D.C.: The World Bank, pp. 37–44.

Banks, Gary, and Jan Tumlir, 1986. The Political Problem of Adjustment. *The World Economy* 9:141–152.

Barzel, Yoram, 1985. Transaction Costs: Are They Just Costs? *Journal of Institutional and Theoretical Economics* 141:4–16.

Baumgartner, T., and T. R. Burns, 1975. The Structuring of International Economic Relations. *International Studies Quarterly* 19:126–159.

Ben-Porath, Yoram, 1980. The F-Connection: Family, Friends, and Firms and the Organization of Exchange. *Population and Development Review* 6:1–30.

Benjamin, Roger, and Raymond Duvall, 1985. The Capitalist State in Context. In Roger Benjamin and S. Elkin, eds., *The Democratic State*. Lawrence, Kansas: University of Kansas Press, pp. 19–57.

Benson, Bruce L., 1989. The Spontaneous Evolution of Commercial Law. *Southern Economic Journal* 55:644–661.

Bergsten, C. Fred, and William R. Cline, 1983. Trade Policy in the 1980s: An Overview. In William R. Cline, ed., *Trade Policy in the 1980s*. Washington, D.C.: Institute for International Economics, pp. 59–98.

Bhagwati, Jagdish, 1990. Aggressive Unilateralism: An Overview. In Jagdish Bhagwati and Hugh T. Patrick, eds., *Aggressive Unilateralism: America's 301 Trade Policy and the World Trading System*. Ann Arbor: University of Michigan Press, pp. 1–45.

Bhagwati, Jagdish, and V. K. Ramaswami, 1963. Domestic Distortions, Tariffs, and the Theory of Optimum Subsidy. *Journal of Political Economy* 71:44–50.

Bohara, Alok K., and William H. Kaempfer, 1991. A Test of Tariff Endogeneity in the United States. *American Economic Review* 81:952–960.

Brams, Steven J., Ann E. Doherty, and Matthew L. Weidner, 1991. Game Theory and Multilateral Negotiations: The Single European Act and the Uruguay

Round. Paper for "International Multilateral Negotiations" Conference. Laxenburg, Austria: International Institute for Applied Systems Analysis.

Brennan, Geoffrey, and James Buchanan, 1985. *The Reason of Rules*. Cambridge, Mass.: Cambridge University Press.

Buchanan, James M., 1965. An Economic Theory of Clubs. *Economica* 32:1–14.

Bueno de Mesquita, Bruce, 1978. Systemic Polarization and the Occurrence and Duration of War. *Journal of Conflict Resolution* 22:241–267.

Bull, Hedley, 1977. *The Anarchical Society*. London: Macmillan.

Buzan, Barry, 1984. Economic Structure and International Security: The Limits of the Liberal Case. *International Organization* 38:597–624.

Caldwell, Bruce J., 1991. Clarifying Popper. *Journal of Economic Literature* 29:1–31.

Carr, E. H., 1964. *The Twenty Years' Crisis, 1919–1939: An Introduction to the Study of International Relations*. New York: Harper Torchbooks.

Cassing, James, Timothy McKeown, and Jack Ochs, 1986. The Political Economy of the Tariff Cycle. *American Political Science Review* 80:843–862.

Casson, Mark, 1987. *The Firm and the Market: Studies on Multinational Enterprise and the Scope of the Firm*. Cambridge, Mass.: MIT Press.

Caves, Richard E., 1974. The Economics of Reciprocity: Theory and Evidence on Bilateral Trading Arrangements. In W. Sellekaerts, ed., *International Trade and Finance: Essays in Honor of Jan Tinbergen*. White Plains, N.Y.: International Arts and Sciences Press, pp. 17–54.

Caves, Richard E., 1976. Economic Models of Political Choice: Canada's Tariff Structure. *Canadian Journal of Political Science* 9:278–300.

————, 1982. *Multinational Enterprise and Economic Analysis*. Cambridge: Cambridge University Press.

Cline, William R., 1983. 'Reciprocity': A New Approach to World Trade Policy? In William R. Cline, ed., *Trade Policy in the 1980s*. Washington, D.C.: Institute for International Economics, pp. 121–158.

Coase, R.H., 1988. R. H. Coase Lectures. *Journal of Law, Economics, and Organization* 4:3–48.

Coase, Ronald, 1984. The New Institutional Economics. *Journal of Institutional and Theoretical Economics* 140:229–231.

Cohen, Benjamin J., 1990. The Political Economy of International Trade. *International Organization* 44:261–281.

Colander, David C., ed., 1984. *Neoclassical Political Economy: The Analysis of Rent-Seeking and DUP Activities*. Cambridge, Mass.: Ballinger.

Commission of the European Communities, 1985. *Completing the Internal Market: White Paper from the Commission to the European Council*. Brussels.

Commons, John, 1934. *Institutional Economics*. New York: Macmillan.

————, 1950. *The Economics of Collective Action*. Madison: University of Wisconsin Press.

Contractor, Farok J., and Peter Lorange, eds., 1988. *Cooperative Ventures in International Business: Joint Ventures and Technology Partnerships between Firms*. Lexington, Mass.: Lexington Books.

Conybeare, John A. C., 1980. International Organization and the Theory of Property Rights. *International Organization* 34:307–334.

———, 1983. Tariff Protection in Developed and Developing Countries: A Cross-Sectional and Longitudinal Analysis. *International Organization* 37:441–468.

———, 1984. Public Goods, Prisoners' Dilemmas and the International Political Economy. *International Studies Quarterly* 28:5–22.

———, 1986. Trade Wars: A Comparative Study of Anglo-Hanse, Franco-Italian, and Hawley-Smoot Conflicts. In Kenneth A. Oye, ed., *Cooperation under Anarchy*. Princeton: Princeton University Press, pp. 147–172.

———, 1987. *Trade Wars*. New York: Columbia University Press.

Cooper, Richard N., 1987. Trade Policy as Foreign Policy. In Robert M. Stern, ed., *U.S. Trade Policies in a Changing World Economy*. Cambridge, Mass.: MIT Press, pp. 291–336.

———, 1989. Europe Without Borders. *Brookings Papers on Economic Activity*, no. 2:325–340.

Cooter, Robert, and Thomas Ulen, 1988. *Law and Economics*. Glenview, Illinois: Scott, Foresman.

Corden, W. Max, 1984. The Normative Theory of International Trade. In Ronald W. Jones and Peter B. Kenen, eds., *Handbook of International Economics*, vol.1. Amsterdam: North-Holland, pp. 63–130.

Cornes, Richard, and Todd Sandler, 1986. *The Theory of Externalities, Public Goods, and Club Goods*. Cambridge: Cambridge University Press.

Cowhey, Peter F., and Edward Long, 1983. Testing Theories of Regime Change: Hegemonic Decline or Surplus Capacity? *International Organization* 37:157–188.

Cox, R. W., 1983. Gramsci, Hegemony, and International Relations: An Essay in Method. *Millennium: Journal of International Studies* 12:162–175.

Craswell, Richard, and John E. Calfee, 1986. Deterrence and Uncertain Legal Standards. *Journal of Law, Economics, and Organization* 2:279–303.

Cuddington, John T., and Ronald I. McKinnon, 1979. Free Trade versus Protectionism: A Perspective. In *Tariffs, Quotas and Trade: The Politics of Protectionism*. San Francisco: Institute for Contemporary Studies, pp. 3–23.

Culbert, Jay, 1987. War-Time Anglo-American Talks and the Making of the GATT. *The World Economy* 10:381–408.

Czinkota, Michael R., and Ilkka A. Ronkainen, 1988. *International Marketing*. Chicago: Dryden Press.

Dam, Kenneth W., 1970. *The GATT: Law and the International Economic Organization*. Chicago: University of Chicago Press.

Deardorff, Alan V., and Robert M. Stern, 1987. Current Issues in Trade Policy: An Overview. In Robert M. Stern, ed., *U.S. Trade Policies in a Changing World Economy*. Cambridge, Mass.: MIT Press, pp. 15–76.

Dessler, David, 1989. What's at Stake in the Agent-Structure Debate? *International Organization* 43:441–474.

Destler, I. M., 1986. *American Trade Politics*. Washington, D.C.: Institute for International Economics.

Deutsch, Karl W., and J. David Singer, 1964. Multipolar Power Systems and International Stability. *World Politics* 16:390–406.

Dixit, Avinash, 1987. How Should the United States Respond to Other Countries' Trade Policies? In Robert M. Stern, ed., *U.S. Trade Policies in a Changing World Economy.* Cambridge, Mass.: MIT Press, pp. 245–282.

Doran, Charles F., 1971. *The Politics of Assimilation.* Baltimore: Johns Hopkins University Press.

Dorfman, Robert, 1991. Review Article: Economic Development from the Beginning to Rostow. *Journal of Economic Literature* 29:573–591.

Dornbusch, Rudiger, 1990. Policy Options for Freer Trade: The Case of Bilateralism. In Robert Z. Lawrence and Charles L. Schultze, eds., *An American Trade Strategy.* Washington, D.C.: The Brookings Institution, pp. 106–134.

Dow, Gregory K., 1987. The Function of Authority in Transaction Cost Economics. *Journal of Economic Behavior and Organization* 8:13–38.

Duncan, George T., and Randolph M. Siverson, 1982. Flexibility of Alliance Partner Choice in a Multipolar System: Models and Tests. *International Studies Quarterly* 26:511–538.

Durkheim, Emile, 1933 [1893]. *The Division of Labor in Society.* New York: Free Press.

Eden, Lorraine, 1991. Bringing the Firm Back In: Multinationals in IPE. *Millennium.*

Eden, Lorraine, and Fen Osler Hampson, 1990. Clubs are Trump: Towards a Taxonomy of International Regimes. Carleton University: Center for International Trade and Investment Policy Studies Discussion Paper.

Eden, Lorraine, and Maureen Appel Molot, 1991. From Silent Integration to Strategic Alliance: The Political Economy of North American Free Trade. Carleton University: Norman Paterson School of International Affairs Working Paper.

Edgeworth, Francis, 1925. Papers Relating to Political Economy. Cited in Viner (1975 [1937]).

Ekelund, Robert B., Jr., and Robert D. Tollison, 1981. *Mercantilism as a Rent-Seeking Society.* College Station, Texas: Texas A&M Press.

Ellickson, Robert C., 1991. *Order Without Law.* Cambridge, Mass.: Harvard University Press.

Elliott, E. Donald, Bruce A. Ackerman, and John C. Millian, 1985. Toward a Theory of Statutory Evolution: The Federalization of Environmental Law. *Journal of Law, Economics, and Organization* 1:313–340.

Elster, Jon, 1979. *Ulysses and the Sirens: Studies in Rationality and Irrationality.* Cambridge: Cambridge University Press.

———, 1983. *Explaining Technical Change.* Cambridge: Cambridge University Press.

Emerson, Michael, et al., 1988. *The Economics of 1992: The EC Commission's Assessment of the Economic Effects of Completing the Internal Market.* Oxford: Oxford University Press.

Encarnation, Dennis J., and Louis T. Wells, Jr., 1985. Sovereignty en Garde: Negotiating with Foreign Investors. *International Organization* 39:47–78.

Evans, Peter B., 1989. Declining Hegemony and Assertive Industrialization: U.S.-Brazil Conflicts in the Computer Industry. *International Organization* 43:207–238.

Field, Alexander J., 1981. The Problem with Neoclassical Institutional Economics. *Explorations in Economic History* 18:174–198.

Finger, J. Michael, 1987a. Antidumping and Antisubsidy Measures. In J. Michael Finger and Andrzej Olechowski, eds., *The Uruguay Round: A Handbook on the Multilateral Trade Negotiations.* Washington, D.C.: The World Bank, pp. 153–162.

———, 1987b. Introduction. In J. Michael Finger and Andrzej Olechowski, eds., *The Uruguay Round: A Handbook on the Multilateral Trade Negotiations.* Washington, D.C.: The World Bank, pp. 1–3.

Finger, J. Michael, and Paula Holmes, 1987. Unilateral Liberalization and the MTNs. In J. Michael Finger and Andrzej Olechowski, eds., *The Uruguay Round: A Handbook on the Multilateral Trade Negotiations.* Washington, D.C.: The World Bank, pp. 52–58.

Finlayson, Jock A., and Mark W. Zacher, 1981. The GATT and the Regulation of Trade Barriers: Regime Dynamics and Functions. *International Organization* 35:561–602.

Friedman, David, 1977. A Theory of the Size and Shape of Nations. *Journal of Political Economy* 85:59–77.

Frohlich, Norman, Joe A. Oppenheimer, and Oran R. Young, 1971. *Political Leadership and Collective Goods.* Princeton: Princeton University Press.

Galanter, Marc, 1981. Justice in Many Rooms. *Journal of Legal Pluralism* 19:1–47.

Gallarotti, Giulio, 1985. Toward a Business-Cycle Model of Tariffs. *International Organization* 39:155–188.

Gallick, Edward C., 1984. Exclusive Dealing and Vertical Integration: The Efficiency of Contracts in the Tuna Industry. Bureau of Economics Staff Report, U.S. Federal Trade Commission, Washington, D.C.

Garnett, John, 1981. The Role of Military Power. In Michael Smith, Richard Little, and Michael Shackleton, eds., *Perspectives on World Politics.* Kent: Croom Helm London, pp. 63–75.

Garrett, Geoffrey, 1990. The European Internal Market: The Political Economy of Regional Integration. Paper for the Ford Foundation Workshop on Multilateralism.

Gatignon, Hubert, and Erin Anderson, 1988. The Multinational Corporation's Degree of Control over Foreign Subsidiaries: An Empirical Test of a Transaction Cost Explanation. *Journal of Law, Economics, and Organization* 4:305–336.

Gilpin, Robert, 1975. *U.S. Power and the Multinational Corporation: The Political Economy of Foreign Direct Investment.* New York: Basic Books.

———, 1981. *War and Change in World Politics.* Cambridge: Cambridge University Press.

———, 1987. *The Political Economy of International Relations.* Princeton: Princeton University Press.

Goldberg, Victor, and John R. Erickson, 1987. Quantity and Price Adjustment in Long-term Contracts: A Case Study of Petroleum Coke. *Journal of Law and Economics* 30:369–398.

Goldschmidt, Walter, 1966. *Comparative Functionalism*. Berkeley: University of California Press.

Goldstein, Judith, 1989. The Impact of Ideas on Trade Policy. *International Organization* 43:31–72.

Gordon, Wendell, 1967. Orthodox Economics and Institutionalized Behavior. In Carey C. Thompson, ed., *Institutional Adjustment*. Austin: University of Texas Press, pp. 41–67.

Gowa, Joanne, 1986. Anarchy, Egoism, and Third Images. *International Organization* 40:167–186.

———, 1988. Public Goods and Political Institutions: Trade and Monetary Policy Processes in the United States. *International Organization* 42:15–32.

———, 1989a. Bipolarity, Multipolarity, and Free Trade. *American Political Science Review* 83:1245–1256.

———, 1989b. Rational Hegemons, Excludable Goods, and Small Groups: An Epitaph for Hegemonic Stability Theory? *World Politics* 41:307–324.

Grandy, Christopher, 1989. Can Government Be Trusted to Keep Its Part of a Social Contract? New Jersey and the Railroads, 1825–1888. *Journal of Law, Economics, and Organization* 5:249–270.

Granovetter, Mark, 1985. Economic Action and Social Structure. *American Journal of Sociology* 91:481–510.

Grey, Rodney de C., 1983. A Note on U.S. Trade Practices. In William R. Cline, ed., *Trade Policy in the 1980s*. Washington, D.C.: Institute for International Economics, pp. 243–257.

Grieco, Joseph M., 1990. *Cooperation Among Nations: Europe, America, and Non-Tariff Barriers to Trade*. Ithaca, N.Y.: Cornell University Press.

Grilli, Vittorio, 1989. Financial Markets and 1992. *Brookings Papers on Economic Activity*, no. 2:301–324.

Grunberg, Isabelle, 1990. Exploring the 'Myth' of Hegemonic Stability. *International Organization* 44:431–477.

Haas, Ernst, 1958. *The Uniting of Europe*. Stanford: Stanford University Press.

———, 1964. *Beyond the Nation-State*. Stanford: Stanford University Press.

———, 1975. *The Obsolescence of Regional Integration Theory*. Berkeley: University of California Institute of International Studies.

Haas, Ernst B., 1990. *When Knowledge is Power: Three Models of Change in International Organizations*. Berkeley: University of California Press.

Haggard, Stephan, and Beth A. Simmons, 1987. Theories of International Regimes. *International Organization* 41:491–517.

Hall, John A., and G. John Ikenberry, 1989. *The State*. Minneapolis: University of Minnesota Press.

Hamilton, Gary G., and Nicole Woolsey Biggart, 1988. Market, Culture, and Authority: A Comparative Analysis of Management and Organization in the Far East. *American Journal of Sociology* 94 (Supplement):S52–S94.

Hamilton, Walton, 1932. Institutions. In E. R. A. Seligman and A. Johnson, eds., *Encyclopedia of the Social Sciences*, vol. 8. New York: Macmillan, pp. 84–89.

Hanke, Steven H., 1983. U.S.-Japanese Trade: Myths and Realities. *The Cato Journal* 3:757–769.

Hansen, John Mark, 1990. Taxation and the Political Economy of the Tariff. *International Organization* 44:527–551.

Hardin, Russell, 1982. *Collective Action*. Baltimore: Johns Hopkins University Press for Resources for the Future.

Harris, Richard, 1989. "Market Access" in International Trade. In Robert M. Stern, ed., *Trade and Investment Relations Among the United States, Canada, and Japan*. Chicago: University of Chicago Press, pp. 263–284.

Hart, Michael M., 1987. The Mercantilist's Lament: National Treatment and Modern Trade Negotiations. *Journal of World Trade Law* 21:37–62.

Hathaway, C. Michael, and Sandra Masur, 1990. The Right Emphasis for U.S. Trade Policy for the 1990's: Positive Bilateralism. Working Paper.

Haufler, Virginia, 1991. The Framework for Foreign Investment and the New Economics of Organization. Paper presented at the Annual Conference of the International Studies Association, Vancouver, B.C., Canada.

Heckscher, Eli, 1919. The Effects of Foreign Trade on the Distribution of Income. *Ekonomisk Tidskrift* 21:497–512.

Helleiner, G. K., 1977. Transnational Enterprises and the New Political Economy of U.S. Trade Policy. *Oxford Economic Papers* 29:102–116.

Hennart, Jean-Francois, 1982. *A Theory of Multinational Enterprise*. Ann Arbor: University of Michigan Press.

Hipple, F. Steb, 1990a. Multinational Companies and the Growth of the U.S. Trade Deficit. *International Trade Journal* 5:217–234.

———, 1990b. The Measurement of International Trade Related to Multinational Companies. *American Economic Review* 80:1263–1270.

Hirschman, Albert O., 1945. *National Power and the Structure of Foreign Trade*. Berkeley: University of California Press.

Hobbes, Thomas, 1962 [1651]. *Leviathan*. New York: Macmillan.

Hodgson, Geoffrey M., 1988. *Economics and Institutions: A Manifesto for a Modern Institutional Economics*. Philadelphia: University of Pennsylvania Press.

———, 1991. Economic Evolution. *Journal of Economic Issues* 25:519–533.

Hoekman, Bernard, 1989. Determining the Need for Issue Linkages in Multilateral Trade Negotiations. *International Organization* 43:693–714.

Hoekman, Bernard M., and Michael P. Leidy, 1990. Policy Responses to Shifting Comparative Advantage: Designing a System of Emergency Protection. *Kyklos* 43:25–51.

Holmstrom, Bengt, 1982. Moral Hazard in Teams. *Bell Journal of Economics* 13:324–340.

Hufbauer, Gary Clyde, and Joanna Shelton Erb, 1984. *Subsidies in International Trade*. Washington, D.C.: Institute for International Economics.

Hymer, Stephen, 1976. *The International Operations of National Firms: A Study of Direct Foreign Investment*. Cambridge, Mass.: MIT Press.

Ikenberry, G. John, 1986. The State and Strategies of International Adjustment. *World Politics* 39:53–77.

———, 1988. Conclusion: An Institutional Approach to American Foreign Economic Policy. *International Organization* 42:219–243.

Ikenberry, G. John, and Charles A. Kupchan, 1990. Socialization and Hegemonic Power. *International Organization* 44:283–315.

Ikenberry, G. John, et al., 1988. Introduction: Approaches to Explaining American Foreign Economic Policy. *International Organization* 42:1–14.

Imlah, Albert H., 1958. *Economic Elements in the Pax Britannica: Studies in British Foreign Trade in the Nineteenth Century.* Cambridge, Mass.: Harvard University Press.

International Organization, 1988. The State and American Foreign Economic Policy. Special issue.

Irwin, Douglas A., 1988. Welfare Effects of British Free Trade: Debate and Evidence from the 1940s. *Journal of Political Economy* 96:1142–1164.

Jackson, John H., 1987a. The Constitutional Structure for International Cooperation in Trade in Services and the Uruguay Round of GATT. Seminar Discussion Paper No. 207, Department of Economics, University of Michigan.

———, 1987b. Multilateral and Bilateral Negotiating Approaches for the Conduct of U.S. Trade Policies. In Robert M. Stern, ed., *U.S. Trade Policies in a Changing World Economy.* Cambridge, Mass.: MIT Press, pp. 377–412.

———, 1990. *The World Trading System.* Cambridge, Mass.: MIT Press.

Jackson, Robert H., 1987. Quasi-States, Dual Regimes, and Neoclassical Theory: International Jurisprudence and the Third World. *International Organization* 41:519–549.

Jacquemin, Alexis, and André Sapir, 1991. Europe Post–1992: Internal and External Liberalization. *American Economic Review Papers and Proceedings* 81:166–170.

James, Scott C., and David A. Lake, 1989. The Second Face of Hegemony: Britain's Repeal of the Corn Laws and the American Walker Tariff of 1946. *International Organization* 43:1–30.

Jervis, Robert, 1982. Security Regimes. In Stephen D. Krasner, ed., *International Regimes.* Ithaca: Cornell University Press, pp. 173–194.

———, 1988. Realism, Game Theory and Cooperation. *World Politics* 60:317–349.

Johnson, Harry G., 1965. An Economic Theory of Protectionism, Tariff Bargaining, and the Formation of Customs Unions. *Journal of Political Economy* 73:256–283.

Jones, Kent, 1984. The Political Economy of VER Agreements. *Kyklos* 37:82–101.

Jones, L. B., 1986. The Institutionalists and 'On the Origin of Species': A Case of Mistaken Identity. *Southern Economic Journal* 52:1043–1055.

Jones, Ronald W., 1971. A Three-Factor Model in Theory, Trade, and History. In Jagdish Bhagwati, et al., eds., *Trade, Balance of Payments, and Growth.* Amsterdam: North-Holland, pp. 3–21.

Jones, Ronald W., and J. Peter Neary, 1984. The Positive Theory of International

Trade. In Ronald W. Jones and Peter B. Kenen, eds., *Handbook of International Economics*, vol. 1. Amsterdam: North-Holland, pp. 1–62.

Joskow, Paul L., 1985. Vertical Integration and Long-term Contracts: The Case of Coal-Burning Electric Generating Plants. *Journal of Law, Economics, and Organization* 1:33–80.

———, 1987. Contract Duration and Transactions Specific Investment: Empirical Evidence from Coal Markets. *American Economic Review* 77:168–185.

———, 1988. Asset Specificity and the Structure of Vertical Relationships: Empirical Evidence. *Journal of Law, Economics, and Organization* 4:95–118.

Journal of Economic Issues, 1987. Special issues.

Journal of Institutional and Theoretical Economics, 1984, 1985, 1986, 1987. Special issues.

Kalt, Joseph P., and M. A. Zupan, 1984. Capture and Ideology in the Economic Theory of Politics. *American Economic Review* 74:279–300.

Kaplow, Louis, 1990. Optimal Deterrence, Uninformed Individuals, and Acquiring Information about Whether Acts are Subject to Sanctions. *Journal of Law, Economics, and Organization* 6:93–128.

Kemp, Murray C., and H. Y. Wan, Jr., 1972. The Gains from Free Trade. *International Economic Review* 13:509–522.

Keohane, Robert O., 1984. *After Hegemony: Cooperation and Discord in the World Political Economy*. Princeton: Princeton University Press.

———, ed., 1986a. *Neorealism and Its Critics*. New York: Columbia University Press.

———, 1986b. Reciprocity in International Relations. *International Organization* 40:1–27.

———, 1988a. International Institutions: Two Approaches. *International Studies Quarterly* 32:379–396.

———, 1988b. Reciprocity, Reputation, and Compliance with International Commitments. Paper presented at the 1988 Annual Meeting of the American Political Science Association, Washington, D.C., September 1–4.

———, 1990. Multilateralism: An Agenda for Research. *International Journal* 45:731–764.

Keohane, Robert O., and Joseph S. Nye, Jr., eds., 1970. *Transnational Relations and World Politics*. Cambridge, Mass.: Harvard University Press.

———, 1975. International Integration and Interdependence. In Fred I. Greenstein and Nelson W. Polsby, eds., *Handbook of Political Science*, vol. 8. Reading, Mass.: Addison-Wesley, pp. 363–414.

———, 1987. *Power and Interdependence* Revisited. *International Organization* 41:725–753.

Kindleberger, Charles P., 1973. *The World in Depression*. Boston: Little, Brown.

———, 1975. The Rise of Free Trade in Western Europe. *The Journal of Economic History* 35:20–55.

———, 1981. Dominance and Leadership in the International Economy. *International Studies Quarterly* 25:242–254.

———, 1986. Hierarchy Versus Inertial Cooperation. *International Organization* 40:841–847.

Klein, Benjamin, 1980. Transaction Cost Determinants of 'Unfair' Contractual Relations. *American Economic Review* 70:356–362.

————, 1988. Vertical Integration as Organizational Ownership: The Fisher Body-General Motors Relationship Revisited. *Journal of Law, Economics, and Organization* 4:199–213.

Klein, Benjamin, Robert G. Crawford, and Armen A. Alchian, 1978. Vertical Integration, Appropriable Rents, and the Competitive Contracting Process. *Journal of Law and Economics* 21:297–326.

Klein, Benjamin, and Keith Leffler, 1981. The Role of Market Forces in Assuring Contractual Performance. *Journal of Political Economy* 89:615–641.

Kobrin, Stephen J., 1980. Foreign Enterprise and Forced Divestment in the LDCs. *International Organization* 34:65–88.

————, 1984. Expropriation as an Attempt to Control Foreign Firms in LDCs: Trends from 1960 to 1979. *International Studies Quarterly* 28:329–348.

Krasner, Stephen D., 1976. State Power and the Structure of International Trade. *World Politics* 28:317–347.

————, 1979. The Tokyo Round: Particularistic Interests and Prospects for Stability of the Global Trading System. *International Studies Quarterly* 25:242–254.

————, 1982a. Regimes and the Limits of Realism: Regimes as Autonomous Variables. In Stephen D. Krasner, ed., *International Regimes*. Ithaca, N.Y.: Cornell University Press, pp. 355–368.

————, 1982b. Structural Causes and Regime Consequences. In Stephen D. Krasner, ed., *International Regimes*. Ithaca, N.Y.: Cornell University Press, pp. 1–21.

————, 1984. Approaches to the State. *Comparative Politics* 16:223–246.

Krauss, Melvyn B., 1972. Recent Developments in Customs Union Theory: An Interpretive Survey. *Journal of Economic Literature* 10:413–436.

Kreps, David, and Robert Wilson, 1982. Reputation and Imperfect Information. *Journal of Economic Theory* 27:253–279.

Kronman, Anthony T., 1978. Mistake, Disclosure, Information, and the Law of Contracts. *Journal of Legal Studies* 7:1–34.

————, 1985. Contract Law and the State of Nature. *Journal of Law, Economics, and Organization* 1:5–32.

Kronman, Anthony T., and Richard A. Posner, 1979. *The Economics of Contract Law*. Boston: Little, Brown.

Krueger, Anne O., 1974. The Political Economy of the Rent-Seeking Society. *American Economic Review* 64:291–303.

Krugman, Paul, 1983. New Theories of Trade Among Industrial Countries. *American Economic Review Papers and Proceedings* 73:343–347.

————, 1987. Is Free Trade Passé? *Journal of Economic Perspectives* 1:131–144.

Lake, David A., 1983. International Economic Structures and American Foreign Policy, 1887–1934. *World Politics* 35:517–543.

————, 1988. *Power, Protection, and Free Trade*. Ithaca, N.Y.: Cornell University Press.

————, 1991. British and American Hegemony Compared: Lessons for the Current Era of Decline. In Michael Fry, ed., *History, the White House, and the Kremlin: Statesmen as Historians.* London: Pinter Publishers, pp. 106–122.

Langlois, Richard N., 1986. Rationality, Institutions, and Explanation. In Richard N. Langlois, ed., *Economics as a Process.* Cambridge: Cambridge University Press, pp. 1–25.

———, 1988. What Was Wrong With the 'Old' Institutional Economics? (And What is Still Wrong With the 'New'?) Working paper, Department of Economics, University of Connecticut.

Lavergne, Real P., 1983. *The Political Economy of U.S. Tariffs.* New York: Academic Press.

Lawrence, Robert Z., and Robert E. Litan, 1990. The World Trading System After the Uruguay Round. Working Paper.

Leibenstein, Harvey, 1987. *Inside the Firm.* Cambridge, Mass.: Harvard University Press.

Levi, Margaret, 1988. *Of Rule and Revenue.* Berkeley: University of California Press.

Lipsey, R. G., 1960. The Theory of Customs Unions: A General Survey. *Economic Journal* 70:496–513.

Lipson, Charles, 1984. International Cooperation in Economic and Security Affairs. *World Politics* 37:1–23.

———, 1985. *Standing Guard: Protecting Foreign Capital in the Nineteenth and Twentieth Centuries.* Berkeley: University of California Press.

Llewellyn, Karl N., 1931. What Price Contract? *Yale Law Journal* 40:704–751.

Lodge, Juliet, 1990. Plurilateralism and the Single European Act. Working Paper. University of Hull, England: European Community Research Unit.

Macaulay, Stewart, 1963. Non-Contractual Relations in Business. *American Sociological Review* 28:55–70.

MacBean, A. I., and P. N. Snowden, 1981. *International Institutions in Trade and Finance.* London: George Allen & Unwin.

MacDonald, G. M., 1984. New Directions in the Economic Theory of Agency. *Canadian Journal of Economics* 17:415–440.

MacNeil, Ian R., 1974. The Many Futures of Contracts. *Southern California Law Review* 47:691–816.

———, 1978. Contracts. *Northwestern University Law Review* 72:854–906.

Magee, Stephen P., W. A. Brock, and Leslie Young, 1989. *Black Hole Tariffs and Endogenous Political Theory.* Cambridge: Cambridge University Press.

Magee, Stephen P., and Leslie Young, 1987. Endogenous Protection in the United States, 1980–1984. In Robert M. Stern, ed., *U.S. Trade Policies in a Changing World Economy.* Cambridge, Mass.: MIT Press, pp. 145–195.

Malinowski, Bronislaw, 1944. *A Scientific Theory of Culture and Other Essays.* Chapel Hill: University of North Carolina Press.

Maoz, Zeev, and Dan S. Felsenthal, 1987. Self-Binding Commitments, the Inducement of Trust, Social Choice, and the Theory of International Cooperation. *International Studies Quarterly* 31:177–200.

Martin, Lisa L., 1991. Interests, Power, and Multilateralism. Paper presented at the Annual Meeting of the American Political Science Association, Washington, D.C.

Masten, Scott E., 1984. The Organization of Production: Evidence from the Aerospace Industry. *Journal of Law and Economics* 27:403–417.

———, 1988. A Legal Basis for the Firm. *Journal of Law, Economics, and Organization* 4:181–198.

Masten, Scott E., James W. Meehan, Jr., and Edward A. Snyder, 1989. Vertical Integration in the U.S. Auto Industry: A Note on the Influence of Transaction Specific Assets. *Journal of Economic Behavior and Organization* 12:265–273.

Mayer, Wolfgang, 1981. Theoretical Considerations on Negotiated Tariff Adjustments. *Oxford Economic Papers* 33:135–153.

McGinnis, Michael, 1986. Issue Linkage and the Evolution of International Cooperation. *Journal of Conflict Resolution* 30:141–170.

McKeown, Timothy J., 1983. Hegemonic Stability Theory and 19th Century Tariff Levels in Europe. *International Organization* 37:73–91.

———, 1984. Firms and Tariff Regime Change: Explaining the Demand for Protection. *World Politics* 36:215–233.

———, 1991. A Liberal Trade Order? The Long-Run Pattern of Imports to the Advanced Capitalist States. *International Studies Quarterly* 35:151–171.

McMillan, John, 1990. Strategic Bargaining and Section 301. In Jagdish Bhagwati and Hugh T. Patrick, eds., *Aggressive Unilateralism: America's 301 Trade Policy and the World Trading System.* Ann Arbor: University of Michigan Press, pp. 203–216.

Merton, Robert, 1947. Manifest and Latent Functions. In *Social Theory and Social Structure.* New York: Free Press, pp. 19–84.

Milgrom, Paul R., Douglass C. North, and Barry R. Weingast, 1990. The Role of Institutions in the Revival of Trade: The Law Merchant, Private Judges, and the Champagne Fairs. Hoover Institution Working Paper in Political Science P–90–1.

Milgrom, Paul, and John Roberts, 1982. Predation, Reputation, and Entry Deterrence. *Journal of Economic Theory* 27:280–312.

Millar, T. B., ed., 1984. *Current International Treaties.* New York: New York University Press.

Milner, Helen, 1988a. Anarchy and Interdependence. Working paper, Department of Political Science, Columbia University.

———, 1988b. *Resisting Protectionism: Global Industries and the Politics of International Trade.* Princeton: Princeton University Press.

———, 1988c. Trading Places: Industries for Free Trade. *World Politics* 60:350–376.

Milner, Helen, and David B. Yoffie, 1989. Between Free Trade and Protectionism: Strategic Trade Policy and a Theory of Corporate Trade Demands. *International Organization* 43:239–272.

Milward, A., 1984. *The Reconstruction of Western Europe, 1945–51.* London: Methuen.

Mitrany, David, 1948. The Functional Approach to World Organization. *International Affairs* 24:350–363.

Mitrany, David, 1966. *A Working Peace System*. Chicago: Quadrangle Books.

Moe, Terry M., 1984. The New Economics of Organization. *American Journal of Political Science* 28:739–777.

Monteverde, Kirk, and David Teece, 1982. Supplier Switching Costs and Vertical Integration in the Automobile Industry. *Bell Journal of Economics* 13:206–213.

Moravcsik, Andrew, 1991. Negotiating the Single European Act: National Interests and Conventional Statecraft in the European Community. *International Organization* 45:19–56.

Morgenthau, Hans J., 1967 [1948]. *Politics Among Nations*. New York: Knopf.

Mulherin, J. Harold, 1986. Complexity in Long-term Contracts: An Analysis of Natural Gas Contract Provisions. *Journal of Law, Economics, and Organization* 2:105–117.

Neale, Walter C., 1987. Institutions. *Journal of Economic Issues* 21:1177–1206.

Ness, Gayl D., and Steven R. Brechin, 1988. Bridging the Gap: International Organizations as Organizations. *International Organization* 42:245–273.

North, Douglass C., 1981. *Structure and Change in Economic History*. New York: Norton.

———, 1990. *Institutions, Institutional Change and Economic Performance*. Cambridge: Cambridge University Press.

North, Douglass C., and Barry R. Weingast, 1988. Constitutions and Commitment: The Evolution of Institutions Governing Public Choice in 17th-Century England. Working paper.

Nye, Joseph S., Jr., 1988. Neorealism and Neoliberalism. *World Politics* 40:235–251.

Ohlin, Bertil, 1933. *Interregional and International Trade*. Cambridge, Mass.: Harvard University Press.

Olson, Mancur, 1965. *The Logic of Collective Action: Public Goods and the Theory of Groups*. Cambridge, Mass.: Harvard University Press.

Onuf, Nicholas, and Frank F. Klink, 1989. Anarchy, Authority, Rule. *International Studies Quarterly* 33:149–174.

Ostrom, Elinor, 1990. *Governing the Commons: The Evolution of Institutions for Collective Action*. Cambridge: Cambridge University Press.

Oye, Kenneth A., ed., 1986a. *Cooperation under Anarchy*. Princeton: Princeton University Press.

———, 1986b. Explaining Cooperation under Anarchy: Hypotheses and Strategies. In Kenneth A. Oye, ed., *Cooperation Under Anarchy*. Princeton: Princeton University Press, pp. 1–24.

Palay, Thomas, 1984. Comparative Institutional Economics: The Governance of Rail Freight Contracting. *Journal of Legal Studies* 13:265–287.

———, 1985. Avoiding Regulatory Constraints: Contracting Safeguards and the Role of Informal Agreements. *Journal of Law, Economics, and Organization* 1:155–176.

Parsons, Talcott, 1937. *The Structure of Social Action*. New York: McGraw-Hill.

Patterson, Gardner, 1983. The European Community as a Threat to the System.

In William R. Cline, ed., *Trade Policy in the 1980s*. Washington, D.C.: Institute for International Economics, pp. 223–242.

Piccioto, Sol, 1984. Political Economy and International Law. In Susan Strange, ed., *Paths to International Political Economy*. London: George Allen and Unwin, pp. 164–182.

Pincus, Jonathan J., 1977. *Pressure Groups and Politics in Antebellum Tariffs*. New York: Columbia University Press.

Plato, 1974. *The Republic*. New York: Penguin Books.

Polanyi, Karl, 1944. *The Great Transformation*. New York: Rinehart.

Pollak, Robert A., 1985. A Transaction Cost Approach to Families and Households. *Journal of Economic Literature* 23:581–608.

Pomfret, Richard, 1988. *Managed Trade: The Economics of Discriminatory International Trade Policies*. Oxford: Basil Blackwell.

Powell, Robert, 1991. The Problem of Absolute and Relative Gains in International Relations Theory. *American Political Science Review*, forthcoming.

Pratt, John W., and Zeckhauser, Richard J., eds., 1985. *Principals and Agents: The Structure of Business*. Cambridge, Mass.: Harvard Business School Press.

Puchala, Donald J., and Raymond F. Hopkins, 1982. International Regimes: Lessons from Inductive Analysis. In Stephen D. Krasner, ed., *International Regimes*. Ithaca, N.Y.: Cornell University Press, pp. 61–91.

Putnam, Robert D., 1988. Diplomacy and Domestic Politics: The Logic of Two-Level Games. *International Organization* 42:427–460.

Putterman, Louis, 1986. *The Economic Nature of the Firm*. Cambridge: Cambridge University Press.

Radcliffe-Brown, A. R., 1935. On the Concept of Function in Social Science. *American Anthropologist* 37:394–402.

Ramstad, Yngve, 1989. Book Review of Geoffrey Hodgson's *Economics and Institutions*. *History of Economics Society Bulletin* 11:304–313.

Ray, Edward J., and Howard P. Marvel, 1984. The Pattern of Protection in the Industrialized World. *Review of Economics and Statistics* 66:452–458.

Reich, Robert, 1991. The Myth of "Made in the U.S.A." *Wall Street Journal*. July 5.

Rejai, Mostafa, and Cynthia H. Enloe, 1969. Nation-States and State-Nations. *International Studies Quarterly* 13:140–158.

Rhodes, Carolyn, 1989. Reciprocity in Trade: The Utility of a Bargaining Strategy. *International Organization* 43:273–299.

Ricardo, David, 1971 [1817]. *The Principles of Political Economy and Taxation*. Baltimore: Penguin.

Richardson, J. David, 1987. Comment. In Robert M. Stern, ed., *U.S. Trade Policies in a Changing World Economy*. Cambridge, Mass.: MIT Press, pp. 287–290.

———, 1990. The Political Economy of Strategic Trade Policy. *International Organization* 44:107–135.

Rogowski, Ronald, 1989. *Commerce and Coalitions: How Trade Affects Domestic Political Alignments*. Princeton: Princeton University Press.

Rosecrance, Richard, 1986. *The Rise of the Trading State.* New York: Basic Books.

Rubin, Paul, 1978. The Theory of the Firm and the Structure of the Franchise Contract. *Journal of Law and Economics* 21:223–233.

Ruggie, John Gerard, 1983. International Regimes, Transactions, and Change. In Stephen D. Krasner, ed., *International Regimes.* Ithaca, N.Y.: Cornell University Press, pp. 195–231.

Rugman, Alan M., 1981. *Inside the Multinationals.* New York: Columbia University Press.

Rummel, Rudolph J., 1966. Some Dimensions in the Foreign Behavior of Nations. *Journal of Peace Research* 3:201–223.

Russett, Bruce, 1985. The Mysterious Case of Vanishing Hegemony: Or, Is Mark Twain Really Dead? *International Organization* 39:207–232.

Samuelson, Paul A., 1939. The Gains from International Trade. *Canadian Journal of Economics and Political Science* 9:195–205.

———, 1954. The Pure Theory of Public Expenditure. *Review of Economics and Statistics* 36:387–389.

———, 1955. A Diagrammatic Exposition of a Theory of Public Expenditure. *Review of Economics and Statistics* 37:350–356.

———, 1971. Ohlin Was Right. *Swedish Journal of Economics* 73:365–384.

San Francisco Chronicle, 1990. GATT Near Pact on Ways to End Rows. April 21, pp. B1, B24.

San Francisco Examiner, 1990. Lithuania's Fight Just Starting. March 11, p. A6.

Sandholtz, Wayne, and John Zysman, 1989. 1992: Recasting the European Bargain. *World Politics* 42:95–128.

Sandler, Todd, and Jon Cauley, 1977. The Design of Supranational Structures. *International Studies Quarterly* 21:251–276.

Sapir, A., and L. Lundberg, 1984. The U.S. Generalized System of Preferences and Its Impacts. In Robert E. Baldwin and Anne O. Krueger, eds., *The Structure and Evolution of Recent U.S. Trade Policy.* Chicago: University of Chicago Press, pp. 191–231.

Schattschneider, E. E., 1935. *Politics, Pressures, and the Tariff.* New York: Prentice-Hall.

Schelling, Thomas C., 1980. The Intimate Struggle for Self-Command. *The Public Interest* 60:94–118.

Schonhardt-Bailey, Cheryl, 1991. Specific Factors, Capital Markets, Portfolio Diversification, and Free Trade: Domestic Determinants of the Repeal of the Corn Laws. *World Politics* 43:545–569.

Schott, Jeffrey, J., and Gary Clyde Hufbauer, 1991. Scoring the Uruguay Round: Pass, Fail, or Incomplete? In Robert E. Baldwin and J. David Richardson, eds., *The Uruguay Round and Beyond: Problems and Prospects.* Cambridge, Mass.: National Bureau of Economic Research, pp. 1–23.

Schotter, Andrew, 1986. The Evolution of Rules. In Richard N. Langlois, ed., *Economics as a Process.* Cambridge: Cambridge University Press, pp. 117–133.

Sebenius, James K., 1983. Negotiation Arithmetic: Adding and Subtracting Issues and Parties. *International Organization* 37:281–316.

Seyfert, Wolfgang, 1985. A Weberian Analysis of Economic Progress. *Journal of Institutional and Theoretical Economics* 141:170–183.

Shafer, Michael, 1983. Capturing the Mineral Multinationals: Advantage or Disadvantage. *International Organization* 37:93–120.

Shugart, William F., II, 1990. *The Organization of Industry*. Homewood, Illinois: Irwin.

Simon, Herbert, 1961 [1947]. *Administrative Behavior*, 2nd ed. New York: Macmillan.

———, 1978. Rationality as Process and as Product of Thought. *American Economic Review Papers and Proceedings* 68:1–16.

Singer, J. David, 1961. The Level-of-Analysis Problem in International Relations. In Klaus Knorr and Sidney Verba, eds., *The International System: Theoretical Essays*. Princeton: Princeton University Press, pp. 77–92.

Smith, Adam, 1937 [1776]. *An Inquiry into the Nature and Causes of the Wealth of Nations*. New York: Random House.

Snape, Richard H., 1988. Is Non-discrimination Really Dead? *The World Economy* 11:1–18.

Snidal, Duncan, 1985. The Limits of Hegemonic Stability Theory. *International Organization* 39:579–614.

———, 1991. Relative Gains and the Pattern of International Cooperation. *American Political Science Review* 85:701–726.

Snyder, Glenn H., 1984. The Security Dilemma in Alliance Politics. *World Politics* 36:461–495.

Snyder, Glenn H., and Paul Diesing, 1977. *Conflict Among Nations: Bargaining, Decision Making and System Structure in International Crises*. Princeton: Princeton University Press.

Stegemann, Klaus, 1989. Policy Rivalry among Industrial States: What Can We Learn from Models of Strategic Trade Policy? *International Organization* 43:73–100.

Stein, Arthur A., 1984. The Hegemon's Dilemma: Great Britain, the United States, and the International Economic Order. *International Organization* 38:355–386.

Stern, Robert, and Bernard Hoekman, 1987. The Codes Approach. In J. Michael Finger and Andrzej Olechowski, eds., *The Uruguay Round: A Handbook on the Multilateral Trade Negotiations*. Washington, D.C.: The World Bank, pp. 59–66.

Stigler, George J., 1971. The Economic Theory of Regulation. *Bell Journal of Economics and Management Science* 2:3–21.

———, 1974. Free Riders and Collective Action: An Appendix to Theories of Economic Regulation. *Bell Journal of Economics and Management Science* 5:359–365.

Stoessinger, John, 1981. The Anatomy of the Nation-State and the Nature of Power. In Michael Smith, Richard Little, and Michael Shackleton, eds., *Perspectives on World Politics*. Kent: Croom Helm London, pp. 25–36.

Stolper, Wolfgang, and Paul A. Samuelson, 1941. Protection and Real Wages. *Review of Economic Studies* 9:58–73.

Strange, Susan, 1979. The Management of Surplus Capacity: Or, How Does Theory Stand up to Protectionism 1970s Style? *International Organization* 33:303–334.

———, 1982. *Cave! Hic Dragones*: A Critique of Regime Analysis. In Stephen D. Krasner, ed., *International Regimes*. Ithaca, N.Y.: Cornell University Press, pp. 337–354.

———, 1985. Protectionism and World Politics. *International Organization* 39:233–260.

———, 1987. The Persistent Myth of Lost Hegemony. *International Organization* 41:551–574.

———, 1988. *States and Markets*. New York: Basil Blackwell.

Strange, Susan, and Roger Tooze, eds., 1980. *The International Politics of Surplus Capacity*. London: Butterworth.

Stuckey, John, 1983. *Vertical Integration and Joint Ventures in the Aluminum Industry*. Cambridge, Mass.: Harvard University Press.

Takacs, Wendy E., 1981. Pressures for Protectionism: An Empirical Analysis. *Economic Inquiry* 19:687–693.

Taussig, Frank W., 1931. *The Tariff History of the United States*. New York: Putnam.

Taylor, Paul, 1982. Intergovernmentalism in the European Communities in the 1970s: Patterns and Perspectives. *International Organization* 36:741–766.

———, 1983. *The Limits of European Integration*. New York: Columbia University Press.

Telser, Lester A., 1980. A Theory of Self-enforcing Agreements. *Journal of Business* 27:27–44.

Temin, Peter, 1976. *Did Monetary Forces Cause the Great Depression?* New York: Norton.

The Economist, 1990. Policing Europe's Single Market. January 20, pp. 69–70.

Tirole, Jean, 1988. *The Theory of Industrial Organization*. Cambridge, Mass.: MIT Press.

Tollison, Robert D., 1982. Rent Seeking: A Survey. *Kyklos* 35:575–602.

Tollison, Robert D., and Thomas D. Willett, 1979. An Economic Theory of Mutually Advantageous Issue Linkage in International Negotiations. *International Organization* 33:245–249.

Tsoukalis, Loukas, and António da Silva Ferreira, 1980. Management of Industrial Surplus Capacity in the European Community. *International Organization* 34:355–376.

Turner, Jonathan H., and A. Maryanski, 1979. *Functionalism*. Menlo Park, California: Benjamin-Cummings.

Tyson, Laura, and John Zysman, 1983. American Industry in International Competition. In John Zysman and Laura Tyson, eds., *American Industry in International Competition*. Ithaca, N.Y.: Cornell University Press, pp. 15–59.

Ullmann-Margalit, Edna, 1977. *The Emergence of Norms*. Oxford: Clarendon Press.

United States International Trade Commission, 1985, 1986, 1987, 1988. *Operation of the Trade Agreements Program.* Washington, D.C.: United States Government Printing Office.

USA Today, 1991. Europe Group Flexes Muscle, June.

Vernon, Raymond, 1982. International Trade Policy in the 1980s. *International Studies Quarterly* 26:483–510.

Viner, Jacob, 1975 [1937]. *Studies in the Theory of International Trade.* Clifton, N.J.: Augustus M. Kelley.

Wagner, R. Harrison, 1983. The Theory of Games and the Problem of International Cooperation. *American Political Science Review* 77:330–348.

———, 1988. Economic Interdependence, Bargaining Power, and Political Influence. *International Organization* 42:461–484.

Wall Street Journal, 1985. European Officials Push Idea of Standardizing Telecommunications—But Some Makers Resist. April 10, p. 32.

———, 1986a. Gatt Knows Who the Trade Sinners Are, but It Doesn't Matter. January 2, p. 1.

———, 1986b. World Trade Stays Strong Despite Talk about Protectionism. September 1, p. 1.

———, 1990a. Bulk of U.S. Imports Are Said To Be Shipments between Firms and Affiliates. October 15.

———, 1990b. GATT Riddance? December 12, p. A16.

———, 1991a. EC States Warned on Progress. June 12.

———, 1991b. U.S.-Canada Panel Rejects Challenge in Pork Trade Case. June 17.

Wallace, Helen, and Adam Ridley, 1985. *Europe: The Challenge of Diversity.* London: Routledge & Kegan Paul.

Wallerstein, Immanuel, 1980. *The Modern World System: Mercantilism and the Consolidation of the European World Economy, 1600–1750.* New York: Academic Press.

Waltz, Kenneth N., 1959. *Man, The State, and War: A Theoretical Analysis.* New York: Columbia University Press.

———, 1964. The Stability of a Bipolar World. *Daedalus* 93:881–909.

———, 1979. *Theory of International Politics.* New York: Random House.

Wendt, Alexander E., 1987. The Agent-Structure Problem in International Relations Theory. *International Organization* 41:335–370.

Williamson, Oliver E., 1981. The Economics of Organization: The Transaction Cost Approach. *American Journal of Sociology* 87:548–577.

———, 1983. Credible Commitments: Using Hostages to Support Exchange. *American Economic Review* 73:519–540.

———, 1985a. *The Economic Institutions of Capitalism: Firms, Markets, Relational Contracting.* New York: Free Press.

———, 1985b. Reflections on the New Institutional Economics. *Journal of Institutional and Theoretical Economics* 141:187–195.

———, 1988. The Logic of Economic Organization. *Journal of Law, Economics, and Organization* 4:65–93.

Winship, Christopher, and Sherwin Rosen, eds., 1988. Organizations and Institutions. *American Journal of Sociology* 94(Supplement).

Winters, L. Alan, 1987. Reciprocity. In J. Michael Finger and Andrzej Olechowski, eds., *The Uruguay Round: A Handbook on the Multilateral Trade Negotiations.* Washington, D.C.: The World Bank, pp. 45–51.

Wittman, Donald, 1991a. Nations and States: Mergers and Acquisitions; Dissolutions and Divorce. Working Paper.

———, 1991b. Wars and Mergers between Sovereign States: The Role of Credible Commitments. Working Paper.

Wolf, Martin, 1986. Fiddling While GATT Burns. *The World Economy* 9:1–18.

Wolff, A. W., 1983. Managed Trade in Practice: Implications of the Textile Arrangements. In William R. Cline, ed., *Trade Policy in the 1980s.* Washington, D.C.: Institute for International Economics, pp. 363–391.

Wonnacott, Paul, 1987. *The United States and Canada: The Quest for Free Trade.* Washington, D.C.: Institute for International Economics.

Wonnacott, Ronald J., and Paul Wonnacott, 1981. Is Unilateral Tariff Reduction Preferable to a Customs Union? The Curious Case of the Missing Foreign Tariffs. *American Economic Review* 71:704–714.

Yarbrough, Beth V., and Robert M. Yarbrough, 1985a. Free Trade, Hegemony, and the Theory of Agency. *Kyklos* 38:348–364.

———, 1985b. Opportunism and Governance in International Trade: After Hegemony, What? Paper presented at the National Bureau of Economic Research Conference on the Political Economy of Trade Policy, MIT Endicott Center, Dedham, Mass.

———, 1986a. Reciprocity, Bilateralism, and Economic 'Hostages': Self-enforcing Agreements in International Trade. *International Studies Quarterly* 30:7–21.

———, 1986b. Specific Investment and Customs Unions: Relational Contracting in International Trade. Paper presented at the Annual Meeting of the Southern Economic Association, New Orleans, La.

———, 1986c. Specific Subcontracting and Industrial Organization in Japan: Some Empirical Evidence on the Transaction-Costs Approach. Working paper, Department of Economics, Amherst College.

———, 1987a. Cooperation in the Liberalization of International Trade: After Hegemony, What? *International Organization* 41:1–26.

———, 1987b. Institutions for the Governance of Opportunism in International Trade. *Journal of Law, Economics, and Organization* 3:129–139.

———, 1987c. Using Power to Support Exchange. Paper presented at the Annual Meeting of the American Political Science Association, Chicago.

———, 1988. The Transactional Structure of the Firm: A Comparative Survey. *Journal of Economic Behavior and Organization* 10:1–28.

———, 1989. Monitoring, Side-Payments, and Hold-Outs: Opportunism on the Part of the Principal. Working paper, Department of Economics, Amherst College.

———, 1990a. Economic Integration and Governance: The Role of Preferential Trade Agreements. *Journal of International Economic Integration* 5:1–20.

Yarbrough, Beth V., and Robert M. Yarbrough, 1990b. International Institutions and the New Economics of Organization. *International Organization* 44:235–259.

———, 1991a. Security and Trade: The Strategic Organizational Approach. Paper presented at the American Political Science Association Annual Meetings, Washington, D.C.

———, 1991b. *The World Economy: Trade and Finance*, second edition. Chicago: Dryden Press.

Yeager, Leland B., and David G. Tuerck, 1983. Realism and Free-Trade Policy. *The Cato Journal* 3:645–666.

Yoshino, M. Y., and Thomas B. Lifson, 1986. *The Invisible Link*. Cambridge, Mass.: MIT Press.

Young, Oran R., 1978. Anarchy and Social Choice: Reflections on the International Polity. *World Politics* 30:241–263.

———, 1982. Regime Dynamics: The Rise and Fall of International Regimes. In Stephen D. Krasner, ed., *International Regimes*. Ithaca, N.Y.: Cornell University Press, pp. 93–113.

———, 1989. The Politics of International Regime Formation. *International Organization* 43:349–376.

AUTHOR INDEX

SUBJECT INDEX

adaptation, 20, 40, 121
access. *See* market access
adjustment costs, 8, 53
agent-structure problem, 12n.34, 117–120
agreements, design of, 13, 31, 44–45, 66
agreements, self-enforcing. *See* self-enforcing agreements
alternatives, 22–29, 40, 54n.23, 56, 58–59, 65, 121–122, 137–138
anarchy, 13–15, 20–21, 118, 125–126, 130, 132, 139, 144
anonymity, 49, 114, 121–122, 126, 132
antidumping duties (AD), 35n.55, 79, 99–100, 102, 143, 147
arbitration, 49, 62, 65, 102. *See also* dispute settlement
arm's-length transactions, 11n.34, 29–34, 56–57
asset specificity. *See* relation-specific investment
asymmetric information, 21n.4, 26, 45, 54n.23
asymmetry of interests, 26
automobile industry, 15n.53, 25, 28, 29n.36, 30n.39, 37, 59n.39, 71, 77n.32, 78n.37, 83n.62, 138

Baltic states. *See* Soviet republics
beggar-thy-neighbor policies, 52, 83
Bilateral Investment Treaty (BIT), 65–66, 82
bilateral monopoly, 28, 45
bilateral trade, 75n.22
bilateral trade policy, 4–7, 13, 17–19, 41–42, 56, 65–66, 68–86, 89–94, 96, 105, 111, 125, 135–137, 142, 144–145, 147n.31; definition of, 6n.14, 68, 75n.20, 75n.22, 82n.55, 89, 101n.76
binding precommitments, 54, 69–72, 101. *See also* commitments
"black-box" approaches, 112–113, 122, 132
blocs, trade, 5, 103–106, 144, 146–147
bonds, performance, 70, 79–80, 88, 147

bounded rationality, 20–21, 116–117, 121, 124, 126, 133
breach of contract. *See* contracts
bribes, 47, 52–54, 63, 66, 90n.14, 104–105, 140
Britain, 4–5, 7, 12, 17–18, 27, 32–33, 41, 55–60, 66–67, 94, 135, 136n.7, 140, 145
"building blocs," 104
business-cycle theories, 9–10, 12n.35, 12n.40, 13, 43n.4, 111

Calvo doctrine, 35n.52
Canada-U.S. Automotive Products Trade Act, 15n.53, 28, 78n.37
Canada-U.S. Free-Trade Agreement, 6, 72n.10, 82, 86, 89, 99–103, 105–106, 111, 135n.3, 136, 142–143
Canadian trade, 99–103
Canadian investment policy, 101, 143
capture theories, 83, 129n.77
"carrots," 52–54, 62–63, 66, 104n.88, 141. *See also* bribes, side-payments
centralized authority. *See* anarchy
change, institutional, 112n.2, 128. *See also* institutional forms
cheating, 14–15, 20, 31, 46, 62, 64, 74, 80, 84–85, 114. *See also* opportunism; reneging
closure, market, 25n.23, 28, 52n.17, 53, 59–60, 72–76
Cobden-Chevalier treaty, 4n.7, 56
codes, GATT, 46–48, 62, 82–83, 93n.30
collateral, 15, 79–80
collective action, 118, 128
commercial risk, 30
commercial treaties, 38
commitments, 35, 45, 54, 69–72, 80, 89, 101, 122, 132, 135, 139, 147
Common Agricultural Policy (CAP), 91, 94
comparative advantage, 8, 28, 49, 87, 88n.7, 88n.8, 109, 123, 137
comparative-institutional analysis, 119, 127, 147n.30
compensation, 47, 52–54, 63, 66